VOID

Library of
Davidson College

MANDEL'SHTAM'S POETICS:

A CHALLENGE TO POSTMODERNISM

ELENA GLAZOV-CORRIGAN

Mandel'shtam's Poetics:

A Challenge to Postmodernism

UNIVERSITY OF TORONTO PRESS
Toronto Buffalo London

© University of Toronto Press Incorporated 2000
Toronto Buffalo London
Printed in Canada

ISBN 0-8020-4737-8

Printed on acid-free paper

Canadian Cataloguing in Publication Data

Corrigan, Elena
  Mandel'shtam's poetics : a challenge to postmodernism

  Includes bibliographical references and index.
  ISBN 0-8020-4737-8

  1. Mandel'shtam, Osip, 1891–1938 – Criticism and interpretation. I. Title.

  PG3476.M355Z577 2000   891.71′3   C00-930860-1

JACKET ILLUSTRATION: Sculpture of Mandel'shtam (red wood, 70 × 80 cm) by Grigorij Aleksandrovich Israilevitch (1924–1998)

This book has been published with the help of a grant from the Humanities and Social Sciences Federation of Canada, using funds provided by the Social Sciences and Humanities Research Council of Canada.

University of Toronto Press acknowledges the financial assistance to its publishing program of the Canada Council for the Arts and the Ontario Arts Council.

University of Toronto Press acknowledges the financial support for its publishing activities of the Government of Canada through the Book Publishing Industry Development Program (BPIDP).

To my father, Yuri Yakovlevich Glazov (1939–1998), with love

    Когда я спал без облика и склада,
Я дружбой был, как выстрелом, разбужен.

    When I slept without a face or a form
I was awakened by friendship as by a shot.

OSIP MANDEL'SHTAM, 8–12 August 1932

Contents

FOREWORD xi
ACKNOWLEDGMENTS xv

Mandel'shtam: A Biographical Note 3

Introduction 5

1 Meaning and Blank: The First Decade of Mandel'shtam's Poetics 13
  1 Binary Opposition in Mandel'shtam's Early Essays, 1913–1915 13
  2 Evidence of the Growing Theoretical Crisis 22

2 The Word in Mandel'shtam's Poetics 29
  1 The Word as Stone, 1913–1919 29
  2 The Word as Inner and Outer Reality, 1921–1922 32
  3 The Word as Space, 1925 35
  4 The Word as Journey into the Patterns of Communication, the 1930s 38

3 The Word in Action: The Hypnotic Power of Poetry 40
  1 Tangible Intensification and Hypnotism, 1913–1919 40
  2 The Double Effect of Poetry, 1921–1924 42
  3 The Catastrophic Essence of Poetry, 1921–1932 49
  4 Signal-Waves of Meaning, 1930 51

viii Contents

4 The Participation of the Reader   54
  1 The Dialogical Nature of Poetry, 1913 and After   54
  2 The Escape of the Poetic Voice, 1924 and After   56
  3 The Reading Process as Metamorphosis   60

5 Periodization in the Transmutation of the Poetic Landscape. Metamorphosis of the Addressee in the 1930s   68
  1 The Hybrid Nature of Poetic Discourse   68
  2 The Beginning of the Reading Process; Entrance into Matter. The Addressee as Completed Past.   72
    2.1 The beginning of the process: movement initiated near the tangible remnants of 'intelligible life'   73
    2.2 The crack [*proval*]   74
    2.3 Death as the result of entrance   76
    2.4 Reading as awareness of intertextuality   77
    2.5 The reversal of time   78
    2.6 The construction of the organ of transmission and reception   78
    2.7 Language as command   79
    2.8 The ghost of the past as addressee   80
  3 Expression as an Instinctual Escape from the Inferno. The Addressee as Instinctual Response   81
    3.1 Impregnation of the rock   81
    3.2 Literal expression   82
    3.3 Expression as a form of hidden structure   82
    3.4 Metamorphoses of instinctual formations   83
    3.5 The instinctual self as addressee   85
  4 The Living Geography of the Text; Impression as Coloration of the Parts. The Reader as Addressee   86
    4.1 Acquaintance with the parts   87
    4.2 Colour as expression or squeezing of the vegetable dyes   87
    4.3 Colour as speed, and thus apprehension of further movement or transformation   89
    4.4 Coloration of the poetic text as imagination and its limitations   90
    4.5 The reader as addressee   91
  5 From Colour to Wave-Impulse as a Common Textual Characteristic. The Addressee as Co-traveller or Co-inventor   92
    5.1 Identification of the common characteristics: the shift from the notion of colour to the traces of light   93

   5.2 The image of sailing   94
   5.3 The self-erasing surface   96
   5.4 The limits of language   98
   5.5 The co-discoverer as addressee   99
6 Music as Verification of the Final Direction of the Poetic Impulse. The Addressee as Figure of Authority within a Concert-like Setting   100
   6.1 The progression from reason to faith   101
   6.2 Music and chemistry   103
   6.3 The conductor's baton   103
   6.4 A further addressee: the concert-like circumstance of the presence of authority   105
7 Preliminary Conclusions   107
TABLE Changing Stages in the Apprehension of the Poetic Landscape: Communication as Simultaneous Performance of Differentited Strategies   108

6 Conclusion: The Theoretical Implications of Mandel'shtam's Poetics   111

1 A Few Preliminary Observations on the Problem of Contextualizing Mandel'shtam   112
2 The Polemical Focus of Mandel'shtam's Mature Poetics: The Hybrid Nature of Poetry as a Reinterpretation of the Aristotelian Concepts of Form and Matter   118
3 The Hybridization of Impulse and *Materia* as an Implicit Debate with the Russian Formalists   121
4 An Assessment of the Theoretical Validity of Mandel'shtam's Impulse for Modern Poetics: Mukařovský and Pasternak   127
5 The Continual Transformation of Poetic Communication and Its Organic Structure   130
6 The Difference between Writing and Reading, Author and Addressee, within the Differentiated Levels of Poetry   132
7 Intertextuality and the Previous Poetic Tradition in the Context of Poststructuralist Poetics   140
8 Poetry as Reflexology of Speech   146

NOTES   149
REFERENCES   177
INDEX   189

Foreword

The quality of this book that perhaps first captures the eye of the reader is the balance it carefully establishes between caution and courage. Indeed, if a topic conceals within itself as many difficulties, dangers, and unexpected twists as does the subject of this work, then it demands from the author a conscious preparedness for risk. Mandel'shtam is the virtuoso of precisely planned, diametrically opposed judgments pronounced in the very same period of his life, and often in the very same text. Within a single line a word may stand seemingly perpendicular to its neighbours, and this is no passing fancy, but the very essence of Mandel'shtam's poetic position. His poetry is radically opposed to both classicism and the avant-garde, while remaining in intense proximity to each. We sense this dynamic tension between logical poles in the poet's poems and prose writings. The blind swallow with clipped wings will return at any moment to the grotto of shadows – yet still it has not returned. Bright tender green shoots on the dilapidated streets of Petersburg promise that a future virgin forest will cover the modern city – but there is still a place for city dwellers and for a friend, and the old world is alive more than ever. Meanwhile, all this takes place at a single point grounded in the distance between those grammatical rules that govern future and present.

Anyone who dares to write about such a poet without anticipating the risks of the enterprise is predestined to a doubtful harvest. The fact that sober clear-sightedness and an awareness of the necessary risks have guided this book from its inception is already a witness to its quality. It is also reassuring that the introduction clearly formulates the task: 'to uncover the structure and consistency of Mandel'shtam's apparently impenetrable and disconnected theoretical discourse.' The unity within disconnected threads – this is really the essence of Mandel'shtam's thought, and we shall never see the unity, often astonishing and always unexpected, unless we confront directly the consistent absence of external links and transitions.

The second guarantee of the high level of this work is the precision with which Elena Glazov-Corrigan excludes all easy conclusions based either upon biographical data (including psychological and psychoanalytic suppositions) or upon the political history of the poet's country. The complexity of this task is intensified by the fact that Mandel'shtam – while by no means qualified for the post of *poetus doctus* (the post he assumes in the works of Ralf Dutli) – constantly reveals unexpected gaps in his own knowledge and, simultaneously, equally unexpected depths of erudition, as well as that extremely sharp intuitive grasp of the textual essence, which could be spurred into existence by Mandel'shtam's quickest glance through a book, or by his ability to catch concepts from the smoke-filled air of thoughtful conversations. Thus, for the most part, the critic cannot assume the right to postulate with confidence the poet's knowledge or ignorance of a particular text. We lack the opportunity to glance over Mandel'shtam's shoulder as he reads (a procedure easily carried out for most of the symbolists). And if – in accordance with Mandel'shtam's famous statement that the biography of the *raznochinets* consists of the books he has read – the critics succumb to the temptation of an excessively biographical methodology, they may well become embroiled in the confident but somewhat misplaced play of intertextual determinants for every atom of the poet's difficult texts. This method was unfortunately legitimated by a careless reference by the poet himself, in the *Conversation about Dante*, to the memory-saturated keyboard of references, a remark that encouraged his investigators in their methodological excesses, which have so often threatened to clog up the breathing passages of Mandel'shtam scholarship. But even this common version of misplaced biographical zeal is alien to the present work. Glazov-Corrigan, having displayed a satisfactory awareness of both the biographical and historical approaches in her introduction, retains throughout a naturalness of approach most unusual in our day. Her work concentrates on the 'universals' (to which the Middle Ages, so pleasing to Mandel'shtam, were dedicated) rather than exchanging them for the extraneous. The discussion is dedicated throughout to 'the structure and the consistency of Mandel'shtam's theoretical discourse' and not to anything else.

Nor does the author succumb to another short-circuit temptation: a preference for biographical exploration of art over biography as such. Her carefully formulated decision, clearly stated in the introduction, is to avoid approaching Mandel'shtam's theoretical writings as if they were commentaries on his poems. It is clear that Mandel'shtam never pursued such goals, nor did he suffer any unintentional loss of rational control; by contrast, *littérateurs* love to pursue the examination of their own potential and to bypass the potential of poetry and poetic discourse. Mandel'shtam was too sensitive to the texts of other writers to remain caught in the closed circle of his personal needs. The 1923 article 'Vulgata. Notes about Poetry' supplies a striking example of this with comic and even grotesque overtones, but still an example that demonstrates the very substance of Mandel'shtam's manner of thought about literature. The article discusses Pasternak as the great secularizer of the Russian poetic word, one who reoriented poetry from the 'liturgical' speech of the intelligentsia towards its own 'homespun in-rootedness' and the drastic energy of its consonants. Mandel'shtam here is so captured by his own thought that, in order to sharpen the contrast, he aggressively characterizes the practice of 'the minor dictionary' [that is, the employment of ordinary rather than highly rhetorical language] as 'that unfortunate state in which the poet fails to trust his kindred soil and cannot roam freely everywhere.' To exemplify this, Mandel'shtam mentions Sologub, Akhmatova (who was hurt by the remark), and Kuzmin. All of this is truly astounding, for this judgment is diametrically opposed to his own discourses *pro domo mea*: Mandel'shtam could not fail to have known that as a practising poet himself he was an analogue, not of Pasternak, but of Sologub (on whom he bestowed unqualified praise in 1924). Moreover, Mandel'shtam's own vocabulary – even with the notable exceptions that support and strengthen the rule – is, of course, a typical example of a 'minor dictionary,' in which the absence of certain elements is almost more revealing than the presence of others, and where the highest value is accorded to the ability to express the unheard by means of the most common linguistic tools (as in Caesar's Latin or Racine's French). Hence, in order to express this most important quality of the early Pasternak, Mandel'shtam is radically deflected from his own concerns, and forgets 'the extraneous I,' as he observes in one of his poems. This example, although striking and particularly demonstrative, hardly constitutes an exception.

Thus, the limits placed upon the themes of this book are faultlessly justified and executed with precision and consistency. It is all the more interesting that even within these boundaries the author has so much to offer, and that the intensity of the analysis does not diminish but grows tangibly with each succeeding chapter. In keeping with this intensification, the analytic treatment of the *Conversation about Dante* in chapter 5 serves as the most successful exponent of the aptness of the author's chosen methodology. We equally commend the dynamic movement of the last sections towards wider theoretical perspectives. The exposition of the theoretical implications of Mandel'shtam's poetics that concludes this study confirms in the best possible manner the enterprise as a whole.

SERGEI AVERINTZEV
University of Vienna

Acknowledgments

Every book has a prehistory, and since this one is no exception, I shall start my acknowledgments by going back in time. In 1966 Nadezhda Mandel'shtam's memoirs were circulating via Samizdat in Russia and came eventually into our household. The passionate, bitter voice of the poet's widow introduced or perhaps confirmed the beginning of a new stage in our lives, that included my father's signing petitions against the repressions within the Soviet Union, losing his job in 1968, living for four years as a blacklisted academic, and in 1972 coming to the West. Those were unforgettable years, punctuated at times by poignant isolation. The friendship that united the family was cemented by the presence of the voices not only of living but also of departed interlocutors, and the poetry of Osip Mandel'shtam became an inalienable part of our lives. Many years later, during my studies at the University of Toronto, I returned to Mandel'shtam in order to see whether he could help me with articulating that sense of friendship we had received from poetry in general and his poetry in particular.

For these reasons this book was always meant to be a continuation of my conversations with my father, Yuri Glazov, but he is no longer here, and I can no longer tell him the simplest of the phrases that were so habitually exchanged just two years ago. So with this book I want to say to my father that I am deeply grateful for his example of courage, dignity, and love, which became intensified a hundredfold because of the knowledge and love of poetry he so joyously shared with his children. On his deathbed my father repeated to himself Mandel'shtam's poems. The famous lines 'Sisters heaviness and tenderness' were with us during those last days, and friendship with the poet was alive till the end. My own book is then just another page of a story that started so imperceptibly many years ago when my father first told me about this piercing writer who seemed to make one search for a totally new path.

Whatever the prehistory, this made little difference to the academic discourse practised during my doctoral years, and I want to acknowledge the unfailing critical vigilance of my supervisor, Lubomir Dolezel, who, in the face of Mandel'shtam's emotional and passionate poetics, remained unshaken in his devotion to the objective scientific language of Czech structuralism. The thesis emerged as we talked through our differences and I am grateful for the experience of a real dialogue in the middle of this fruitful tension. This acknowledgment would not be complete unless I remind my readers that the creative struggle between student and supervisor took place against the background of a poststructuralism that opposed itself in equal measure to the scientific rigour of structuralism and the emotionalism of metaphoric nuancing, preferring instead to ascribe to all utterances the strategies of power, rhetoric, and manipulation. Every passionate creative battle requires a peacemaker, and ours was right next door – Peter Nesselroth, then the Chairman of the Comparative Literature Department. Against the prevailing fashions of the time, Peter accepted that I had a cogent argument, and the first part of my thesis received the seal of approval. For me, Peter, your help bears the force of legend.

Christopher Barnes and Wladimir Krysinski, the appointed readers for the defence, enthusiastically accepted my thesis and gave me many valuable suggestions. I also owe a huge debt of gratitude to Mario Valdes, who suggested that I forward the manuscript to the University of Toronto Press, into the able hands of Ron Schoeffel. That manuscript was a more comprehensive study of Mandel'shtam and T.S. Eliot. Slowly with the succession of new readers a new book emerged, focused exclusively on Mandel'shtam's place in the world of postmodern poetics. Thus, I thank the readers both for the Press and for the Social Sciences and Humanities Research Council of Canada, and I specifically want to acknowledge the invaluable support and encouragement of Ron Schoeffel, who made it so much easier to return yet again to a new set of revisions. In time, my copyeditor, Joan Bulger, took over from Ron the role of directing and formalizing the manuscript, and even over the distance that separated us I experienced with gratitude her knowledgeable guidance.

For a political immigrant who had at one time lost the right of entry into her country, the reaction of that country's scholars is coloured by deep uncertainty and apprehension. Sergei Sergeievich Averintzev received my work with warm support, and I acknowledge with deep gratitude his helpful corrections and suggestions, and, of course, the Foreword he has written for this book. The family of the painter and sculptor Grigorij Aleksandrovich Israilevich gave me a trusting and warm reception in St Petersburg, and Grigorij Aleksandrovich sent me the pictures of his sculpture dedicated to Mandel'shtam, so that I could use them in my book. I regret that I did not have time to thank him personally: he collapsed and died in the hospital before the photographs arrived in Canada. I feel honoured to be able to acknowledge his and his family's kindness and support.

A revised version of part of my article entitled 'Meaning and Blank: A Theoretical Impasse in the Early Prose Writings of Osip Mandel'shtam,' published in *Slavic Almanach* 5: nos 7–8 (1999): 165–86, is reprinted here with the kind permission of the journal.

The last set of acknowledgments is directed to the people who constitute my life. My mother's help was invaluable as she accepted an unacceptably busy daughter and trusted that eventually all would be well. I am deeply grateful for her understanding. I want to thank my typist, Jane Morris, who believed in this work even if she did not always follow the argument and who was continually accepting yet another revision with the best humour possible. I equally want to thank my stepmother, Marina, for our friendship, which goes all the way back to our Moscow apartment, for her belief in me, and for her gift of babysitting through many summers, and I thank my children, John, Yuri, Maria, and Sarah, for their love and support. Last but not least, I want to thank Kevin Corrigan who understood more years ago than I would like to count that I was in search of a system of poetics which was just out of my reach. Kevin read carefully Mandel'shtam's *Conversation about Dante*, and said: 'Elena, this is simple; the physical step of the journey turns into the foot of the metre, and both are coordinated in every new step of thought, every new stanza on the page. A physical journey carries the trace of the intelligible step.' Well, Kevin, both of us have walked this journey. Thank you.

ELENA GLAZOV-CORRIGAN
December 1999

MANDEL'SHTAM'S POETICS:

A CHALLENGE TO POSTMODERNISM

Mandel'shtam: A Biographical Note

Osip Mandel'shtam belongs to that formidable pleiad of extraordinary Russian poets born in or around the last decade of the nineteenth century, poets whose work and lives became inseparable from the cataclysmic history of post-revolutionary Russia: Vladimir Maiakovsky (chosen by Stalin as the first and best poet of the Revolution), Boris Pasternak, Marina Tsvetaeva, Anna Akhmatova. In *Safe Conduct* Pasternak singled out Maiakovsky not as the best but as a twin brother of this newborn country, both poet and country pervaded by the strangeness of the epoch itself. Mandel'shtam's strangeness, however, went beyond that of his land or his time, and for this reason, perhaps, the age was not kind to him and found no laurels for the poet during his lifetime.

Osip Mandel'shtam was born in Warsaw on 15 January 1891 into the family of a Jewish leather tradesman. Shortly after his birth the family moved to Pavlovsk, a town just outside St Petersburg. The children's education was highly valued in the family, and in 1900 Mandel'shtam was sent to Tenishev School, one of the best of St Petersburg's educational institutions. In 1907 he went abroad, studied in Paris, and then visited Switzerland and Italy.

Soon after his return in 1910 Mandel'shtam entered St Petersburg University and quickly became a notable figure among the young poets of the city. Not only did he appear at the lectures and poetry readings held in the famous tower of the symbolist poet Viacheslav Ivanov, but he also joined forces with Nikolai Gumilev and Anna Akhmatova, and thus the acmeist movement was born. Opposing itself to symbolism and to the emerging futurism, acmeism proclaimed its allegiance to the freedom of the word to be and to mean what it is, which gave the young poets a sufficient platform to strike in all directions with vehemence, energy, and bravado. Happy years ensued, which involved poetic friendships, reading poetry, meeting, debating, and reciting at the Stray Dog Cafe. Two books of poetry brought Mandel'shtam a solid sense of achievement: *Stone* (1913) and *Tristia* (published in 1922). Initially Mandel'shtam welcomed the Revolution with hope and aspiration. He met Nadezhda Khazina in 1919, and the two became inseparable as they faced together the new social and political climate that pervaded Russia.

What took place between 1920 and 1937 has been the subject of many biographical studies and archival investigations. Although his third and last book of poetry, *Poems*, appeared in 1928, by late 1930 (which also happened to be the year of Maiakovsky's suicide) Mandel'shtam began the life of a literary pariah, who managed to write poetry and essays despite highly unfavourable conditions. Sporadically he even managed to achieve a sense of peace, only to lose it again in the real and imaginary episodes of intimidation visited upon him by the literary establishment upon which he necessarily relied for his material well-being. His satiric poem about Stalin, which he recited to several friends and acquaintances in the winter of 1933, led to a night-long search and then arrest in the early hours of 14 May 1934 and subsequently a series of interrogations in the Lubyanka prison in Moscow. A sentence 'to isolate, but preserve' – that is, a three-year exile to Cherdyn, near the Ural Mountains – was virtually a miraculous reprieve. The place of exile was later changed to the town of Voronezh, and this meant that Mandel'shtam's inevitable execution was postponed until further notice. The Mandel'shtams returned from exile in May 1937; his second arrest came on 2 May 1938.

On 2 August 1938 the poet was sentenced to five years' hard labour for counter-revolutionary activities. Mandel'shtam's prison convoy stopped at the transit centre near Vladivostok where at the beginning of December the camp was ravaged by a typhoid epidemic. One of the last surviving recollections of Mandel'shtam depicts the poet shivering from fever and cold and killing lice with his bare fingers. Mandel'shtam's death is dated 27 December 1938. The official cause of death was 'heart failure and sclerosis.'

Mandel'shtam's wife, Nadezhda, dedicated the rest of her life to the preservation of his manuscripts and his memory. If it had not been for her efforts and those of his family's close friends, his late work, like his life itself, would have been completely obliterated.

Born on the western frontier of the Russian empire, the poet met his death in Russia's far east, measuring even in this the extremes of a country whose language and poetry would from this time on bear the imprint of his work.

Introduction

Given the apparent impenetrability or the intentionally chaotic nature of Mandel'shtam's prose writings about poetry, contemporary scholarship must eventually confront the following question: do Mandel'shtam's observations on poetry make a substantial contribution to poetics? Ours is not an age that grants privileged status to what the writer has to say about the writing process. Even according to that benign man of letters Northrop Frye, 'The poet's task is to deliver the poem in as uninjured a state as possible, and if the poem is alive, it is equally anxious to be rid of him, and screams to be cut loose from his private memories and associations, his desire for self-expression and all the other navel-strings and feeding tubes of his ego' (Frye 1963, 11). Poets, then, are to enter into theory on a par with other investigators and readers of literature, and if they wish to succeed, they must pay close attention to the established metalanguages, be they scientific, political, philological, or philosophical. On a sinister note, one may remember that in Mandel'shtam's native land Soviet writers needed to have much more than an university degree in political literacy to proffer their opinions in print on the essential nature of art.

All in all, the twentieth century was not propitious for Mandel'shtam's entrance into contemporary poetics. His short life, his homelessness, the Soviet ban on the publication and free discussion of his work, his arrest and death, the whole mind-wrenching story which in the last several decades has been documented in a growing number of studies – all seem to play havoc with the established critical consensus that literary work and a writer's biography have at best only an accidental connection. In spite of postmodern poetics Mandel'shtam's poetry was read and continues to be read in the context of his tragic biography, but his biography has also postponed for half a century his entrance into the debates of literary theory. Furthermore, the historical circumstances of Mandel'shtam's life constitute only a partial cause of the poet's absence from modern-day poetics. The character of the man himself and the manner of his writing contributed greatly to the perception that he was too erratic, too impressionistic, and too impulsive a thinker to deserve the status of a theoretician.

Indeed, in which theoretical school would one place Mandel'shtam? Among the scientific investigators of the text, or among tenacious and laborious students of the philosophy of aesthetics? Not if we listen to his own voice: 'I have no manuscript, no notebooks, no archives. I have no handwriting, for I never write. I alone in Russia work with my voice, while all around me consummate swine are writing. What the hell kind of writer am I?' (II, 183; 317). Even less so if we listen to Nadezhda Mandel'shtam's description of the contents of his bookcase: 'Despite his interest in the philosophy of culture and biology, M. could not stomach Hegel (any more than Kant), and his enthusiasm for Marx had not outlasted his school years. Just before his arrest in 1934 he had declined Engels' *Dialectic of Nature* when it was offered to him as a gift by Lezhnev, the former editor of *Rossia*, to which M. had once contributed' (1970b, 241).

Should one then include Mandel'shtam the theoretician among the Russian formalists, most of whom he knew well? He certainly had an intellectual and personal friendship with both Yurij Tynianov (Levin et al. 1974/5) and Victor Shklovsky, and it was Shklovsky's family in particular who looked after the ostracized Osip and Nadezhda before Mandel'shtam's final arrest in May 1938. Yet, although Mandel'shtam's debt to the formalists is a complex issue, even a cursory glance at his relationship with them precludes him from being classified as one of them. An irrevocable historical fact stands at the centre of his relationship with the formalists: the philosophical and literary battle between Mandel'shtam's acmeists and the futurists (who were close friends of the formalists) became dangerously politicized in the 1920s, when the former futurists emerged as spokesmen for the new Soviet art and made Mandel'shtam a target for their attacks against antimodernist archaisms. Something of this bitter history appears in Nadezhda Mandel'shtam's memoirs when she speaks in the 1960s about Roman Jakobson's rather late acceptance of her husband: 'Nor was he recognized by the avant-garde. To the end of his life Aseyev cursed anybody who dared as much as mention M.'s name in his presence ... The group whose purity was so zealously guarded by Kirsanov also included Roman Jakobson and the

Aragon family. They too seem to be wavering a little nowadays, but this is all jiggery-pokery, a matter of tactics, I would happily see them return to their normal state of hostility to Mandel'shtam' (1974, 335–6). Old history aside, Mandel'shtam was clearly aware of the real significance of formalism, and at times he must have been very close to the formalists in their attempts to make poetics a modern scientific discipline. His essays of the early 1920s point simultaneously to his attraction and yet resistance to the school. 'The Literary Moscow' (1922), for example, registers his serious consideration of formalism's achievements, albeit partially prompted by his resentment against Tsvetaeva during yet another of their estrangements: 'Recent experience has shown that the only woman eligible to join the poet's circle with the rights of the new muse is the Russian science [*nauka*] of poetics, summoned to life by Potebnja and Andrei Belyi, and grown mature in the formalist school of Eikhenbaum, Zhirmunsky, and Shklovsky' (II, 327; 146).

Nonetheless, understanding is not equivalent to belonging. Mandel'shtam's theoretical writings exhibit such a flair for similes and metaphors that his very language had to be inimical to the formalists' search for the scientific characteristics of literariness [*literaturnost'*], a literariness which, they believed, 'makes a given work a work of art' (Jakobson 1921, 11). Moreover, while the formalists opposed their own scientific investigations to what they called the 'conglomeration of homespun disciplines' (Jakobson 1921, 11), Mandel'shtam proclaimed his allegiance to a homespun [*domashnyi*] principle of philology and insisted in 'On the Nature of the Word' (1922) that the phenomenon of philology is 'domestic and intimate,' 'a university seminar, the family' (II, 249; 123). Clearly at the immediate level of appearances at least, one cannot classify Mandel'shtam among the scientific investigators of literary discourse.

Still, Mandel'shtam's lengthy (and yet paradoxically creative) five-year crisis began in 1924, just prior to Trotsky's attack on the formalists in *Literature and Revolution* (1924), a work that initiated their public silencing. In the 1930s Mandel'shtam himself faced ever-increasing harassment, and finally labour camp and death. Mandel'shtam's ideas returned posthumously to philology in the 1970s and 1980s, the years when the Western and eventually Eastern European literary fields were no longer dominated by scientific formalism, but rather adopted the free and not so free play of poststructuralism. While Mandel'shtam cannot be considered a proponent of or exemplary spokesman for either of these two theoretical schools (which frame his absence from literature and philology), nevertheless both movements throw light upon some of his otherwise puzzling pronouncements.

Much of what would have been exasperating and unacceptable to the ear of the formalists sounds by the end of the century decidedly, even fashionably, postmodern. Indeed, one cannot read through many passages of Mandel'shtam's theoretical work without recognizing such commonplaces of poststructuralist metalanguage as the Derridian emphasis on orality in contrast to the written word, and on the dissemination of *écriture* or writing. Contemporary theoretical preoccupations come into play when we observe Mandel'shtam's emphasis on *absence* rather than *presence* in the literary tradition, or, for example, when we have our first foretaste of what becomes in Roland Barthes *le bruissement de la langue* [the noise of language] as early as 1921 in Mandel'shtam's description of language in *The Noise of Time*. Poststructuralist concepts abound when Mandel'shtam views himself as a marginalized trace, a Russian-Jewish *raznochinets*, or educated member of the intelligentsia, belonging to no definite social class and articulating heterogeneous babble, rather than language:

> A *raznochinets* needs no memory – it is enough for him to tell of the books he has read, and his biography is done. Where for happy generations the epic speaks in hexameters and chronicles I have merely the sign of the hiatus, and between me and the age there lies a pit, a moat, filled with clamorous time, the place where a family and reminiscences of a family ought to have been. What was it my family wished to say? I do not know. It was tongue-tied from birth – but it had, nevertheless, something that it might have said. Over my head and over the head of many of my contemporaries there hangs congenital tongue-tie. We were not taught to speak but to babble – and only by listening to the swelling noise of the age and bleached by the foam on the crest of its wave did we acquire a language. (II, 99; Brown 1965, 122–3)

Indeed, the investigator of Mandel'shtam starts not merely with the hiatus of an exterminated voice but with the loss of what may have been a form-creating intellectual vision. The very character of Mandel'shtam's essays – their lack of clarity and coherence, their impenetrable, thickly metaphoric texture, which may, indeed, be characterized as babbling and tongue-tied – presents, as in the quotation above, a formidable challenge to the easy understanding of Mandel'shtam's poetics. Yet the same qualities that complicate his prose and imbue it with poststructuralist echoes also tend to separate and isolate his writing. The difficulty seems to be as follows: Mandel'shtam introduces such ideas as the noise of time and hiatus or absence not as concepts but as metaphors, using his poetic images as a way of exploring the new inarticulate or 'tongue-tied' territory. His images are not concepts: they are a way of tasting, smelling, feeling the space. However, this very dependence becomes almost a defect in an academic setting, where metaphor is a suspect vehicle for conveying ideological and political presences. In the words of Jacques Derrida, 'a metaphor would be forbidden. The presence/absence of the trace ... carries in itself the problem of the letter and the spirit' (1976, 71). One Mandel'shtam scholar, Gregory Freidin, articulates this poststructuralist suspicion of metaphors and argues that Mandel'shtam's reliance on specific and recurring images arrests the poet's theoretical and philosophical search: 'The ideological frame of reference that Mandel'shtam had absorbed in the course of his life left him and many of his contemporaries with a limited choice' and resulted in his 'inability to reject this procrustean dilemma altogether, to substitute it for another, more varied discourse' (1987, 231). Another recent critic, Nancy Pollack, argues, in contrast, that the thickly metaphoric texture does not so much arrest Mandel'shtam's thought within a particularized ideological context as protect its meaning until the successful reader finally discovers a 'piece of azure concealed in ... clay' (1987, 470) and deciphers the poet's meaning.

The essential aims of this book are to recover something of Mandel'shtam's voice and to resolve a curious tension, and yet suggestive interplay, between Mandel'shtam's writings on poetry and the problematic and challenging field of postmodern poetics. By the early 1930s Mandel'shtam had already predicted that the theory of poetry stood on the threshold of the discovery of a new science, which he named alternatively the physiology of reading or the reflexology of speech, 'a science still not established, of the spontaneous psycho-physiological influence of the word on those who are conversing, on the audience surrounding them, and on the speaker himself, as well as on the means by which he communicates his urge to speak' (II, 404; 434). On a more anecdotal level there is also evidence that the poet seriously claimed that the key to this new science was to be found in his *Conversation about Dante*. The story is preserved that in Voronezh he daily promised a young critic, Sergei Rudakov, that he would give him this key; whether or not Mandel'shtam carried through on his promise is not known, since Rudakov himself was arrested and killed during the war (Gershtein 1983). In this study I have attempted to discern whether the difficult text of the *Conversation about Dante* does actually embody Mandel'shtam's mature poetics.

Mandel'shtam has not lacked critical attention: indeed, his poetry has become celebrated and is much analysed. The studies of Averintzev, Brown, Bukhshtab, Etkind, Freidin, Ginsburg, Ivanov, Harris, Levin, Przybylski, Ronen, Segal, Taranovsky, Timenchik, Toporov, Zholkovsky (the list is by no means complete) have established a coherent critical framework for the understanding of Mandel'shtam's poetry and some of his prose. There has been little investigation of his theoretical works, however, with the notable exception of Pollak's recent study (1995),[1] and, because of Mandel'shtam's manner of writing, no critical consensus on the validity and the appropriateness of his insight into poetry has emerged.

The study of the language of Mandel'shtam's prose has, therefore, come to be the essential focus of this investigation. Two methodological premises, which one may identify with the views of Freidin and Pollack respectively, can be seen as the two contrasting poles between which other approaches to Mandel'shtam's poetics can be located: Freidin's view that the metaphoric density of Mandel'shtam's prose eventually limits his insight, and Pollack's implicit belief that the metaphors protect the vision as if in a hermetic covering. This study sides to some extent with Pollack's work except that, instead of searching for a system of thought located inside a supposed metaphoric density, my investigation traces the transformation of Mandel'shtam's images by means of the chronological order of the prose works and uses this transformation as a key to his poetics.

In other words, this book demonstrates that if Mandel'shtam's poetics is to be found anywhere, it is to be discovered not in the unity of vision underneath the metaphor but rather within the metaphor, which continuously changes and undergoes a series of metamorphoses. Through a proper chronological study of the changes in the symbolic language of Mandel'shtam's theoretical works this book provides a guide to the development and transformation of Mandel'shtam's key theoretical concepts, and a new methodological context for approaching his theoretical works. Incidentally, the book also demonstrates that the *Conversation about Dante* does in fact contain Mandel'shtam's mature poetics, but it situates this final theoretical position not in a single insight but rather in the understanding of poetics as a journey, that is, as an inclusive gathering of the various chronological changes of images and thoughts.

Introduction 11

Such a view of Mandel'shtam's language facilitates the book's primary and essential aim: to place Mandel'shtam's work in poetic theory alongside the concerns of postmodern poetics. A coincidence of many aspects of these theoretical discourses separated by time and place called for comparative study, and in turn dictated the structure of this book. The challenging suggestiveness of Mandel'shtam's observations about his craft also explains why each of the six chapters in this book pursues a specific theoretical problem. The first four chapters trace the changes and problems in Mandel'shtam's thinking, starting from his early essays in 1913 and leading up to the *Conversation about Dante* of 1933. Chapter 1 deals with what would become the central premise of poststructuralism: the binary opposition of absence/presence, and the need to decentre the privileged status of presence and meaning. It is precisely this binary opposition (the poet's first attempt to create a poetics) that resulted in a crisis and logical impasse that Mandel'shtam did not overcome until the early 1930s. Chapters 2, 3, and 4 examine Mandel'shtam's thought regarding three central *loca* of communication: first, the word as such; second, the effect of the poetic word; and third, the patterns of reception; or, in other words, 'sender,' 'message,' and 'addressee.' Again, all three chapters argue that the poet's position on communication can be recovered only in a chronological diary of the changes in the imagery and metaphors that describe these three concepts of poetics.

Chapter 5 is the centre of the book. It shows how the mature transformation of these key concepts does not privilege any single definition of these moments, but instead reintegrates them within a schema of changing landscapes of poetic discourse, each of which is presented as a specific step in the organic development of communication in both poetry and science. Concentrating primarily upon the relationship between *Conversation about Dante* and *Journey to Armenia* (roughly contemporary works, the latter being written during Mandel'shtam's travels to Armenia, arranged for him by Nikolai Bukharin), chapter 5 provides a guide to Mandel'shtam's mature poetics. In contrast to most investigations of Mandel'shtam, which have addressed the impenetrability of his work, this study insists both upon a chronological diary within the theoretical works themselves and upon an internal logic in Mandel'shtam's presentation of images. Chapter 5 is accompanied by a table outlining in schematic form the organizational principle of images in Mandel'shtam's *Conversation about Dante*, images the work shares with the *Journey to Armenia* (108–9 below). Chapter 6 concludes this investigation with a discussion of some of the theoretical implications of Mandel'shtam's work, which it seeks to situate in the context of modern and postmodern poetics.

Since the major focus of this work is to uncover the structure and consistency of Mandel'shtam's apparently impenetrable and disconnected theoretical discourse, I have resisted at every point the temptation to introduce images from his poetry or analyses of individual poems in order to confirm or supplement the emerging theoretical structures. It is my view that Mandel'shtam's theoretical insights should not be compelled in a procrustean fashion to serve the critical investigation of his poetry. His writings on poetry should first establish a coherent philosophical and theoretical groundwork for a poetics. Theory of poetry and criticism of individual poems must, therefore, remain distinct. However, some of the major findings of this study will undoubtedly add to our understanding of Mandel'shtam's poetry and of the art of criticism as such.

This book attempts to restore some of Mandel'shtam's theoretical views to the position in history that they lost because of the tragedy of his age and of his own life. I argue that Mandel'shtam's poetics not only anticipates many of the later developments in poetic theory in the twentieth century but also frequently offers a major challenge to contemporary theory. It has been an impulse of modern-day poetics to limit poetry to the artistic enterprise, relegating poetic images to the merely decorative, or rhetorical, or political. Furthermore, there has been considerable effort to segregate poets from theoreticians. Pasternak in a somewhat different context laments this fact and comments that the poet may be allowed to translate Shakespeare, but not to introduce his translation, since for introductions there is already a specific class of scholars with whom poets cannot compete. Mandel'shtam believes that poets possess insight into poetic structure in an intense but practical fashion. I offer this work as a contribution to the poetics of poets, in the belief that Mandel'shtam's views are not without applicability to the development of modern poetic theories.

1

Meaning and Blank: The First Decade of Mandel'shtam's Poetics

The progression of Mandel'shtam's ideas about poetry can be traced in the transformation of images united by intuitive, metaphoric associations. Within these rich series of metaphoric and imaginative associations Mandel'shtam's early essays develop a binary opposition between word and blank that foreshadows the theoretical development of postmodernism. There is definite if almost imperceptible development, hitherto unrecognized, in Mandel'shtam's position from the theoretical confidence of 'The Morning of Acmeism,' 'Remarks on Chenier,' and 'Peter Chaadaev' to the eventual sense of loss, and even despair, of 'Pushkin and Skriabin,' in which there is so profound an impasse that one may question whether Mandel'shtam ever completed it[1] and suggest instead that the fragments which he published in the 1928 edition were the original form of the essay. In fact, the peculiar nature of these early essays resides in the growing lack of proportion between the maturing power of Mandel'shtam's poetic dramatization and his diminishing confidence in the correctness of his first theoretical position.

1 Binary Opposition in Mandel'shtam's Early Essays, 1913–1915

The notions of absence and presence, so familiar to the investigators of contemporary poetics in the past fifteen years or so, are associated with such different thinkers as Friedrich Nietzsche, Martin Heidegger, Jacques Derrida, and Wolfgang Iser. Heidegger's Nothing and Derrida's deconstruction of the western tradition as an exclusive movement of the metaphysics of presence,[2] although emerging from different philosophical traditions, have helped to form the postmodern approach to the text. In the context of reader-reception theory, and independent of Derrida, Iser reintroduced the privileged position of absence when he proposed that the blank or break (i.e., a suspension in the connectibility of the text which he called, after R.D. Laing, 'no-thing') was the single essential principle for stimulating or intensifying the reader's imagination or, in his words, 'the act of ideation' (Iser 1978, 189). Thus, there is implicit consensus in the field of postmodern poetics that, in order to dislocate the binary opposition of presence and absence, it is the blank and not presence that must be granted a privileged position.

In his theoretical works on literature and poetry Mandel'shtam has not entered into this debate. In the academic world where metaphor is suspect for reintroducing obsolete political concepts,[3] Mandel'shtam's prose relies too exclusively upon metaphoric expression and unusual movements of images to have influenced the debates of postmodern philology. 'Tongue-tied' [*kosnoiazychnaia*] was the description Mandel'shtam chose for his own family because of its peculiar flight from the Jewish tradition into the 'Great Russian speech, impoverished by intellectual clichés' (II, 66; Brown 1965, 82). His own poems, he was hoping, had been 'steadily encroaching on Russian poetry ... eventually to merge with it, thereby altering something of its structure and composition.'[4] His hope notwithstanding, one may observe that Mandel'shtam escaped only partially his parents' fate, repeating instead in the tragedy of his life the ancestral loss of voice: 'What was it my family wished to say? I do not know. It was tongue-tied from birth – but it had, nevertheless, something that it might have said' (II, 99; Brown 1965, 110). The hiatus of an exterminated intellectual vision concealed under the layers of metaphoric covering is bequeathed to the readers of Mandel'shtam's theoretical work. Yet Mandel'shtam's images in their recurrence and transformation may still reveal the story.

A chronological approach to the change and development of major images, themes, and concepts, starting from the very beginning of Mandel'shtam's theoretical writings and from his earliest metaphoric expression, is, therefore, necessary in order to identify a real point of reference in his sea of images, all vaguely suggestive and reminiscent of one another, and to provide a proper basis for the intelligent investigation of how the poet viewed his own craft and how his poetics matured over the years. I shall start therefore at the beginning with four early essays, 'The Morning of Acmeism' (1913), 'Remarks on Chénier' (1914–15), 'Peter Chaadaev' (1915), and 'Pushkin and Skriabin' (1915–19). The ideas and images of these essays are frequently employed by many critics to explain the works of the 1930s, as if the poet's views remained constant throughout.[5] However, if one charts carefully the progression and transformation of images, which initially appear homogeneous and united by intuitive, metaphoric association, one discovers first of all that within the rich series of imaginative associations Mandel'shtam was, at the beginning of his theoretical work, a child of his time for he too developed a binary opposition between word and blank and welcomed unreservedly the Dionysiac powers of rupture. It is, perhaps, more of a surprise to see how, much to his own dismay, he eventually found that the dichotomy between presence and blank (when left undifferentiated) became a source not of power but of irreversible entropy.

The starting point of this study is the image of the poet as conductor in 'The Morning of Acmeism.' The poet does not organize his words according to an intended goal or thought, but simply harmonizes their chorus.[6] Meaning, therefore, is not presented as artificial organization, but rather as an organic harmony within a choral music that springs out of words themselves. Just as the Gothic cathedral of Notre Dame is a 'triumph of physiology, its Dionysian orgy,' so the poem, according to Mandel'shtam, should possess 'the divine physiology, the infinite complexity of our own dark organism' (II, 323; 63). However, the youthful vigour of the essay masks a logical contradiction, for in the same space Mandel'shtam not only compares words to stones, but speaks of writing as building (II, 321–2; 62), thus equating the living complexity of a 'divine physiology' with the inanimate solidity of stone and then with the artifice of cathedrals composed of stones. This implicit contradiction is intensified by his depiction of a poet who, no longer a builder or conductor, is invited to 'prove and prove endlessly' (II, 324; 64). The striking images Mandel'shtam employs make the essay very readable, but the contradictions between inanimate structure, living physiology, and ceaseless performance might well have been responsible for Nikolai Gumilev's rejection of this article as a program statement of acmeism.[7]

The next essay in chronological order, 'Remarks on Chénier,' attacks precisely the equation between the inanimate solidity of stone and unceasing poetic expression. Indeed, solidity and permanence of expression are made responsible for the moral vacuum of the eighteenth century. Such high moral concepts as *la Verité, la Liberté, la Nature, la Déité,* and *la Vertu* are described as no longer possessing any depth of emotion in the eighteenth century, and this lack itself is responsible for the century's atmosphere of ceaseless moralization: 'It was necessary to repeat them [moral categories] indefatigably since, apparently, they all proved to be insufficiently effective' (II, 293; 75). The continued insistence upon the rightness of these high-minded principles is, in fact, an echo of Mandel'shtam's own depiction of the poet in 'The Morning of Acmeism,' who is to 'prove and prove endlessly,' but on this occasion the depiction is cast in an explicitly ironic key: 'The great principles of the eighteenth century were constantly in motion, in a state of mechanical flurry, like a Buddhist prayer wheel' (II, 293; 75). Even the ancient 'golden ball,' a conception of the Good, which is even-natured and solid, is now in doubt. Solidity itself becomes a sign of the onset of decay: 'This absolute solid character of classical morality, which is by no means imperative or hedonistic, even gives occasion to doubt the moral nature of this consciousness: is it not simply hygiene, that is, a prophylaxis of spiritual health?' (II, 293–4; 75).

The word 'imperative' above is central, for starting from the 'Remarks on Chénier' this power associated with poetry becomes linked for Mandel'shtam with the notion of a hypnotism which the poet exercises over reality.[8] Thus, a hypnotic value can be achieved by poetry not when poetry constitutes a solid unity or a ceaseless performance but only when a rupture or disruptive change is permitted to appear in its developing theme. Mandel'shtam illustrates this by arguing that, whereas the over-rationalized tragedy of the eighteenth century has lost its appeal, every aspect of art hitherto ignored has increased its own longevity and dynamism. Accordingly, Chénier is depicted as a true poet for behaving like a lapsed schoolboy, and for being drawn to forgotten, unanalysed subjects: 'All that was alive and healthy was diverted into trifles because they demanded less supervision, while a child with seven governesses (tragedy) grew up into a luxuriant sterile flower precisely because "the great principles" leaned over its cradle. Chénier's poetic course is a departure, almost a flight, from the great principles to the living waters of poetry' (II, 294; 76).

What is characteristic of Mandel'shtam's thought here, and significant for its future development, is his belief that Chénier's flight from the great principles, far from weakening them, actually gives them new life, returning 'flesh and substance' to 'Liberty, Equality, Fraternity' (II, 298; 79). In this Mandel'shtam, as yet indirectly, adopts the Nietzschean position that in order to have an imperative, living character, poetry must include both presence and absence, statement and rupture, permanence and flux.[9] Furthermore, there is already a suggestion that the hypnotic, revitalizing power of poetry springs rather from absence, break, or rupture than from statement or presence.[10] This also explains

Mandel'shtam's depiction of the hypnotic, imperative power of Chénier's iambic metre (i.e., blank or unstressed, followed by emphasis or stress), which 'descends on Chénier like a fury. Imperative. Dionysian. Obsessive' (II, 297; 78). Again the Nietzschean emphasis is clear. Mandel'shtam echoes the fashionable view that the spirit of music springs from the Dionysian element, that is, the unlimited and disruptive principle.[11]

Thus, the technique of alternation between statement and blank explains not only the curious format of the article itself, in which every three sentences (at most) are followed by a break or blank, and then in turn by a new paragraph, and so on, but also the central images of Mandel'shtam's poetry of the period, namely the image of Persephone in *Tristia* (a goddess who spends six months on earth and six months in Hades), an image which accompanies such key motifs as word, life, and Psyche.[12]

Not only does Persephone's proximity to death clearly explain her role in these central topoi, but Mandel'shtam's rather curious depiction of the romantic poets as 'a necklace of dead nightingales' at last becomes comprehensible, as a presence formed out of privation or absence, and Chénier's role in bringing classicism and romanticism together can finally be seen as that of a person who unites presence and absence. 'But the Romantic poetics presupposes an outburst, unexpectedness, it seeks after effect, unanticipated by acoustics, and it itself knows not what the song may cost ... The laws of poetry sleep in its larynx and all of Romantic poetry, like a necklace of dead nightingales, will not convey, will not betray its secrets, does not know its legacy. A dead nightingale cannot teach anyone how to sing. Chénier ingeniously found the middle road between the Classical and Romantic manner' (II, 296; 77). The similarity between this image of the necklace of dead nightingales and the earlier image of stones in the Gothic cathedral permits a comparative exposition of the role of absence or blank. In the 'Morning of Acmeism' Mandel'shtam was clearly interested in the hypnotic power of the song of stones. Here, however, the notion of hypnotism, or the 'essence of sweetness,' is directly associated with a moment of silence as loss, or the moment of the song's arrest.[13] Furthermore, the essence of hypnotism cannot be set out in concrete, 'stony' outlines; it is an outburst, an essence of unexpectedness that is forever out of reach, while all the time, like a bracelet, it lies in one's hand.

The notion that a dynamism proceeds directly from the occlusion of content may help to explain why the major argument of the 'Remarks on Chénier,' namely, the necessary coexistence of presence and absence, is never explicitly stated or introduced. Even the word 'hiatus' within the Alexandrine metre was consciously omitted from the main body of the essay and can be found only in the Addenda (III, 144; 82). According to Mandel'shtam's theory, the argument lives within the essay precisely when it is not stated openly but introduced obliquely as the only link at every level of discussion between observations which are otherwise disjointed: in other words, it lives in the analysis of the poet's subject matter (when, for example, Pushkin is preferred to Chénier for his ability to withdraw from his own passionate sentiment – II, 298; 78); in the depiction of poetic influence; in the discussion of rhythm and metre; in the assessment of intellectual and moral principles; in the manner of the argument's presentation logically and graphically; and even as a matter of poetical practicality when Pushkin is praised for being practical in writing a line, while in the content of the line one again recognizes the subject matter of the essay, presence and absence: 'Zdes' natisk plamennyi, a tam otpor surovyi [Here a fiery onslaught, and there a stern rebuff]' (II, 299; 80). The concept lives because it is absent; it resides literally between the lines.

This analysis of 'Remarks on Chénier' reveals the acute difficulty that underlies any analysis of Mandel'shtam's prose, where the logic of the thought resides in the logic of the image's development, or even in the transmutation of one image into another, but is never formally stated outside the imaginative structure. However, if we adopt the view that the position formulated above does represent the logical progression of 'Remarks on Chénier,' then the development of thought in 'Peter Chaadaev' and 'Pushkin and Skriabin,' otherwise frequently obscure to the point of self-contradiction, is much easier to grasp. For example, it has long been understood that Mandel'shtam praises Chaadaev for identifying Russia's major contribution to the West as its gift of moral freedom. However, there has been no attempt to explain how this positive view can be reconciled with the singularly negative description of Russia as nothingness and dead weight.[14] Similarly, Skriabin's 'Hellenism,' which is described as pre-Christian yet typically Russian in its passion for salvation, has resisted exposition.[15] Both issues become explicable in the light of the theory of statement-blank in 'Remarks on Chénier.'

Mandel'shtam presents Chaadaev as a person of unparalleled integrity, a person organized and unified by one central idea: 'The idea organized his personality, not only his intellect, and gave his personality a structure, an architecture, subordinated it entirely and, as a reward for absolute subordination, granted it absolute freedom' (II, 295; 83). This absolute freedom granted to Chaadaev was, according to Mandel'shtam, the raw, Russian spirit, amorphous and, therefore, incapable of unity. Chaadaev is here presented as a unified movement-thought-statement and Russia, which surrounds him from his birth and throughout his life, is a blank: 'He had enough courage to tell Russia to her face the terrible truth – that she was cut off from universal unity, excommunicated from history, from God's "teacher of the people"' (II, 286; 84). As always in Mandel'shtam, this image is then presented in a series of transformations, and it is particularly striking in its idea of history as a unified structure from which Russia is excluded: 'The fact is that Chaadaev's conception of history excludes the possibility of any access to the historical path. In keeping with this conception one can already be on the historical path prior to its beginning. History was Jacob's ladder, down which the angels descended from heaven to earth. It must be called sacred due to the continuity of the spirit of grace that inhabits it ... Neither the will alone nor good intentions are sufficient to 'begin' history anew. Unity cannot be created, invented or learned' (II, 286; 84). In this passage we have a clear example of the transmutation of the poet's key images, which signal to the reader the changes of thought that have evidently taken place but are never directly stated. Jacob's ladder in this passage is a new presentation of what was in 1913 the Gothic cathedral and in 1914 the necklace of dead nightingales; only on this occasion the two images are blended together and the original structure of stone includes the blanks or breaks as part of its very nature. This is further confirmed by the image of the stones' slumber (no longer a song) in the final passages of the essay: 'every stone slumbers covered by the patina of time and enveloped in its firmament' (II, 290; 88). Russia's freedom brought by Chaadaev to the West must, therefore, bring new life to the stony structures of history, just as the spaces between the rungs of the ladder permit the free movement of thought.

The relationship between history and the passage of time is also depicted as a relationship between a unified movement and a blank. Time outside the generating unity of the 'idea' is nothingness, or mere 'progress,' that is, simple succession: 'Unity cannot be created ... In its absence one has, at best, not history but "progress" – the mechanical movement of a clock hand and not the sacred bond and succession of events' (II, 286; 84). The passage of time blunts Chaadaev's thought. He cannot ascend Jacob's ladder, and the structure of his thought, that is, its gothic, ideal unity, is arrested by time. In fact, within the logic of the image time intermingles with the emptiness of the space, an emptiness initially attacked by Chaadaev's writing: 'Had his Gothic thought resigned itself and ceased to raise its lancet towers to the sky? No, Chaadaev had not resigned himself, although time's blunt file had touched even his thoughts' (II, 287; 85). Even 'standing, not passing' time is depicted as a ring surrounding history or thought. Although Mandel'shtam seeks to distinguish two conceptions of time and to give 'eternal' time the metaphoric overtones of the Aristotelian unmoved mover, the image of time embracing history, just as empty space engulfs the cathedral, becomes in turn equated with the image of an emptiness that is at once destructive and creative:[16] 'Is this not an omnipotent symbol of time – not of the one which passes but of that which is immobile through which everything passes but which itself stands imperturbable and through which and by means of which it is perfected' (II, 286–7; 85).

A similar metaphoric structure (i.e., statement-blank) pervades Mandel'shtam's description of Chaadaev's writings. Mandel'shtam suggests that the fragmentary nature of these writings does not presuppose a fragmented movement of thought. Rather, the presence of Russia in Chaadaev's writings, by means of the presence of breaks between fragments, makes him a true Russian philosopher. In order to emphasize the heaviness and reality of that absence, Mandel'shtam replaces the original image of absence as background or foil [*phon*] in his earlier version with the new image of the prepared canvas which is invisible in the completed painting [*grunt*].[17] 'To understand the form and spirit of the *Philosophical Letters*, it is necessary to imagine that Russia serves as their vast and awesome canvas [*grunt*]. The gaping wasteland among the well-known, written fragments is the missing thought about Russia' (II, 286; 86). However, since the emptiness of Russia also presupposes freedom, a gift that, according to Mandel'shtam, even the pope himself embraces, we are invited to conjecture that Russia's emptiness will make the slumbering stones of the 'Gothic cathedral'[18] wake up and sing: 'This freedom is worth the majesty petrified in architectural forms, it is as valuable as everything the West has created in the realm of material cultures, and I see the Pope himself ... has arisen to greet this freedom' (II, 290; 88). The fragmented presentation of the unified idea is, therefore, a sign of its vitality and dynamism, and in this light Chaadaev's real breakthrough is literally the blanks between fragments: a 'mute thought about Russia.' Thus, Chaadaev, a man who symbolizes unity for Mandel'shtam, is praised for both fleeing from and yet incorporating indefiniteness, for both leaving Russia and returning to it, and therefore for being able to put the blankness of Russia's essence to constructive application; he is 'one completely free man who is able to make use of his freedom' (II, 291; 88).

One cannot determine on the basis of 'Remarks on Chénier' or 'Peter Chaadaev' whether in 1915 Mandel'shtam held to the necessity of blanks only on the level of the presentation of ideas or whether he was inclining towards the idea that any generative structure possesses indefiniteness in its very essence. While the 'solid Good' is presented as an impotent 'golden ball' in 'Remarks on Chénier' and the unified West is found to be lacking in freedom in 'Peter Chaadaev,' the unity of thought still remains 'the immortal spring of undying Rome.' It is clear, however, that although the blank is presented as either negative or highly ambiguous (death, explosion, break, emptiness, raw material, plague, threat, blunt file, suffocating non-being), its role within structure becomes progressively more valuable.[19] While the blank in itself possesses a negative nature, and while those who cannot combine it with a desire for solidity and unity are 'worthy of woe' (II, 292; 89), its presence within a structure allows for freedom. Mandel'shtam even suggests that the playfulness of creativity comes from the blank itself.[20] Again, this is never explicitly stated. Nonetheless, the ending of 'Peter Chaadaev' advocates a return to Russia's blankness as the only possibility for the creative artist. This is all the more significant since Mandel'shtam is aware of the philosophical implications of this appeal. At the opening of the essay the form-matter duality is clearly evoked: 'Still more unusual for Russia was Chaadaev's dualism, the sharp distinction he drew between matter and spirit. In a young country, a country of half-animated matter and half-dead spirit, the grey-haired antinomy of the inert clod and the organized idea was almost unknown' (II, 284; 83).

There is, therefore, a growing tendency in Mandel'shtam, still closely checked and balanced in 'Peter Chaadaev,' to attribute the birth of the creative impulse to the role of the blank, to 'the inert clod' or to matter, if we employ the philosophical context of the article.[21] Mandel'shtam's uncertainty, however, is also evident; this appears particularly in his conception of 'immobile time,' discussed above, which he depicts simultaneously as measure ('through which everything passes'), metre ('by means of which everything is perfected'), surrounding blank or medium ('in which' it is perfected), and even potential source and content (the cumulative effect of the whole image). Thus, he is ultimately uncertain whether the blank and the source are synonymous, but he certainly entertains this possibility on the level of the images he employs.[22]

2 Evidence of the Growing Theoretical Crisis

The essay 'Pushkin and Skriabin,' which has apparently survived only in fragments, was written sometime between 1915 and 1919. In 1921, according to his widow, Mandel'shtam assessed it as his most important article and decried its loss. In 1928, while preparing an edition of his collected essays, he again searched frantically for the manuscript.[23] Perhaps, however, he never had a final copy, and the article remained in unfinished drafts.

The essay is, indeed, one of his most elusive prose works. Arguments supported by one part of the essay are refuted by another. It is more than probable that this essay, whose writing spanned Russia's most turbulent years, reflects the development of views which are becoming progressively more difficult to reconcile. I would argue further that the essay continues its unveiling of the statement-blank theory, which it develops and brings to what we might say is its logical conclusion, which is also effectively a dead-end. The elusiveness of the essay is to be attributed, then, not merely to its fragmentary character but probably to a crisis in Mandel'shtam's own theory, a theory which he nevertheless attempts to retain.

Skriabin's music is clearly intended to represent a 'blank.' It is described as generated by, and consisting in death: 'Seen from this wholly Christian point of view, Skriabin's death astonishes us. It is not only remarkable as the fantastic posthumous growth of the artist in the eyes of the masses but also serves, as it were, as the source of his creative work, as its teleological cause. If one removes the shroud of death from around this creative life, that life will flow freely from its cause, from death, and it will surround death as it surrounds its own sun, and will consume its light' (II, 313; 90). Even the most cursory glance at this article uncovers parallels between the presentation of Skriabin and that of the romantics in 'Remarks on Chénier' and of Russia in 'Peter Chaadaev.' If the romantics were a necklace of dead nightingales who will not betray their secrets, Skriabin is seen as a link between the madness of Hellas and the 'Russian sectarians [*raskol'niki*, i.e., "break-ers"] who burned themselves in their coffins' (II, 256; 91). Like Russia in 'Peter Chaadaev,' Skriabin is mute; he avoids 'voice,' or unity. His music is a siren, but like romantic poetry, a seductive one (the 'blank' has so far always been 'hypnotic,' 'imperative,' 'seductive' in Mandel'shtam's prose): 'The wordless, strangely mute chorus of Prometheus continues as that very same seductive Siren' (II, 317; 93).

In fact, 'Pushkin and Skriabin' reintroduces the whole vocabulary of images familiar to us from the earlier essays. Here, however, Mandel'shtam's subject matter is no longer pliable; it threatens the overall unity of his theory. For example, by contrast with the image in 'The Morning of Acmeism' of the poet conducting a choral symphony and harmonizing words in ceaseless reiteration, we are presented in 'Pushkin and Skriabin' with the image of a 'voiceless symphony,' which cannot be linked or harmonized because Mandel'shtam's principle of unity, the statement-blank, cannot be employed. Without voice (i.e., statement, meaning) how can one connect blank to blank? In order to dramatize this, Mandel'shtam employs the image of the 'siren-piano,' and opposes its music, or Skriabin's music, to the synthetic movement of the Ninth Symphony, 'Beethoven's Catholic Joy.'

The identification of the blank with the 'siren-piano' introduces a more aggressive and sinister note to what was previously a rather passive concept blunting rather than destroying the thought of Chaadaev. By the very force of the image Mandel'shtam clearly confronts the possibility that rupture cannot be a constructive image and is, as Nietzsche predicted in *The Birth of Tragedy*, ultimately destructive of culture as the poet knows it, for the siren, of course, brings about shipwreck as well as madness and loss of coherent unity. Yet there is also the implication that the siren cannot break the unity of Christian art precisely because this art already includes the blank or rupture and also transcends it through Christ's act of redemption (i.e., life, death, and resurrection). The very force of this imagery, however, pushes Mandel'shtam to abandon the notion of culture as stone in favour of a new image of vegetative growth, death, and rebirth. Thus, the earlier image of the Gothic cathedral,[24] exchanged later for Jacob's ladder (a stony structure pervaded by blanks), is left behind altogether because stones evidently cannot admit aggressive breaks or ruptures in a natural manner. This in turn explains the switch from the metaphoric identification of the unity of Christian culture with Rome (a persistent image in all the earlier works associated with the cathedral) to an identification with Hellas as soil and vegetation:[25] 'Hellenism, impregnated with death, is Christianity. The seed of death, having fallen on the soil of Hellas, miraculously flourished: our entire culture has grown from this seed; we reckon our history from the moment when the soil of Hellas accepted that seed. Rome was infertile because the soil of Rome is rocky, Rome being Hellas devoid of grace' (II, 318; 94).

In order to avoid a potentially irreconcilable opposition between Rome and Hellas, Mandel'shtam remains within the framework of this metaphorical opposition between, yet also conjunction of, presence and blank, while attempting to develop new images that might give this opposition an even greater intensity. Skriabin is presented not merely as a Hellene, like Pushkin, but as a mad Hellene, like Dionysus: 'Skriabin's just value for Russia and Christianity derives from his being a *mad [raging] Hellene*' [*bezumstvuiuschii ellin*][26] (II, 314; 91; the emphasis is Mandel'shtam's). In other words, Skriabin is praised for lacking the unity and solidity of Hellenic culture, and for *not being its unifying aspect*, as Pushkin was for Russian culture. He is instead its destructive side, an 'ill-fated Phaedra' or Dionysus. This interpretation is confirmed by Mandel'shtam's insistence at this point that the deep Hellenic madness in Skriabin's 'purely Russian thirst for salvation' (thirst [*zhazhda*], another 'lack' or blank) is not necessary in the Christian world. Skriabin expresses an overwhelming sense of guilt, which should no longer be possible, since humankind has already been redeemed. This sense of guilt, I propose, explains Mandel'shtam's perception of Skriabin as standing outside Christian culture. His desire for redemption is too profound, too hungry, and should not be found in a culture where redemption is freely present: 'Christian art is always an action based upon the great idea of redemption' (II, 314; 91).

In his insatiable passion for redemption and with the guilt of a Phaedra, Skriabin represents a movement of time against its Christian pattern. His music even signifies that time is returning to its pagan past: 'In the fateful hours of purification and storm, we raised Skriabin above us, Skriabin whose sun-heart burns above us, but alas – his is not the sun of redemption but the sun of guilt ... Time can go backwards: witness the entire courts of guilt ... recent history which, with a frightening force, has turned away from Christianity toward Buddhism and theosophy' (II, 314; 90). Yet, according to Mandel'shtam, Skriabin still repeats the movement of Christian redemption by the fact of his death. Even if he behaves as if Christianity were forgotten, his own fate – his confrontation with, and unveiling of, the siren of music, his subsequent death, and his 'fantastic posthumous growth in the eyes of the masses' (II, 313; 90) – proves that the movement of Christian dynamics, life-death-resurrection, is inescapable. 'The myth of long forgotten Christianity' is overcome by Skriabin's creativity and death, which unexpectedly recover the Christian pattern: 'To conquer oblivion even at the price of death: that is Skriabin's motto, that is the heroic aspiration of his art! It is in this sense that I meant Skriabin's death is the supreme act of his creativity for it illuminates him with a blinding and unexpected light' (II, 317–18; 94). As Christianity introduces death into the organic system (i.e., Christianity 'Hellenizes death,' so too does Skriabin: 'Skriabin's art is directly connected with the historical task of Christianity that I call the Hellenization of death, and through that task it acquires its profound meaning' (II, 318; 94).

On the surface, therefore, the theory of the conjunction of presence and blank has been preserved in Skriabin's re-emerging power despite (and, in fact, because of) his death. However, a careful examination also reveals that the pattern has at the same time been profoundly ruptured. The concept of indefiniteness or break, which was first introduced in the 'Remarks on Chénier,' demands here some unexpected concessions. The blank seems to be growing in size. Gone is the picture of the Gothic cathedral, stable in its unity. Poets, instead of standing and singing on its towers, piercing and hypnotizing the emptiness of the sky, are now faced with an abyss which itself possesses the hypnotic power to end art and history as we know them: 'Time is rushing backwards with a roaring splash like the dammed-up waters of mountain falls – and the new Orpheus flings his lyre into the seething foam: there is no more art' (II, 314; 91). Furthermore, the only way to overcome the abyss is to grant it the life of the artist himself. Only in this way will his individuality return Dionysus-like, magnified, to be reintegrated in posthumous fame. However, there is no guarantee that such an abyss, which now requires human sacrifice, will not demand further concessions.

In short, the theory of indefiniteness as a constructive principle has proven to be highly self-destructive. In its many metaphorical transformations in Mandel'shtam's prose the blank proves to be ever more difficult to control. By 1920 even the ideology of the new state makes it impossible for Mandel'shtam to advise artists to follow Chaadaev's creative use of Russia's emptiness-freedom: 'Chaadaev took it as his holy staff and set off for Rome' (II, 291; 88). Russia's "thirst for salvation" has unexpectedly shown that it may not be so pliable at all, and that the desire to go to Rome is last on its list of priorities.

Emptiness, as absence of meaning, of sound, of voice, of force, of energy, of history, of unity, etc., once introduced by Mandel'shtam as a constructive concept has finally become a theoretically uncontrollable force, which is presented in 'Pushkin and Skriabin' as having the potential to bring about the death of Christian culture, and shown to be capable of making all cultural achievements relative in a manner not dissimilar to that expressed in the much more recent debates of postmodern poetics.[27] Deeply challenged by the implications of his own imagery, and no doubt by the everyday human and cultural destruction vividly displayed in Russian political life, Mandel'shtam searches for a theoretical position that will permit the free development of his creative insight without demanding or legitimizing murder or cultural extermination, even if he can sympathize with the tumult and still hope for his own legitimate place in the new society. However, in 1919 there is very little scope for new theoretical development or even for personal sources of renewal. Thus, in 'Pushkin and Skriabin' the poet introduces the motif of free play[28] almost as a plea to end the necessity for extinction. Christian art becomes freedom and play. It is a joyous imitation of Christ, not Skriabin's sacrifice and redemption, since these sacrifices have already taken place once and for all: 'Art cannot be sacrifice, because a sacrifice has been made; it cannot be redemption, because the world along with the artist has already been redeemed' (II, 314; 91). The destruction-blank, then, does not have to be all-encompassing. It may be only the free play of a game or the 'joyous communion with God like some game played by the Father with his children, some blind man's bluff or hide-and-seek of the spirit' (II, 315; 92). Our part is that of observers who are invited to experience catharsis, which becomes 'redemption in art.'

What has normally been considered to be Mandel'shtam's theory of Christian art in 'Pushkin and Skriabin'[29] is more likely to have been constructed as a temporary alternative to the impact of his own developing theory in the context of a parallel and rather sinister development in contemporary events, and out of a desire to minimize their potentially destructive effects. The view that the 'blank' is only a game of the divine spirit, far from being a mature position, is like a child's plea for mercy in a reality becoming daily darker and more sinister. But for the time being the concept of 'some blind man's bluff or hide-and-seek of the spirit' also helps Mandel'shtam to retain his unique, theoretical voice and to prevent his position from sliding into the symbolist abyss. Indeed, theoretical originality and contempt for the symbolist artistic theory of the abyss were a major driving force of acmeism, central to the young Mandel'shtam's poetic identity. After such a crisis one expects in this essay an acknowledgment of a change in the employment of images, but no clear change is discernible. The familiar vocabulary of images and their metaphoric associations remain consistently employed even when they point to an overall logical dead end.

Later in this study I shall trace what happens to Mandel'shtam's poetics after he overcomes the long silence of 1925–9 and regains his voice, and particularly after he discovers Dante and journeys to earthbound Christian Armenia, as Chaadaev had travelled to Rome a century earlier. Two separate and distinct principles of absence emerge in the 1930s: one acts as a positive impulse which, when 'taken by itself, is completely mute' (II, 363; 397) and whose signal-waves of meaning 'vanish, having completed their work (II, 364; 398); and the other is the negative abyss of the *Inferno*. In *Conversation about Dante* one enters the Inferno through a crack or blank by means of which one is 'permitted to see those people laid in open graves' (II, 370; 403). Therein the past, which has been considered dead, lives and teaches, no longer with that 'essence of sweetness' associated in 'Remarks on Chénier' with 'the necklace of dead nightingales' (II, 296; 77), but 'categorically and authoritatively' (II, 370; 403), that is, by means of imperatives and accusations. Escaping from these ghostly merciless judges and surrounded by a growing number of scandals, 'the tormented and downtrodden man' is concealed 'at the very bottom of a sack of mute sounds' (II, 373; 406), which image had once been considered in Mandel'shtam's early work to characterize the hypnotic essence of art.

In the poetics of the early 1920s, however, Mandel'shtam does not yet differentiate between the two absences; instead the binomial principles of meaning and blank continue to live under his metaphors and images, which grow either more confusing or more poignant.[30] Even in the early 1920s he will continue to praise Chénier for his ability to 'combine rationality and furies' while observing in the same essay ('The Nineteenth Century,' 1922), with unequivocal, mordant self-criticism, the self-destructive pattern of that union. The concept of Buddhism, employed in this essay as a pejorative principle about to destroy European culture, operates here as a metaphor for what can no longer be said, namely, for that Russian thirst for annihilation, which loses finally the poet's fascinated devotion:

> Out of the union of the mind and furies a mongrel was born, equally alien to the high rationality of the Encyclopedia and to the Classical raging of the revolutionary storm in Romanticism ... The nineteenth century was the conduit of Buddhist influence in European culture. It was the carrier of an

alien principle, inimical and powerful, against which our entire history has been doing battle ... Latent Buddhism, an inward tendency, a worm-hole. The century did not preach Buddhism, but harbored it within itself, like inner night, like blindness of the blood, like furtive fears and vertigo. (II, 280; 141–2)

2

The Word in Mandel'shtam's Poetics

This chapter traces the changes in Mandel'shtam's conception of the word, from his earlier metaphoric identification of the word with stone and his subsequent partial alienation from that metaphor, to his tendency to see the word as possessing a dual nature, an inner and outer reality, and finally to his recognition that this dual nature does not exhaust the word's essence. This realization is reflected in Mandel'shtam's presentation of the word as an energy flow that strikes consciousness as a series of changing perspectives.

1   The Word as Stone, 1913–1919

Mandel'shtam's earliest tendency is to regard words as tangible material acquisitions – as things. In 'François Villon,' one of his first essays, Mandel'shtam equates the gift of the poet with that of the thief: the quickest way to steal a chicken is to write a poem about it. Given this view, it is not surprising that Mandel'shtam became one of the leading theoreticians of acmeism, a movement opposed to the symbolist technique of using poetry as a ladder to a non-material realm (see, for example, Toporov 1979, 249–52; Meijer 1979). In the 'Morning of Acmeism,' his earliest attempt at a definitive motto-essay,[1] Mandel'shtam proclaims a 'stone age' of poetry, where each word is returned to its unalterable status as a stone.[2] While this comparison generates innumerable possibilities for word games and images of word construction, the central position is clear: in acmeist hands the word becomes a part of material reality, whose continuous and undifferentiated existence is affirmed and pledged at the outset: 'The architect says: I build – therefore, I am right ... we introduce the gothic principle into the relationship of words, just as Sebastian Bach established it in music ... But Tiutchev's[3] stone ... is the word ... Reverently the Acmeists raise this mysterious Tiutchevian stone and make it a foundation stone of their building' (II, 321–2; 62).

In other words, Mandel'shtam in 1913 views poetry as a creation of the world-cathedral (the poem, or the body of the poem) made out of words/stones. This world-cathedral knows no death: it is tangible and yet eternal, a world possibly better than that already existing: 'To build means to conquer emptiness, to hypnotize space. The handsome arrow of the Gothic bell tower rages because its function is to stab the sky, to reproach it for its emptiness' (II, 323; 63). Much work has been done on the recurrent image of stone constructions and cathedrals in Mandel'shtam's poetry,[4] and it is also generally argued that the Gothic cathedral is a central image of all Mandel'shtam's earlier essays. Only in 'Pushkin and Skriabin' (an essay written between 1915 and 1919) is the image of stone rejected as a metaphor for poetry: 'Rome was infertile because the soil of Rome is rocky, Rome being Hellas devoid of grace' (II, 318; 94).[5] The same essay attempts to speak of art (and, thus, poetry) in terms of soil and vegetation.[6]

In 'The Word and Culture' (1921) this new preference for putting the word into an organic-vegetative context, instead of metaphorically equating word with stone, is no longer accompanied by unambiguous enthusiasm. Instead, it is made clear that a shift towards a purely vegetative metaphor is equivalent to the death of culture, and there is a rare mixture of irony and sadness in the eulogy of Petersburg, in which the city is lauded not for its stony architecture but for its grass – 'the first sprouts of the virgin forest that will cover the site of the modern city' (II, 222; 112).

It is also in 'The Word and Culture' that Mandel'shtam moves towards entertaining the possibility of the coexistence of the two metaphors, as he gives poetry two successive definitions, one in a stony context, followed immediately by a second presented in the context of vegetation-earth. In both definitions material reality – either that of stone or that of vegetation and soil – is no longer equated with permanence; it is rather a symbol of the ravages of time.[7] Thus, grass breaks stones, hungry time destroys the state or is destroyed by it (II, 224ff; 114–15), but poetry, either as inscription or as plough, is called to save material objects, all of which carry within them the seeds of self-annihilation and mutual destruction. Inscriptions in stone protect the chaotic materiality of civilizations. Poetry/the plough[8] saves time/soil from the eventual annihilation of the fertile memory hidden in the soil's otherwise inaccessible layers:

Cultural values ornament the State, endowing it with color, form and, if you will, even gender. Inscriptions on State buildings, tombs, and gateways insure the state against the ravages of time.

Poetry is the plough that turns up time in such a way that the abyssal strata of time, its black earth, appear on the surface. (II, 224; 113)

The identification of word and stone should, therefore, be abandoned: the image of the solid stony structure offers no solution against its own possible decay. The word outlives stone; their identification has reached, and disclosed, its limitations.

Yet, surprisingly, word as a finalized solid structure, a stone, a kernel, unexpectedly reappears in 'On the Nature of the Word' (1922), which is considered to follow both chronologically and theoretically upon 'The Word and Culture': 'We don't have an Acropolis. Even today our culture is still wandering and not finding its walls. Nevertheless, each word in Dal's dictionary is a kernel of Acropolis, a small Kremlin, a small winged fortress of nomination, rigged out in the Hellenic spirit for the relentless battle against the formless element' (II, 251; 126). The puzzle consists in the fact that Mandel'shtam preserves the metaphoric identification (word/stone) even after he has found it seriously deficient.[9]

This tendency is particularly evident in Mandel'shtam's treatment of Vasilii Rozanov. The figure of Rozanov in 'On the Nature of the Word' is chosen, among other things, to represent Mandel'shtam's former self as well as his former need to identify word and culture respectively with stone and cathedral. Mandel'shtam's portrayal of Rozanov has bewildered many a critic,[10] yet the logic of this portrayal is typical of the poet: for Mandel'shtam any view (and particularly his own) once held with such intensity is always a genuine insight, however unsatisfactory it may later appear. For this reason Rozanov is invariably treated with much love and sympathy (a point always observed by the critics), but every admiring description of Rozanov finds its culmination in an anticlimactic indifference to his theoretical stance. Rozanov's insight, therefore, is not abandoned, but it is found theoretically unsatisfactory and lacking in a broader perspective:

> One of Rozanov's books bears the title *By the Cathedral Walls*. It seems to me that Rozanov spent his entire life rummaging about in a soft yielding void, groping for the walls of Russian culture ... he could not live without walls, without an Acropolis ... Rozanov's craving for the nut and for whatever wall might symbolize that nut completely determined his fate ... In his indefati-

gable search for the kernel, he nibbled and cracked every word, every utterance, leaving us only empty shells. It comes as no surprise that Rozanov turned out to be an unnecessary and uninfluential writer. (II, 249; 123–4)

In a very original manner does Rozanov define the essence of his nominalism: the eternal cognitive movement, the eternal cracking of the nut which comes to nothing, for there is no way to crack it. (II, 249; 124)

Apart from Mandel'shtam's love for the word/stone metaphor and its vogue among acmeists,[11] his historical and cultural outlook has also much influenced his reluctance to abandon the word/stone identification. In the chaos of Russia's history, language is the country's only solid protection, its only foundation stone. Mandel'shtam, therefore, agrees with Chaadaev that Russia has no delineation, no permanence, no values, yet he specifies that Russian language and literature embody the permanence lacking in all the country's other aspects: 'Chaadaev, in stating his opinion that Russia belongs ... to the unorganized, unhistorical world of cultural phenomena, overlooked one factor – the Russian language' (II, 247; 123).[12] This, in turn, explains his love for Rozanov, who 'could not live without walls, without an Acropolis' (II, 248; 123) and found cultural stability, a stony delineation, in language. This historical view of Mandel'shtam's makes his insistence on the use of the metaphor more comprehensible and shows that an insight into the insufficiency of a particular metaphoric identification does not lead him to reject it. A reshaping of the former identity is a preferable alternative.

The continuing, but transformed, identification of word and stone appears even in Mandel'shtam's last theoretical work, *Conversation about Dante*, in which he argues that the entire poem 'is not a stanza but a crystallographic figure, ... a stereometric body, one continuous development of the crystallographic theme' (II, 376; 409). This identification, differently qualified in so many prose writings, is for Mandel'shtam a clear moment in the perception of poetry. It is not to be abandoned, but to be reapplied within a much larger framework whose various delineations he attempts to uncover, starting from 'The Word and Culture.'

2 The Word as Inner and Outer Reality, 1921–1922

As early as 'The Word and Culture' (1921), alongside his word-stone comparison, Mandel'shtam attempts to give a definition of the word that invokes no material identity. There is a distancing from material identification in his most famous definition of poetry, which is that the word is not controlled by the things it designates and the poem in turn is not controlled by words.[13] Yet even this frequently quoted definition is not Mandel'shtam's final pronouncement on the issue, but rather an indication of a most profound reorientation:[14]

> Is the thing really the master of the word? The word is a psyche. The living word does not designate an object but freely chooses for its dwelling place, as it were, some objective significance, material thing, or beloved body. And the word wanders freely around the thing, like the soul around an abandoned but not forgotten body. (II, 226; 115)

> The poem lives through an inner image, that ringing mold of form which anticipates the written poem. There is not yet a single word, but the poem can already be heard. This is the sound of the inner image, this is the poet's ear touching it. (II, 226; 116)

It is here and in his next essay, 'On the Nature of the Word,' that Mandel'shtam, much influenced by the philosophy of Henri Bergson, attempts to view the word as a relationship, a principle fundamental to communication, and not a thing. The word becomes a manifestation of energy, and the inner source of this energy will always remain different from the word's appearance. However, since the word's appearance is also changing (that is, it can be grasped either as its manifestation on the page, or in its indication of the signified object, or as the audible form), the very status of both inner and outer realities changes with the direction of our approach to the word. Here the quality of the poetic universe is found to be such that, whichever aspect of the word is to be studied (phoneme, meaning, etc.), its relation with other aspects can invariably be presented as a connection between an inner and an outer aspect of the word itself: 'A verbal representation is a complex composite of phenomena, it is a connection, a "system." The significance of the word may be viewed as a candle burning inside a paper lantern, and conversely, its phonetic value, the so-called phoneme, may be located inside the significance, just as that candle may be inside that lantern' (II, 255–6; 129).

The word, therefore, is a relationship,[15] yet Mandel'shtam is wary of viewing it simply as a relationship without tangible identity, without centre, without a sense of unity:[16] 'The movement of an infinite chain of phenomena having neither beginnings nor end is precisely that bad infinity ... it gives an appearance of scientific generalization, but only at the cost of renouncing all synthesis and inner structure' (II, 242; 118). Instead, the word is a relationship which nevertheless possesses an inner centre, its own source of energy independent of the relationship as such. The word is like Bergson's fan, manifested into relationship when opened, yet possessing a single identity when closed: 'a kind of fan whose folds can be opened up in time; however, this fan may also be closed up in a way intelligible to the human mind' (II, 242; 117).[17]

It is difficult to assess the theoretical validity of Mandel'shtam's standpoint. For him definition is always metaphorical, and here the nature of the word is best defined by a metaphor that allows for diffusion – 'the body freely chosen for the dwelling place' – a diffusion of light, an opening of the fan. Each of these metaphors, however, presupposes an existence independent of the word's manifestation in relationship: 'soul freely wandering around the body,' the source of light or warmth, the closed state of the fan. The word, therefore, assumes a series of dual characteristics, each identifying in turn the double reality of the word: its invisible inner centre and its outer wavelike existence manifested as a relationship. In the 1930s Mandel'shtam would apply a wave theory of light to his definition of word and poetry[18] – an invisible source of energy manifested as waves easily perceptible and most easily depicted as waves of a fluid: 'Poetic discourse is a carpet fabric ... ; an extremely durable carpet woven out of fluid.' The ornament on the surface preserves and enacts traces of its origin that otherwise remain invisible (II, 365; 398). In the 1920s, however, he is only implicitly suggesting this duality by working with a set of metaphors that exhibit dual characteristics.

The implications of this dual metaphor (source and manifestation) are felt in every aspect of Mandel'shtam's poetics. Even his depiction of the two philologists, Rozanov and Innokentii Annensky, in 'On the Nature of the Word' continues this dual description, since Rozanov represents the word's inner reality (its kernel) and Annensky its outer limits. The most striking visualization of this duality of the word appears in descriptions of the word as creator of space. Since the invisible source of energy is to be manifested in space and time, it becomes necessary for Mandel'shtam to speak about 'spaciousness,' or the inner space of the word.[19] It is important to observe that this particular view of the word as possessor and creator of inner space explicitly surfaces in Mandel'shtam's theatre articles, which by definition deal with the word as relationship, as pattern of communication, that is, as the dramatic interpretation of the written word.

3 The Word as Space, 1925

The theatre essays were almost all written during Mandel'shtam's prolonged creative impasse between 1923 and 1927, and thus they shed light on the development of his ideas in the period that is most difficult to assess and understand: 'The Moscow Art Theatre and the Word' (1923), 'The Thrust' (1924), a chapter entitled 'Komissarzhevskaia' in *The Noise of Time* (1925), 'Mikhoels' (1926), and 'Iakhontov' (1927). In these works Mandel'shtam speaks about the dramatization of the inner space of the word, the awareness and understanding of whose existence provide a necessary direction for its being read intelligently.

In these essays Mandel'shtam is equally critical of an exclusive interpretative emphasis on either the outer dimension or the inner reality of the word. An emphasis on the dramatic aspects of words constitutes for him their external function, equivalent in its isolation to signs of deafness. Thus, the Moscow Art Theatre, well known for its realism, is criticized for its misdirected desire to 'help' the word in the external world: 'All the work of the Moscow Art Theater went under the banner of distrust in the word and a craving to touch literature ... In reality they touched only themselves' ('The Moscow Art Theater and the Word,' III, 100; 189). The irony for Mandel'shtam resides in the fact that the overemphatic, realistic dramatization of the word disrupts the process of communication; indeed, when the externality of the word, its tangible manifestation, is given sole prominence, the interpreter no longer hears the word; he hears only himself. In this case communication ceases and is exchanged for the new, but useless, text of pitiful conjectures: 'Would it not have been simpler to replace the text of *Woe from Wit* [*Gore ot uma*] with their own psychological directions and conjectures?' (III, 101; 189). Awareness of the duality of the word is, therefore, essential for communication. Once awareness of the inner reality of the word is lost, communication as such ceases to exist.

Again and again Mandel'shtam emphasizes that forgetfulness of the hidden inner reality of the word is equal to deafness: 'The true and righteous pass to theatrical tangibility lies through the word; the direction is hidden in the word. The highest expression is found in the form [*stroenie*] of speech, poem or prose' (III, 100; 189).

In 'The Thrust' ['Vypad'], an essay written a year later, Mandel'shtam again insists that poetical literacy, with its rules for communication, can only be found *inside* the word. In order to understand the text one has to enter verbal space (metaphorically of course – see the *as if* of the following passage): 'In poetic notation, for instance, in contrast to musical notation, there is a large gap, a glaring absence of the multitude of implicit signs, markers and indicators that alone make the text comprehensible and law abiding [*zakonomernyj*]. However, all these signs are no less exact than musical notes or hieroglyphics of dance. The poetically literate reader supplies them himself, as if extracting them from the text' (II, 230–1; 204).

Nevertheless, total dedication to the inner reality of the word also results in an impasse. Vera Komissarzhevskaia, in Mandel'shtam's *The Noise of Time*, clearly embodies this alternative. An actress who founded the only symbolic theatre in Russia is praised by the poet for her ability to enter into the internal dimensions of the word: 'she raised and lowered her voice as it was demanded by the breathing of the form of the words, her acting was three-quarters in words' (II, 101, translation mine): Komissarzhevskaia's alternative, however, is 'the false and impossible oxygen of the theatrical miracle' (II, 101, translation mine), which is barren because it has no manifestation in the tangible dramatic play. Throughout the chapter on Komissarzhevskaia Mandel'shtam invariably depicts her acting as a form of standing still, at its best an alienated arrest of movement: 'To walk and sit she was bored; as it happened she mostly stood ... Yet Komissarzhevskaia had all the gifts of a tragic actress, all in embryonic state ... Komissarzhevskaia ran off from the Russian theatrical world as from a mental hospital – she was free, but the heart of the theatre stopped' (II, 100–1, translation mine).

Mandel'shtam's answer to the impasse both of interpretative purity (attention to the inner reality of the word) and of interpretative deafness (an over-realistic emphasis upon its external reality) appears in two articles written at the very centre of the poet's creative crisis. In his essay on Vladimir Iakhontov (1927), an actor of the one-actor theatre, Mandel'shtam no longer portrays inner space as a silent and hidden receptacle; instead he presents it as an expanding source of energy, a living property of a gifted actor: 'A sense of space is indispensable to any actor: Iakhontov always carries his sense of space with him, tied up in the tailor Petrovich's handkerchief, as it were, or ready to be pulled out of a top hat like a magician's egg ... In his portrayal of the tailor ... Iakhontov is already portraying footmen ... thus expanding his picture to encompass the *entire* theatre, from the tailor's room to the frozen night. At each moment, he conveys an image of a broadly expanding perspective' (III,

111, 113; 267, 268–9). The inner space, however minute, is destined to expand into action within an ever-widening perspective. The energy thus created by re-enactment is the energy that bridges the inner and outer realities of the word and that thus becomes the energy of mutual inclusion or understanding.

The inner reality of the word becomes a source of movement, and as such cannot be at a standstill; it takes over the face of the actor, his movements, his fingertips, and the surrounding space.[20] The notion of the fan in 'On the Nature of the Word' is still implicitly present in this depiction of the actor reading the word's inner design and moving with its ever-increasing energy on the theatrical stage: Iakhontov 'is unique among contemporary Russian actors in that he is able to move about both in the word and in space' (III, 113; 269). An attentiveness to the inner command always results in movement,[21] which is 'a graphically precise and spare picture, a pattern of movement and a design of the word' (III, 112; 267).

The inner space of the word, therefore, is not simply a direction towards an understanding; rather it is a powerful command to enactment. More and more often this inner space is compared to a substratum of energy, dramatic in its essence, consummated in the artistic creation of a growing number of tangible objects within a broadening perspective. In the essay 'Mikhoels' (1926), dedicated to the Jewish actor and director, Mandel'shtam writes of Solomon Mikhoels as a Jewish Dionysus carrying out in his every movement the vibrating energy of an articulated design which arises out of a properly grasped work of art. The ever-widening circularity of this awakened design and its intoxicating and transforming power are depicted in the clearest and most emphatic fashion, even if at this point they are identified with an exclusively Jewish, aesthetic awareness:

> The dancing Jew now resembles the leader of the ancient Greek chorus. All the power of Judaism, all the rhythm of the abstract ideas in dance ... all this extends into the trembling of the hands, into the vibration of the thinking fingers which are animated like articulated speech.
>
> ... Such an actor must be kept off the realistic stage – things will just melt away under his touch. He creates his own props – a needle and thread, a glass of pepper vodka, a mirror, any object from his daily life that he needs – whenever he takes it into his head to do so. (III, 108–9; 261–2)

The word becomes for Mandel'shtam dynamic energy bursting into, and creating, space. In this portrayal he moves beyond a double, contrasting characterization of the word: the word is an energy flow, a transmutation of reality, not merely a dual metaphor. The theatre articles written during the years of Mandel'shtam's artistic crisis present a clear picture of the direction of this new transition. The word is not a thing, nor is it a possessor of space. Its inner reality expands into movement; it reshapes and creates an ever expanding space. We shall find a similar image in *Conversation about Dante,* where the words of poetry are presented as signal-waves of meaning, which create the inner space of the poem, in Dante's case, the three invisible landscapes of the whole universe: *Inferno, Purgatorio,* and *Paradiso.*

4 The Word as Journey into the Patterns of Communication, the 1930s

Tracing the transitions and developments of Mandel'shtam's definitions and depictions of the word according to the chronological order of his works makes it clear that his conception of the word underwent significant changes up to the 1930s. However, it remains problematic how these different definitions of the word can co-exist. Why in the 1930s does Mandel'shtam not single out a particular definition, but continue to operate within this very wide range of what he considers the essential nature of the word? Perhaps Mandel'shtam's temperament, along with the ups and downs of his creative search, gave him a fundamental insight into the nature of the word itself: the word is revealed to consciousness in a variety of ways, and cannot be reduced to a single form or definition.

In this sense Mandel'shtam's theoretical journey became for him an initiation into the journey of our varying perceptions of the word. In *Conversation about Dante* and *Journey to Armenia* he would attempt to outline the rules of the periodization of this journey. To the poet's ear the word is always a command to travel into all the ramifications of its essence. No single vision is a mistake; it becomes a mistake only in its isolation – as a standing still, a cessation of movement. The word calls into movement and is understood only in journey. Therefore, we read in the *Conversation about Dante*: 'In all seriousness the question arises: how many shoe soles, how many oxhide soles, how many sandals did Alighieri wear out during the course of his poetic work, wandering the goat paths of Italy?' (II, 367; 400). The physical journey, the long historical wandering, is also an insight into the intelligible landscape of the word with its precise delineations. The ringing, hidden command of the inner reality of the word is an invitation, and for the poet an obligation, to outline this journey into the complex stages of the word's reality:

> Any given word is a bundle, and meaning sticks out of it in various directions, not aspiring to any single official point ... What distinguishes poetry from automatic speech is that it rouses us into wakefulness in the middle of a word. Then it turns out that the word is much longer than we thought, and we remember that to speak means to be forever on the road. (*Conversation about Dante*, II, 374–5; 407)

The word clearly comprises a whole range of manifestations, relations, and metaphoric identifications. By the 1930s the challenge for Mandel'shtam therefore becomes not the presentation of a single definition but the possibility of outlining the characteristic stages that are disclosed by the journey into the variegated nature of the word itself.

3

The Word in Action: The Hypnotic Power of Poetry

Since poetry for Mandel'shtam is the display of the word in its full reality [*slovo kak takovoe*], the poetic word is invariably described in his work as an intensified experience of language. This chapter outlines Mandel'shtam's varying perceptions of the principles that are involved in this intensification and, thus, in the different metaphorical presentations of the word. The nature of the poetic word is explored, starting from the earlier notions of hypnotism, then turning to the idea of opposed dual commands, and finally examining the word as invitation to follow out its own multidimensional journey.

1 Tangible Intensification and Hypnotism, 1913–1919

Profoundly connected with Mandel'shtam's view of the word is his treatment of the intensification of speech in poetry,[1] no matter which particular metaphoric figure is identified with the word. Thus, in the 'Morning of Acmeism' the comparison between word and stone tends naturally towards viewing poetic verse as intensified reality: 'the poet raises a phenomenon to its tenth power, and the exterior of a work of art deceives us with regard to the monstrously condensed reality contained within. In poetry this reality is the word as such' (II, 320; 61).

Mandel'shtam's later image of the word as a Bergsonian fan also allows for the display of poetry as an intensification of language, for the phenomenon of self-gathering and dispersion becomes reflected in the numerous images of poetry presented in the intensification of the energy flow.[2] Thus Rozanov and Annensky, the two philologists in 'On the Nature of the Word,' are depicted as involved in the process of the intensification or solidification of speech. For Rozanov the word is 'a little Kremlin'; for Annensky the writing of poetry is a preparation for the strongest possible infusion: 'the compression- fermentation of such bitter absinth-saturated verse of a kind no one before or after him would write' (II, 253; 122, translation altered). Thus, from 1922 onwards the notion of condensation- intensification in poetry has a permanent place in Mandel'shtam's oeuvre. The closed state of the fan, the spreading source of light, the strong bitter infusion, the source of spreading warmth – these are the source and goal of civilization: 'Hellenism is ... the humanizing and warming of the surrounding world with the most delicate teleological warmth' (II, 253; 128).[3]

This notion of intensification is connected most directly with another central motif in Mandel'shtam: an awareness of the intrinsic dynamism of poetic verse. An intensified phenomenon becomes an act,[4] a deed, an event.[5] Examples of this are almost too numerous to mention; one of the earliest is the description of Sologub's verse in 'About the Interlocutor' ["O sobesednike"]: 'Sologub's lines continue to live, long after they were written, as events, not merely as tokens of experience which has passed' (II, 240; 73).

What is the source of this dynamic intimation of action in the word as such? As we have seen in chapter 1, Mandel'shtam's initial answer during his acmeist years anticipates the work of Iser (not to mention that of Heidegger, especially in 'What Is Metaphysics'): an invitation to action that cannot be found in the word itself, which is a thingness, a stone, but is rather found in the 'nothingness' of the word.[6] All Mandel'shtam's early essays exhibit this polarity as the very foundation of poetry: for him *the word as meaning* and *the word as effect* do not originate in the same source. Rather the word as statement, meaning, or thought falls on one side of the scale, whereas absence, hypnotism, effect, and command constitute another polarity within the word itself.[7] In all the early works (1914–20) the effect of poetry, referred to as its hypnotic power[8] and understood as command, is consistently described as an obsession whose source is absence, blank, nothingness, or death:

> The laws of poetry sleep in its larynx and all of Romantic poetry, like a necklace of dead nightingales, will not convey, will not betray its secrets, does not know its legacy. ('André Chénier,' II, 296; 77)[9]

> Oh, Legacy of a thinker! Precious scraps! Fragments that end precisely where continuity is most wanted, grandiose beginnings of what we do not

> know ... The gaping wasteland among the well-known, written fragments is the missing thought about Russia ...
> ... Russia was the cause of Chaadaev's thought. What he thought about Russia remained a mystery. ('Chaadaev,' II, 287–8; 85–6)

> If one removes the shroud of death from around this creative life, that life will flow freely from its cause, from death, and it will surround death as it surrounds its own sun, and will consume its light. (Pushkin and Skriabin,' II, 313; 90)

Moreover, this notion that the power of poetry originates in nothingness is not a permanent aspect of Mandel'shtam's poetics;[10] the notion of nothingness appears only in conjunction with his metaphoric description of the word as stone (discussed in chapter 2). Only in the first decade of Mandel'shtam's writings on poetry did he hold that the role of poetry was to rule over both principles – over the materiality and the nothingness of the word – to bring existence and hypnotism together. In this period the goal of the poet, as he states in 'André Chénier' (1914), is to combine the two elements, to follow Pushkin's formula: 'the union of the mind and furies' (II, 297; 78). Yet this view of poetry was subjected to a serious crisis, rendered perhaps even more acute by the irreversibility of the political and social events of the Russian Revolution. Emptiness overpowers meaning. The advent of nothingness, once welcomed for its hypnotic power, may never be arrested. Instead, this advent endangers history, eliminating its calendar and its tradition and jeopardizing all human art: 'The Christian calendar is endangered, the fragile reckoning of the years of our era has been lost – time is rushing backwards with a roaring splash like the damned up waters of mountain falls – and the new Orpheus flings his lyre into the seething foam, there is no more art' (II, 314; 91).

Thus, Mandel'shtam's initial view of the intensification of the nature of the word in poetry results in a profound impasse, for the dualistic principles of materiality and nothingness are found to carry a potential for the destruction of all cultural principles. Moreover, the position that the materiality of the word in poetry is displayed in its fullest intensity whereas the word's nothingness exhibits a hypnotic command is found to be theoretically fruitless.

2 The Double Effect of Poetry, 1921–1924

It is in the 1920s that the reorganization of the theoretical constructive principles takes place.[11] As the metaphor of Bergson's fan enters Mandel'shtam's essays, the notion of word as tangible reality and the idea of the effect of poetry are brought, so to speak, into the same source. Thus, in 'On the Nature of the Word' we read: 'The word in its Hellenistic conception is active flesh consummated in the event' (II, 288; 121).[12] The word, poem, culture, Hellenism – all exist in, act within, and affect the space around them unconditionally; they light up, they warm up, the surrounding space. In other words, from 1922–3 onwards, the notions of essence and existence, of meaning and dynamism, and even of hypnotism in poetry appear as synonyms; that is, they appear as essential characteristics of the same principle.

As noted in chapter 2, however, Mandel'shtam is faced in the 1920s with what seems to be another set of polar principles. Once the conceptual framework of thingness-nothingness has been abolished, the notion of the inner and outer reality of the word gradually develops. This new polar contrast differs from the earlier position in that both aspects of the word (not one, as was formerly the case) have power and, indeed, a hypnotic effect. In the earlier case the hypnotic effect was a direct result of nothingness or absence, never of the thingness itself of the word. In the present case both inner and outer aspects of the word exhibit their effects, and both aspects are also acts.

In the 1920s the inner reality of the poem, constituted by the inner reality of the words, is invariably presented as a collection of growing impulses.[13] It seems that we recognize this inner reality and listen to its directions through a certain kindredness. Its secret life is akin to our own: 'Hellenism [i.e., a hidden source of Russian culture] is any kind of stove near which a man sits treasuring its heat as something akin to his own internal body warmth' (II, 253–4; 128). In contrast, the poem's external reality, its visible surface or thingness, is invariably described as exhibiting an arresting effect and a control of movement.[14] This arrest is encountered by the reader, as it were, in a contest. Mandel'shtam's metaphor identifying this effect is 'raging,' and later 'literary wrath' [*literaturnaia zlost'*].[15]

It is necessary at this point to make the following qualification: although I am speaking about a particular view of the effect of poetry, this view is never stated explicitly in Mandel'shtam's essays. Instead, the reader is confronted with highly impressionistic patterns of description, but there is nevertheless a fundamental repetition in the use of images and metaphors. The metaphors, invariably striking and powerful, are equally puzzling and challenging. What follows is once again a careful chronological reconstruction of a particular vision never stated overtly in the oeuvre itself, but always played out in recognizable patterns of description. Mandel'shtam presents poetry as an inner, hidden source of power, which manifests itself in, but is not reducible to, its visible configurations. This is a view that in fact guided (whether consciously or unconsciously) the patterning of his own work and that yet retained its hiddenness, to be displayed only in the repetitive series of metaphors on the surface of the text.

The description of these two effects of poetry – a kindredness of the impulse and a call to rage or contest – appears in Mandel'shtam's essays consecutively, the notion of kindredness and love being particularly characteristic of the early 1920s and that of anger or *zlost'* becoming increasingly prominent around 1925.

The image of poetry as an active form of discourse displaying an unconditional effect appears for the first time in 'The Word and Culture.' This unconditional effect is identified with love, which is for Mandel'shtam (as I shall argue below) an intense recognition of kindredness. Mandel'shtam turns to Catullus, a proverbial lover/poet, and speaks about the notion of command, imperative voice, obligation, and the unceasing hypnotism of poetry. Quoting Catullus' line (with the verb in the present subjunctive) '*volemus*' [let us fly], Mandel'shtam plays on the notion of the subjunctive and its undeniably imperative address, obviously intending to present these qualities as characteristics of poetry per se: 'I chose a Latin line because it is clearly perceived by the Russian reader as a category of obligation: the imperative rings more vividly in it. Such an imperative characterizes all poetry that is Classical. Classical poetry is perceived as that which must be, not as that which has already been' (II, 224; 114).[16] Poetry, therefore, and good (that is, classical) poetry in particular, exhibits a commanding effect that is simultaneously a recognition of beloved objects as one's own, discovered in what, nevertheless, belongs to someone else.[17] In the continuation of the Catullus passage Mandel'shtam carefully follows the notion of an obligatory command with a description of a state which is as unconditional and absolute as the recognition of a familiar and dear scene: 'When in the stillness of the night a lover gets tangled up in tender names and suddenly remembers that all this already was: the words and the hair and the rooster crowing outside his window, exactly as it had been in Ovid's *Tristia,* then the profound joy of recurrence seizes him, a dizzying joy' (II, 224–5; 114).

It is plausible to suppose that here Mandel'shtam is experimenting with Shklovsky's principle of defamiliarization.[18] Shklovsky's 'seeing as if anew' is turned into recollection and is interpreted by the poet not merely as a technical device but as a pattern of communication, most successful because the hidden command is as instantaneous as the recognition of a familiar object and as joyous as the recognition of the beloved.

It is only within these interconnections of meanings that the startling descriptions of Rozanov's philology in 'On the Nature of the Word' finally come into focus. Rozanov, 'an unnecessary and uninfluential writer,' nevertheless feels the inner life of language and the hypnotic power of words. Thus, his attraction to literature is real; he is drawn by love and is a 'philologist,'[19] a term that Mandel'shtam uses with explicit intention: one who is moved by the power or love of words.[20] According to Mandel'shtam, Rozanov's sensitivity to literature is determined by his recognition of literature as his home.[21] Rozanov, 'the anarchistic, nihilistic spirit,' who 'recognized only one authority: the magic of the language, the power of the word' (II, 248; 122), is sensitive to the command of language as one is sensitive to the nuances[22] of the conversations in one's family. Poetry attracts with the same unconditional power as the beloved intonations of conversations at home. Thus, one of Mandel'shtam's most perplexing descriptions finally becomes clear: the inner life of poetry is always a kindred attraction, and therefore, ultimately, an intangible nuance of beloved and respected familiarity:

> Rozanov's attitude towards Russian literature was most unliterary. Literature is a social phenomenon, while philology is domestic, intimate ... Philology is a family because every family is held by [*derzhitsia na*] its own intonations, its personal references and by its own special meanings of words defined in parenthesis. The most casual utterance within a family takes on nuances of its own. Moreover, such limitless, individual and purely philological nuancing characterizes the atmosphere of family life. Hence, I would derive Rozanov's propensity for the domestic quality of life, which so powerfully informed the whole tenor of his literary activity, from the philological nature of his soul. (II, 249; 123–4, translation altered)

The inner life of poetry exhibits an unconditional, personal attraction, a hypnotic drawing into literature as into a family (often compared by Mandel'shtam to the circulation of blood), without which culture ceases to be.[23] Even more significant here is the fact that the exact identification of the source of this attraction cannot be located; as a nuance or intonation it can be recognized but never clearly identified as a tangible locus.

Again, it is reasonable to suppose that this observation that the essence of poetry is an act or a state rather than a device marks Mandel'shtam's disagreement with the formalists, for whom literary analysis was defined as the quest for the precise formal characteristics of defamiliarization, or, in the words of Boris M. Eikhenbaum, a search for 'special artistic devices acting upon perceivers so as to force them to experience form' (1978, 13). But for Mandel'shtam one experiences art not because one is forced to do so by a device, but because one encounters a well-known beloved presence. Another example of this depiction of artistic attraction as family recognition within the inner life of culture appears in the essay 'Mikhoels' (1926), which was written about the same time as Eikhenbaum's defence of formalism, quoted above, a defence summarizing for the last time the formalist platform in the face of Trotsky's attack. The passage from 'Mikhoels' reiterates the familial kindred understanding of art, first so powerfully articulated by Mandel'shtam in his depiction of Rozanov. However, 'Mikhoels' offers perhaps the most striking presentation of the imperative command in the inner world of culture (and poetry) to be recognized as a blood relative, or a deeply familiar presence. Mikhoels's Jewishness is described as this attraction, and the familiar identification among kindred people is simultaneously presented as a metaphor for the inner attraction of all art.[24] Jewishness, two Jews recognizing each other, is treated as an insight into the inner life of an aesthetic principle, as an immediate and joyful recognition of kindredness that cannot be outmoded or forgotten. Mikhoels's Jewish theatre rejoices at the sight of every Jew, pulls him into the factory of the theatre's art, and then transforms him into its visible product, its hardened surface: 'This paradoxical theatre ... becomes intoxicated like a woman at the mere sight of a Jew and immediately begins to draw him into its workshop – into the porcelain factory to be baked and hardened ... into a group ... [which] dances like modest young maidens clasping hands in a circle' (III, 107; 261).

However, the inner 'laboratory' of poetry and its attraction as the recognition of home[25] are balanced by the opposite effect of the outer life of the poem, which calls its reader to a contest. Again this notion appears first in 'On the Nature of the Word' and it sounds, indeed, somewhat eccentric. Annensky, a poet-philologist, is presented by Mandel'shtam as a contrast to Rozanov: 'In the same way that Rozanov represents the domestic Hellenism of God's fools and of the poor in Russian literature, Annensky represents heroic Hellenism, martial philology' (II, 252; 126). Annensky's fight[26] with the treasures of western literature cannot as yet be fully identified with the rage, contest, and conflict characteristic of Mandel'shtam's later descriptions of the reception of the literary text and its guardianship, but it is clearly an initial appearance of this element. The conflict is presented here as Annensky protecting Russian soil from western patterns: 'In a most original manner, Annensky grasped in his talons all that was foreign, and still soaring high in the sky arrogantly dropped his plunder, allowing it to fall as it would. And the eagle of his poetry which had seized as its prey Euripides, Mallarmé, Leconte de Lisle, brought us nothing but a handful of dry grass ... When Annensky kept vigil, everyone was sleeping' (II, 252–3; 126–7). As strange as this account of Annensky's profound knowledge of romance literature may seem,[27] it already possesses in embryonic form all of Mandel'shtam's subsequent descriptions of the reader's contest with the external power of poetry. Annensky's fight, indeed, takes place at the outer limits of the evoked landscape: it is either taking place high above[28] (i.e., the eagle 'soaring high in the sky') or at the furthest geographical boundaries: 'Annensky's lyric poetry and his tragedies can be compared to wooden fortifications, the walled towns far out in the steppes' (II, 252; 126). The implication of the image is that one reaches the outer limits of poetry, that is, its design and form, only with courage and strength and by means of conflict or contest.

In 1924 this is exactly how Mandel'shtam presents Fiodor Sologub's thematic closeness to Tiutchev. The outer limits of poetry are now represented not merely as a battlefield under apparent control, but also in terms of coldness, even ice – an image that will appear in several key descriptions in *The Noise of Time*.[29] Sologub is praised for his ability first to reach the height of Tiutchev's themes, and then to humanize them, to bring them literally inside, down to the level of the familiar, into one's own home. Thus, Sologub is described as a courageous mountaineer, who can melt the perpetual snow of Tiutchev's poetry:

> in time we came to understand Sologub's poetry as a science of action, a science of will, a science of courage and love.
>
> Sologub's poetry flowed from Tiutchev's Alpine summits, like limpid mountain streams. These streams babbled so close to our domicile, to our home ... This is a descent into the valley to the level of life and habitation. It is a descent of the snowy, ethereally cold deposits of Russian poetry (per-

haps too immobile and egoistical in their icy indifference and accessible only to a courageous reader)   (II, 356; 207)

The last chapter of *The Noise of Time*, 'In a Fur Coat above One's Station,' develops these notions of contest, courage, conflict, into an almost sardonic note of literary rage [*literaturnaia zlost*]. Literature can be understood only through fighting and anger, yet it remains a source of love and warmth. Here Mandel'shtam brings the inner and outer notions of poetry together in an amazing portrayal of his first teacher of literature who, as may be expected, is always ferociously angry: 'He differed from the other witnesses of literature precisely in this angry astonishment. He had a kind of feral relationship to literature, as if it were the only source of animal warmth ... He was a Romulus who hated his wolf mother and, hating her, taught others to love her' (II, 104–5; Brown 1965, 128).

It is also clear that the emphasis on anger and ferocious rage as well as icy cold temperatures in *The Noise of Time* (1925)[30] represents not only a theoretical insight but also Mandel'shtam's own painful and angry bewilderment about his position in the new Soviet state. The energetic, brilliant, and impulsive writer discovers that his intellectual journey only takes him further and further away, however inadvertently, from the by now well-charted course of Soviet literature. Ferocity and anger, as well as the recognition of home in the literature of the past, were utterly unwelcome in the new Soviet state. In 1930, after five years of near-silence, Mandel'shtam again restates his position in *The Fourth Prose*, in which he insists that any writer who does not hear the contest-call of literature, or its challenge to battle, is a hateful and contemptible cultural adjunct: 'I divide all of world literature into authorized and unauthorized works. The former are all trash, the latter – stolen air. I want to spit in the face of every writer who first obtains permission and then writes. I want to beat such writers over the head with a stick' (II, 182; 316). The poetic text literally attracts with love, yet it also precipitates disagreement. Poetry liberates the dynamism of the word – this fact is clear in Mandel'shtam's essays of the 1920s. But the discussion still remains highly metaphorical and is particularly obscure in its elucidation of the process of the intensification of dynamism or its liberation.

Mandel'shtam has a definite perception of the two opposite effects of poetry, or two contrasting imperatives, each identified with either the inner or the outer life of poetic expression. However, a clearer explanation of *how* this perception is achieved, or displayed, is needed, for it is never directly stated in the essays. As is always the case with Mandel'shtam's work, an answer can be found only by a careful sifting and juxtaposition of his images in their chronological order, and here we must now turn to the images of catastrophe.

3   The Catastrophic Essence of Poetry, 1921–1932

The catastrophic essence of art is perhaps the most difficult concept in Mandel'shtam's writing in the 1920s.[31] It is unclear, fragmentary, and yet central.[32] It is asserted most emphatically in 'Badger Hole' (1922), where the Revolution (and its thematic treatment) is called 'the highest form of musical tension and the catastrophic essence of culture' (II, 317; 138). There is an echo of this image in a newspaper article, 'Human Grain' (1922), in which catastrophe is cited as the cause of an earthquake extending into politics and into the origin of culture (Fleishman 1982, 453–5).[33] We find the same notion in the *Conversation about Dante* (1933), where Mandel'shtam compares the *Commedia* to a great crystallographic body and asserts: 'Granular admixtures and veins of lava indicate a singular shift or catastrophe as the common source of formation' (II, 413; 407, translation altered). The concept, therefore, is long-standing and important in Mandel'shtam's poetics, and demands careful examination.

One may approach this notion directly from the equation of revolution and catastrophe. In the essay 'Iakhontov,' where the actor's attentiveness to the word has been described among other images as a fight ('He is a living reader; he stands on an equal footing with the author, arguing with him, disagreeing with him, fighting with him,' III, 114; 269), Mandel'shtam also states that revolution has liberated the word: 'A revolution was required to liberate the word in the theatre' (III, 114; 269). We have already seen, however, that in 'Badger Hole' Mandel'shtam calls revolution the catastrophic essence of art. Revolution, therefore, does to culture what poetry does to the word: it intensifies the hidden tension and displays it in its full power. This explains Mandel'shtam's depiction of Blok, whose 'catastrophic temperament' ('The poet's spiritual temperament is inclined to catastrophe,' II, 275; 137) allows the poet to hear the music of revolution long before it can be manifested in any visible or audible form: 'It is impossible not to be astonished by Blok's historical sensitivity. Even long before he implored us to listen to the music of revolution, Blok heard the subterranean music of Russian history, where the most highly attuned ear caught only a syncopated pause' (II, 272; 134). The juxtaposition of these images allows us to conclude that for Mandel'shtam the contrast between the outer stillness, on the one hand, and the fullness of the subterranean music (that is, a highly charged, invisible, and inaudible inner structure), on the other, results not only in the storm, the earthquake, the shift of ground,[34] but also in the birth of poetry, or catastrophe – literally *kata* [going downwards into] and *strophe* [turn, dance, movement, conversion]. Further, in the Catullus passage in 'The Word and Culture' the birth of the poem is depicted as the poet's *entanglement* in the multiplicity of beloved names within a surrounding stillness (II, 224–5; 114). The poem is presented as a birth, an escape, or even an awareness of this rich, ringing life through the narrow entrance of metre, structure, or form: 'poetic speech may be compared to a piece of amber in which a fly still buzzes, having long been buried under layers of resin' ('Some Notes on Poetry,' II, 260–1; 165).

The catastrophic essence of poetry is a form-creation in which the hidden aspect of the word comes to full dynamic display. Yet Mandel'shtam's thought undergoes another significant transformation in his essays of the 1920s. The earlier essays (around 1922) all signify his acceptance of the Revolution, and his view of poetry as a powerful manifestation of a hidden and suppressed dynamism. It is around this time that Mandel'shtam was much attracted to the futurists, whose work he viewed as the unleashing of an intensified substratum.[35] In these terms precisely he describes the work of Pasternak: 'In Pasternak's poetry this "burning salt" of some speeches, this whistling, crackling, rustling, sparkling, splashing, this fullness of life, this fullness of sound, this flood of images and feelings emerges with unprecedented force' (II, 264; 168). Yet after 1922 Mandel'shtam seems to value the ability of the poet (and poetry in general) to control the awakened lava, to effect 'the solidification of the morphological lava under the semantic crust' (II, 261; 166).[36] It is at this time that Mandel'shtam re-evaluates the works of the symbolists, praising their ability to direct and control the rich, living mass of poetry.[37] Poetry, therefore, is catastrophic in its essence because it uncovers the energy underneath an apparent stillness.[38] In the 1930s Mandel'shtam will compare this quality to the scientific use of the microscope. Yet the process of merely uncovering the hidden turbulence is insufficient. The poet is able to hear the living lava of the language, yet the role of art is both to permit and to contain the lava's release. The conclusion of Mandel'shtam's essay on Blok, 'Badger Hole,' formerly obscure, can now be explained.[39] The arresting, shaping power of poetry prevents a catastrophe, for art literally *contains* catastrophe by encompassing and sealing it. From the images of other essays, especially those of warmth and love, it now becomes clear that for Mandel'shtam the process of shaping is also care and love (*philology*): 'The poet's spiritual temperament is inclined to catastrophe. Cult and culture presuppose a hidden, protected source of energy, a measured and expedient motion: "the love which moves the sun and all the luminaries." Poetic culture arises from the attempt to avert catastrophe, to make it dependent on the central sun of the whole system, be it love, of which Dante spoke, or music, at which Blok finally arrived' (II, 275; 137).

This confirms my thesis that there is a demonstrable but implicit duality of the inner/outer aspects of poetry and their effects in Mandel'shtam's view of poetry in the 1920s. The outer surface, whose role is to arrest the movement, or to impede the kindred impulse, reinforces the notion of the sealing of the internal catastrophe as a function of art. The notion of catastrophe, therefore, is initially embedded in Mandel'shtam's double pattern of describing poetry. By 1925, however, he must have realized that his characterization of the imperative power of poetry relies too heavily on the artificial nature of this depiction of the inner and outer space of the word, each exhibiting an opposite effect. As the notion of Bergson's fan – a self-gathering and dispersion – fades and the metaphor of the word as a journey, or alternatively a pilgrim, emerges, Mandel'shtam finds it necessary to extend the description of the effects of poetry, not limiting them to the display of contrasting commands, whose very duality suggests an imposed, and therefore artificial, insight.

4 Signal-Waves of Meaning, 1930

By the end of the 1920s the opposition between the rich, diversified impulses within poetry, on the one hand, and the solidified, external surface, on the other, is no longer strictly delineated and emphasized. Moreover, the metaphoric presentation of the living internal mass of impulses begins to be identified in an increasingly explicit manner with the image of waves.[40] In turn, the image of waves within the inner dimensions of poetic expression begins to assume a central place, and in the 1930s it is finally presented no longer as a descriptive metaphor but as a theoretical insight supported by (or even founded upon) the discoveries of modern physics concerning the wave origin of sound and light. For Mandel'shtam in *Conversation about Dante* and *Journey to Arme-*

nia: 'Dante can be understood only with the help of quantum theory' (III, 183; 446). The very nature of poetry and culture is constituted by, and displays its origin as, a succession of quantum-waves: 'the purely European passion [is] for periodic undulating movements, the very same close listening to sound and light waves found in all our theory of sound and light, in all our scientific study of matter, in all our poetry and music' (II, 390; 421). In the 1930s, therefore, the surface of the poem is no longer presented as tranquil, or solid, or frozen. Rather, it appears as an endless series of imperceptible explosions.[41] The text literally moves as a succession of waves, while the impulses[42] that constitute the poetic texture move quickly and imperceptibly from the source of their origin to their textual manifestation. The earlier presentation of the external surface of poetry as 'consolidated morphological lava' (II, 261; 166), 'a piece of amber in which a fly still buzzes' (II, 260; 165), is succeeded by the notion of poetry as a durable, fluid carpet, where an inner life is displayed in endlessly changing surface configurations. The movement of the waves is never arrested; rather, the movement is played out in outer and inner dimensions alike: 'It [poetry] is an extremely durable carpet, woven out of fluid: a carpet in which the currents of Ganges, taken as a fabric theme, do not mix with the samples of the Nile or the Euphrates, but remain multicoloured, in braids, figures and ornaments ... Ornament is good precisely because it preserves traces of its origin as a piece of nature enacted. Whether the piece is animal, vegetable, steppe, Scythian, or Egyptian, indigenous or barbarian, it is always speaking, seeing, acting' (II, 365; 398). This notion of the quantum-wave at the origin of poetic expression brings a significant alteration into Mandel'shtam's depiction of the effect of the poetic text. There is no longer a clear distinction between the outer and the inner dimensions of poetry and the specific contrast of their effects.[43] Instead, Mandel'shtam presents waves of meaning that awaken the reader into action and disappear before the precise nature of their command can be analysed: 'The signal-waves of meaning vanish having completed their work; the more potent they are the more yielding and the less inclined to linger' (*Conversation about Dante*, II, 364; 398). The command here is directly related to the notion of the word as pilgrim: the signal-wave of meaning awakens one to action,[44] yet the character of the action changes once the pilgrimage has begun. It is most important to observe in this context that the speed of the command is not so much that of a quick attack but rather of a quick yielding: the text is like the keys of a piano, quick and yielding to the performer's power and, therefore, teaching him new levels of understanding and agility. A successful understanding is 'not at all passive, reproducing or paraphrasing ... Semantic adequacy is equivalent to the feeling of having fulfilled a command' (II, 364; 398).

In this preliminary presentation of Mandel'shtam's position I have concentrated on his depiction of poetry in his essays of the 1930s as an initiation of movement, a movement which is then presented along successive levels of complexity. The precise nature of the signal-command upon each particular level will be outlined in chapter 5, which deals specifically with the periodic stages of the changing landscape of the unveiling poetic texture. At this point we may conclude that the command of poetry is to awaken the reader to a series of actions that comprise the whole range of physical and intellectual involvement:[45] 'In Dante philosophy and poetry are constantly on the go, perpetually on their feet. Even a stop is a variety of accumulated movement ... The metrical foot is an inhalation and exhalation of the step. Each step draws a conclusion, invigorates, syllogizes' (II, 367; 400).

The effect of poetry, therefore, does not originate in nothingness, as Mandel'shtam seemed to think in his early essays, nor does it exhibit a series of dualistic contrasts. Its effect contains all of these moments, but its range is much more complex and varied. Mandel'shtam must have searched from 1925 onwards for a system of thought the nature of which was not simply that of artificially constructed and assumed patterns, but which comprises most genuine aspects of human experience and which allows, therefore, for a wide diversity of insights into the effect of poetry. Following the logic of the images to which Mandel'shtam invariably returns when he speaks of poetry, we can see that he arrives naturally at a new configuration of the poetic vision in so far as he comes to regard poetry as not merely an effective expression but as an organic territory that both contains and displays radically differing patterns of communication.

4

The Participation of the Reader

The principles involved in listening to, and receiving, the vibrant word of poetry also formed a necessary part of Mandel'shtam's interest in the phenomenon of poetic communication. This chapter will trace Mandel'shtam's thought about the patterns of the reception of poetry, starting from the notion of poetry as dialogue, then moving to the idea of reception as flight in pursuit of a word that eludes capture, and ultimately coming to his final position that the processes involved in reception extend from an instinctual, organic response to a highly complex activity, all the stages of which can be represented by means of an equation between the reading process and organic growth.

1 The Dialogical Nature of Poetry, 1913 and After

Even Mandel'shtam's earliest essays address the issue of poetic communication. 'François Villon' (1910), 'Morning of Acmeism' (1913), and 'About the Interlocutor' (1913) all discuss the reader and his presence in the configurations of the poetic text. Although these works scarcely present a coherent theoretical position in themselves, they nevertheless exhibit insights crucial for the understanding of the poet's later development. Their importance becomes clear when in 1925 Mandel'shtam begins to formulate the context in which these views can be grounded and properly developed.

Already in 1910, in his essay on Villon, Mandel'shtam asserts without hesitation that the lyric poet is hermaphroditic, and that this bipolarity in his make-up is necessary for the sake of the inner dialogue of poetic expression. Furthermore, Mandel'shtam develops this notion of an inner dialogue in his assertion of the dynamic nature of poetry, which addresses numerous interlocutors and reaches a potentially endless number of readers. Mandel'shtam gives the process of acquiring readers a vertical, rather than a horizontal, orientation. In fact, he likens the dialogical structure of Villon's poetry to the architecture of the Gothic cathedral whose movement upwards parallels the vertical succession of acquired addressees: 'This is no anemic flight on the waxen wings of immortality; it is an architecturally founded Ascension, corresponding to the tiers in the Gothic cathedral ... Perhaps ... somewhere in his soul there lurked an untamed but profoundly feudal sense of a God above God' (II, 308–9; 59, translation altered).

In 1913, in 'About the Interlocutor,' Mandel'shtam gives a subtle reformulation of the same argument, this time in a novel and provocative manner. Poetry, he asserts, cannot address a close neighbour, for the poet knows in advance his acquaintance's reaction and 'will not be astonished at his astonishment' (II, 239; 72). The element of surprise, which brings joy into the texture of poetry, can be achieved only if 'the distance of separation erases the feature of the loved one,' for only from a distance can the poet 'feel the desire to tell his interlocutor something important' (II, 239; 72). He argues, furthermore, that if the poet feels disdain for the reader, it will be mirrored in the reader's response to the poem, whereas his joy and surprise will again be shared by the reader, for 'there is only one thing that pushes us into the addressee's embrace: the desire to be astonished by our own words, to be captivated by their originality and unexpectedness' (II, 239; 72). Poetry, therefore, can only address the unknown, for this in turn shapes the content of the discourse, making the distancing of the addressee a necessary law of poetry. Moreover, the poet's lack of trust in the presence of this providential interlocutor will always result in a lack of trust in himself (II, 240; 73). This mirroring of moods and attitudes, and the inverse proportion between the distance of the interlocutors on the one hand and the intimacy of the address on the other, constitute in the dialogical nature of poetry a state that is nothing less in stature 'than, without fantasizing, exchanging signals with the planet Mars' (II, 239; 72).

The 'Morning of Acmeism' is much less precise in its discussion of the dialogical principle of poetry. The notion of joyful cooperation among the stones of the cathedral (II, 322; 62) may imply an intention to see poetic discourse as a chorus of polyphonic voices, but this is nowhere explicitly stated. Later essays, up to the 1920s, are even less specific about the status of the addressee in the texture of poetic discourse. Mandel'shtam's preoccupation with 'nothingness' as a source of hypnotism gives us grounds to suppose that, if the poem addresses anyone externally, it is no longer a distant interlocutor or a neighbouring voice, but the emptiness of the blank, which it hypnotizes and pierces by the employment of the same blank in its own unveiling. Thus, a poem exercises power over external indefiniteness by drawing this indefiniteness inside its own structured unity.

What is most surprising about these views is their variety. Mandel'shtam starts his career as an essayist simultaneously arguing for the dialogical principle of poetry and attempting to identify its addressee. The concept proves to be elusive, however, and, what is perhaps worse, susceptible to considerable differentiation. It is clear that these concepts cannot be properly broached until several other key characteristics of poetic discourse are elucidated, and Mandel'shtam's initial excitement about the notion of the addressee disappears around 1915.

2 The Escape of the Poetic Voice, 1924 and After

Mandel'shtam returns in an explicit manner to the discussion of the reader's role in the poetic texture only around 1924,[1] but this renewed interest could well have been predicted from his writings of the early 1920s. Its immediate cause seems at least twofold: first, the affective nature of poetry, which he had so clearly emphasized, was leading him to a consideration of the patterns of reception; second, the death of culture that he had witnessed, and was continuing to witness, and the intellectual anaemia of Soviet youth caused Mandel'shtam to see reading as an almost medicinal process:[2] 'The word born deep in the womb of speech-consciousness serves the deaf and dumb, the inarticulate, the cretins and degenerates of the word' ('Vypad,' 1923, II, 231; 204). Perhaps, the intrinsic dynamism of the word would be able to undo these ills, for a culture that might no longer be able to write could still read.

Mandel'shtam's difficulty lies in the description of the process. All of his theoretical prose in the 1920s is highly metaphorical, and here he approaches a topic that demands a much more direct and precise treatment. Yet throughout the mid-1920s his portrayal of the reading process and the reader's consciousness remains allusive and allegorical. Nevertheless, a careful examination of several key passages will permit us to grasp the force and direction of his thought.

It seems likely that while Mandel'shtam presented the contrast between the inner and outer aspects of poetry, he entertained the possibility of treating as synonymous and equivalent both the inner character of poetic discourse and the consciousness of the reader. As a result the controlling power of the solidified outer structure might have been presented as limiting and directing the inner dynamism not only of the poetry but also of the reader's response. This suggestion is only partially correct, however. Mandel'shtam does indeed set out parallel descriptions of the inner world of poetry and the consciousness of the reader. For example, the depiction of Iakhontov's stage portrayal of the reading process (1927) repeats almost idea for idea the presentation of the inner dynamism of Khlebnikov's often inaccessible prose (1923). On Khlebnikov's verse Mandel'shtam writes: 'He gave us examples of marvellous prose ... the result of an incessant stream of images and ideas pushing each other out of consciousness. Each line he wrote is the beginning of a new long poem' ('Storm and Stress,' 178). On Iakhontov's acting he writes: 'In other pieces Iakhontov's montage emerges as a harmonious literary whole, precisely reproducing [tochno vosproizvodiashchii] the internal world of the reader in which a variety of literary works coexist side by side, often colliding with each other or pushing one another into the background' (III, 122; 268). The natural next step would be to develop the idea that the outer aspect of poetry directs these inner impulses of the reader's consciousness, controlling and sealing the awakened effect and shaping the response in a manner similar to its formation of the inner world of poetry, where it contains and controls catastrophe. It is precisely this step, however, that Mandel'shtam does not take. Instead, the reader's subjugation to the controlling power of poetic discourse is portrayed in an emphatically negative fashion.

The Noise of Time, in particular, outlines the danger of this subjugation. Semion Nadson, a poet beloved of Russian students at the end of the nineteenth century,[3] is presented as a great victor in an enterprise marked by continuous failures. He exercised remarkable control over his audience. However, the power of his immobile, wooden voice over the burning, living consciousness of his readers is described as the suicide of the century, as the century's unanimous loss of its desire to live, and Nadson's role of leader is bitterly satirized: 'But what actually happened was that the intelligentsia with Buckle and Rubenstein and *led by the enlightened personalities – who in their beatific idiocy had completely lost the way* – resolutely turned to the practice of self-burning. Like high tar-coated torches the adherents of the People's Will Party burned for all people to see, while Sofja Perovskaia and Zheliabov, and all of them, all of provincial Russia and all of the students, smouldered in sympathy: not one single green leaf was to be left' (II, 60–1; Brown 1965, 84–5).

However, *The Noise of Time* also depicts two brilliant musicians, Iosif Hofmann and Ian Kubelik, whose virtuosity is portrayed as an *inability* to control their audience; they are praised precisely for their failure to direct the inner life of the audience. Indeed, it is the absence of similarity between the musicians' power and the audience's response that is emphasized in the description of the reception of their music: 'But what in their performance was clear and sober served only to enrage and incite to new frenzies the crowd that clung to the marble columns, hung in clusters from the gallery, sprouted from the flowerbeds of the orchestra, and thickened hotly on the stage. Such was the power in the rational and pure playing of these two virtuosi' (II, 73; Brown 1965, 96). What, we may ask, is wrong in Nadson's power over his audience? Is not his uninspired face what was lauded in 1922 as the 'consolidation of morphological lava'? Why should the musicians be praised for their inability to standardize an audience's response?

Here we come to the very heart of that so-difficult-to-trace reorientation of Mandel'shtam's ideas. As we have seen in chapter 3, the idea of a surface consolidation of growing impulses guided much of Mandel'shtam's work on poetry in the 1920s. Yet we have also seen that a change was taking place: the notion of consolidation was giving way to that of a fluid carpet representing the surface of the poetic text. The consolidation or standardization of the reader's consciousness by the poetic text, therefore, cannot be expected to be developed in this context. And Mandel'shtam's treatment of the power of the poetic text over the reader's understanding is, indeed, somewhat unexpected. In 1924, in the two essays 'Vypad' and 'For the Anniversary of F.K. Sologub,' Mandel'shtam suggests implicitly that the health of poetry consists not in the exercise of a solidifying control over its readers but in its ability to avoid being grasped by the listener and enveloped in the patterns of his consciousness.

In 'Vypad,' when he laments the ignorance of the simple Russian people, Mandel'shtam states that it is comforting that the meeting between poetry and people has not yet been carried out. On a superficial level the statement can be read as the rather awkwardly expressed, but nonetheless perfectly natural, desire of a Soviet poet to be read by the working class. But the wider context in which this new image occurs (poetry is compared to a ray of light, instead of to the plough as in the 1922 image) implies that the meeting between the light and the 'masses' of earth (but also 'social masses') will result in the death of light because of the density of the layers of the earth. Thus, this complex passage suggests that it is in its avoidance of these levels and in its, so to speak, postmortem penetration of them that the longevity of poetry consists:

> Perhaps the most comforting thing about the general state of Russian poetry is the people's sheer ignorance of their own poetry.
> The masses [*massy*], that is, those levels [*sloi*] in which the morphology of language grows, strengthens, and develops, have retained a wholesome philological sense, and have not yet encountered individualist Russian poetry.[4] Poetry has still not reached its readers. Perhaps it will reach them only after the extinction of those poetic luminaries which have sent their rays to that distant and as yet unattainable destination. (II, 232; 204–5, translation altered)

The only other surviving essay of 1924, 'On the Anniversary of F.K. Sologub,' substantiates this reading. Sologub is presented as a poet who never addressed his contemporary public. In what seems to be an almost impenetrable series of metaphors[5] Mandel'shtam implies that Sologub's most transparent speech [*prozrachnyi golos*] will escape the grasp of a contemporary tongue-tied public [*kosnoiazychie*],[6] burn their sluggish nature,[7] and be understood only in future, transparent generations when the light of poetry will not be extinguished. Indeed, Sologub's poetry explicitly avoids the contemporary generation: 'To the future all the poetry of Sologub is addressed.'

I propose that these intentionally ambiguous passages play out the pattern they describe: the ability of the poet to escape the grasp of the reader. We should remember that all the images of reading in 1925 and 1926 imply a fight between the reader and the poet, and that the reader of *The Noise of Time* is always in a fighting mood, whereas Iakhontov, who 'plays out the reader,' stands on an equal footing with the author, arguing with him, disagreeing with him, fighting with him' (III, 114; 269).

The idea that the power of poetry resides in its escape from the reader explains, in turn, why Hofmann and Kubelik, the two musicians in *The Noise of Time*, are praised for their inability to control their listeners directly. It is the escape of their music that has moved the audience to Dionysiac frenzy: the mastery of the artist does not control; it escapes, provoking the listener into pursuit rather than controlled obedience. The poet Nadson, in contrast, meets his reader face to face, and through his absolute control initiates the suicidal urge to conform, but the voice of the poet does not survive this total union with the reader's consciousness. Thus, it is no longer possible to discern Nadson's voice:

'Do not laugh at Nadsonism; it is the enigma of Russian culture and the essentially incomprehensible sound of it, for we do not understand and hear as they understood and heard' (II, 59–60; Brown 1965, 83–4). Nadson's voice has been grasped and encompassed and consumed. This, for Mandel'shtam, is the fate of a very lucky but inferior poet.

Thus, by 1930 Mandel'shtam had, as it were, the rudiments of a theory of communication that went totally against all the demands of his age. In contrast to Maiakovsky, who had proclaimed that the survival of poetry resides in its ability to meet the contemporary reader face to face, Mandel'shtam found himself insisting that poetry's survival could only reside in its obliqueness and in its ability both to outmanoeuvre the reader and at the same time to present him with a ringing inner life, drawing the reader into the familiar nuances of home and yet escaping, and thus provoking the reader to pursuit. This in turn awakens the reader's inner world, layer by layer; the substratum begins an organic life in the mind of the reader, and the echoes of each poetic word 'collide with one another or push one another into the background' (II, 122; 268). At this point the description of the process (so disjointedly thrown into the pages of Mandel'shtam's manuscripts) breaks down. Mandel'shtam speaks about the growth of inner impulses, and the fight between author and reader. The notion of laws that govern the reader's understanding is also suggested at this point, but not developed (see, for example, the symbolists as law-givers in 'Vypad').

Mandel'shtam, therefore, moves into the 1930s with a somewhat unsettling theoretical stance. Even if we momentarily disregard the sociopolitical implications of his view (so clearly unneeded in the Soviet state), he carries into the new decade a troublesome burden of unresolved ideas. The early essays that he included in his 1928 edition of *On Poetry* present the role of the addressee in varying, almost mutually exclusive, patterns of visualization. His essays of the 1920s depict poetic speech as simultaneously drawing in the reader with its familiar intonation and yet also provoking him to a contest. However, while the imperative power of poetry is stressed, these essays also portray poetic communication as the necessity for the poet to outmanoeuvre the consciousness of the reader. It is my belief that in his last two major works Mandel'shtam discovered a way to unite these strands of insight into a new, complex, and yet taut framework.

3 The Reading Process as Metamorphosis

In both *Journey to Armenia* (1933) and *Conversation about Dante* (written in 1933, but not published in Mandel'shtam's lifetime) Mandel'shtam stresses that the theory of poetry stands on the threshold of the discovery of a new science, which he alternately calls the physiology of reading or the reflexology of speech. The present embryonic state of this future science reflects, according to Mandel'shtam, his own difficulty in outlining the process with precision. In the 1930s he himself gives three descriptions of the reading process. Each is strikingly different, and each is presented within radically dissimilar metaphorical settings. It is clear, then, that even in the 1930s, no single, clear, unifying depiction can be found.

Let us examine these three descriptions in more detail. The *Conversation about Dante* presents the science that is to deal with the reading process as akin to modern physics (the wave-theory of sound and light), whereas the physiology of reading is depicted as an artistic principle in *Journey to Armenia* and as an organic pattern in the rough draft of that work. Here are the passages in question:

Conversation about Dante
His 'reflexology of speech' is astonishing – a science still not established, of the spontaneous psycho-physiological influence of the word on those who are conversing, on the audience surrounding them, and on the speaker himself, as well as on the means by which he communicates his urge to speak, that is by which he signals with a light his sudden desire to express himself. Here he comes closest to approaching the wave theory of sound and light, determining their relationship.   (II, 404; 434)

Journey to Armenia
Let us speak about the physiology of reading. It is a rich, inexhaustible and seemingly forbidden theme. Of all the objects of the material world, of all the physical bodies, a book is the object which inspires man with the greatest degree of confidence. A book firmly established on a reader's desk is like a canvas stretched on its frame.   (II, 163; 366)

Journey to Armenia, early draft
The physiology of reading still remains to be studied. Moreover, this subject differs radically from bibliography, and must be related to the organic phenomena of nature. A book in use, a book established on a reader's desk is like a canvas stretched on its frame.   (III, 165; 393)

These major differences in the descriptions of the reading process have much in common with the greatly varying visualizations of the addressee in the early essays. However, in the 1930s Mandel'shtam discontinues his search for a homogeneous unifying principle; instead, he accepts and develops the position that the process under examination possesses not one pattern but a variety of patterns. As always in Mandel'shtam, this breakthrough is not explicitly stated; it is left to the reader to deduce the new pattern of thinking from a variety of striking, and at first somewhat bewildering, passages.

The scattered discussions of the process of reading in both *Conversation about Dante* and *Journey to Armenia* concentrate upon the difficulty of outlining this uncharted territory: reading is an act that leaves no trace and produces no visible alterations. The reading process is an elucidating act of understanding. By calling the process fulfilling (where 'fulfilling' [*ispolnenie*] allows for two meanings: 1 / creative performance and 2 / obedience to the command), Mandel'shtam stresses the fact that upon its completion the process involved in reading is immediately forgotten, and that this forgetfulness is an essential part of its nature. As the waves of the text are imperceptible in their quick yielding, the process of reading and the elucidation of understanding are imperceptible acts always accompanied by a willing amnesia: 'Imagine something intelligible, grasped, wrestled from obscurity, in a language *voluntarily and willingly forgotten* immediately after the clarifying act of understanding-fulfilling is completed [*sovershilsja projasnjajushchij akt ponimanija-ispolnenija*]' (II, 364; 348, translation altered). In the manuscript of the *Conversation about Dante*, Mandel'shtam calls this act 'idiotic in its essence,' that is, an individual or idiosyncratic act unfilled by self-reflexivity (cf. Greek *idiotês*). Again, by employing the double-entendre of *ispolnenie*, and by playing on the notion of 'filling in' [*zapolnenie*], he identifies the process as an unfilled (i.e., uncharted) gap between hearing and articulation.[8] It is in this unfilled gap that the source of creativity [*ispolnitel'stvo*] lies, yet it remains a gap, a blank:[9] 'There exists a middle activity between hearing and articulation. This activity is the closest to the performance [or fulfilling – *ispolnitel'stvo*] and contains, as it were, its very heart. Unfilled interval between listening and articulation is idiotic in its essence. Material is not matter' (III, 182; 445, translation altered). Thus, the act of reading-fulfilment is identified as a source of the artistic gift – 'this activity is the closest to the performance' – yet it has to be approached as a blank, a gap, an uncharted locus of forgetfulness. The experiences in question are forgotten as an integral part of their very unveiling. The unfilled interval is no longer the blank of Mandel'shtam's earlier works, but rather the discovery of a potential for creativity as yet unrealized, in which Mandel'shtam situates the proper material (that is, not simply matter) for the future individual artistic performance, a material not to be equated with blank matter.

Journey to Armenia continually returns to the notion of forgetfulness and attempts to reconstruct its landscape, or rather its transformation into the act of recollection. It is here that a major breakthrough takes place: Mandel'shtam starts to entertain the possibility of regarding this process as semi-forgetfulness followed by recollection. Invariably the transformation is described as an organic process,[10] similar in its patterns to the emerging of a plant from a seed hidden in the soil: 'Without suspecting it, we are all carriers of an enormous embryological experiment: indeed, the very process of remembering, crowned with the victory of memory's effort, is astonishingly similar to the phenomenon of growth. In both instances, there is a sprout, an embryo, either some facial feature or character trait, a half-sound, a name ending, something labial or palatal, some sweet pea on the tongue, which does not develop out of itself, but only responds on an invitation, only stretches forth, justifying our expectation' (II, 155; 359). The possibility of approaching reading as an organic process, that is, as the material of physiology, a science – 'the physiology of reading' – was for Mandel'shtam an invaluable insight, a personal celebration: 'Since that time when my friends – no, that's too strong, I should say, "acquaintances," lured me into their circle of natural scientists, a broad green glade arose, before my eyes. A new door opened before me into a bright and active field' (III, 161; 390, translation altered).[11] Moreover, he views this new pattern of thinking in which the intellectual process (reading) becomes an organic process (growth) as an act of the foremost importance, a return to the very source of the intellectual activity of the mind: 'We approach the mysteries of organic life. Indeed, the most difficult thing for an adult is making the transition from inorganic thought (the mode in which we have been trained during the most active period of our lives, when thought is but an adjunct to action) to the first form [*pervoobraz*] of organic thinking' (III, 161; 390, translation altered).

It seems, therefore, that Mandel'shtam insists that the secrets of reading, or the patterns of reading-reception, cannot be uncovered without the alignment of these processes with organic patterns. The processes of reading and of biological development were never equivalent for the poet; yet he insists in the *Conversation about Dante* that poetic discourse 'plays out nature,' that is, manifests organic secrets in the very patterns of the transformations of poetry.

Once an alignment between reading and organic patterns is found, Mandel'shtam can proceed towards an understanding of the process of growth that he invokes in the description of embryonic transformation/recollection cited above (II, 155; 359). Once the equation between reading and growth has been accepted, growth begins to be perceived not as a purely biological, organic function but rather as a display of the invisible forces at work in the universe. The plant comes out of the earth; its origin is organic, yet as it grows it answers the invitation of the magnetic charges of the cosmos, thus becoming a playground for, and participator in, forces that transcend the plant's immediate biological status: 'A plant is a sound extracted by the wand of a termenvox,[12] which pulsates in a sphere oversaturated with wave processes. It is the envoy of a living storm permanently raging in the universe akin in equal measure to stone and lightning. A plant in the world is an event, a happening, an arrow, hardly some boring, bearded "development"!' (II, 154; 359). As reading and growth are understood to share similar patterns, the process of growth is presented as surpassing in its unveiling the purely biological network of interchanges.

If we have here uncovered Mandel'shtam's pattern of thinking as he approaches the secrets of poetic discourse and its reception, it will be possible to grasp several other key passages scattered in what otherwise seems to be a rather whimsical fashion in the manuscripts, the drafts, and the final versions of *Conversation about Dante* and *Journey to Armenia*. If reading is a process of growth, whose source and character of unveiling are an uncharted blank, and if growth in its turn carries the imprint of other forces in the surrounding universe, then it becomes clear why Mandel'shtam insists in his notebooks that this is not a development but a metamorphosis, an act of never-ending transformation: it is not an adjustment to a particular state but a process of differentiation, or participation in different states (that is why Mandel'shtam depicts Maiakovsky as being qualitatively different from his critics). Growth is an interplay and periodization of radically different stages; biological similarity does not explain the full extent of these transformations. Moreover, growth always outdistances and contrasts with the preceding stage of its development; it is a process that is always in conflict with its environment and with its former stage of identification:

> What is more, Growth is a metamorphosis [literally werewolf: *oboroten'*], not a reformer. Apart from that, it is a folklore fool, weeping at weddings and

laughing at funerals – you carry it, carry, and there is more left. It is not for nothing that we are most tactless at the age when our voices are cracking.

Critics of Maiakovsky have a relationship to him proportionate to that of the old woman (who used to cure Hellenes of internal hernias) to Heracles. (III, 155; 385 translation altered)

All this explains Mandel'shtam's somewhat bewildering observations (scattered throughout various drafts) on the process of reading or understanding, which was for him a process of growth. Growth for Mandel'shtam, however, is metamorphosis, a process of transformation, and it too must characterize the process of reading since growth and reading are one and the same. Thus, the notion of metamorphosis becomes a characteristic of the processes involved in reading. And, indeed, in Mandel'shtam reading is the initiation of a series of radical transformations; we actually follow in our responses along a pattern reminiscent of the great chain of being.[13] In reading we discover the stages of our kindred association with the changing levels of organic and intelligible life. A key paragraph on reading in Mandel'shtam, therefore, finally comes into focus: 'When we are completely immersed in the activity of reading, we marvel above all at our generic [*rodovye*] attributes. We experience, as it were, the ecstasy of classifying ourselves in various ages and stages [*ispytyvaem kak by vostorg klassifikacii svoikh vozrastov*]' (III, 166; 394). In other words, the poetic landscape and the reader's response change, according to the growth of our recollection, from the state of inanimate objects (stone), to those of plants and animals, and ultimately to the configuration and laws of the intelligible world.[14] Mandel'shtam never states this directly (but of course it is his temperament not to state anything directly, and, besides, the sociopolitical atmosphere was becoming hostile), yet such a view explains much of his writings on the naturalists (*Journey to Armenia*, 'On the Naturalists'), which follow closely in tone, image, and manner the 'journey' with Dante along the vertically changing landscape of Dante's *Commedia*. Mandel'shtam's descriptions of the naturalists and of the different levels of Dante's universe give an outline of the same process. Each step with Dante along the changing landscape of the *Conversation about Dante* is for Mandel'shtam an uncovering of the changing patterns of the poetic texture and of its reception which correspond to the organic patterns of growth, at least in so far as their infernal and purgatorial stages are concerned. Only an interpretation such as this can explain why Mandel'shtam was so impressed with Belyi's view (which was certainly a description of the changing states of consciousness) 'that the *Inferno*, taken as a series of problems, is given up to solid state physics ... where in various guises – sometimes in the historical drama, sometimes in the mechanics of landscape dreams – we find analyzed gravity, weight, density, the acceleration of falling bodies ... and finally, the human gait or step, as the most complex form of movement regulated by consciousness' (see Mandel'shtam's rough notes for *Conversation about Dante*, III, 184; 446–7; Mandel'shtam struck up a close friendship with Belyi in the 1930s and discussed with him at length his views on poetry).

Thus, in following Dante, 'this great strategist of transformations and hybridizations' (II, 364; 397), Mandel'shtam sets out the changing landscape of the poetic texture, which he describes as 'the poetic material which creates its instruments in passing and in passing erases them' (II, 404; 433). He also sets out the changing landscape of the reader's participation in the poetic (or reading) process.[15] If reading is indeed a process that involves radically different patterns, all of which cannot be fully remembered, and if the order of succession of these different patterns can be found, then the variety of radically different insights into the nature of the word's reception can finally be accounted for. They will no longer be contradictory, but will be encompassed within a much more comprehensive differentiating process. The radically differing stages of reading are a part of human growth. The difficulty of outlining the processes involved resides in the fact that growth is always imperceptible. The paradox lies in the fact that growth is change and, thus, involves perception (i.e., change as the perception of difference), yet growth as change also escapes perception, since it eludes conscious awareness of the act. Only at this stage can Mandel'shtam begin to reassemble and reintegrate the different insights into the nature of communication that characterize his earlier writing.

In the 1930s Mandel'shtam also returns to the long-dormant concept of the status of the addressee in the poetic text. He can finally overcome his earlier inability to identify the precise delineations of this changing interlocutor, for the addressee too is a part of this metamorphosis. When Mandel'shtam, throughout the *Conversation about Dante*, calls poetic discourse *obrashchaiushchaiasia* and *obratimaia poeticheskaia materiia* [converting and convertible poetic texture], he is suggesting a wide variety of meanings by employing the active and passive as well as reflexive adverbial adjectives of the verb *obratit*,' which means 'conversion,' or 'turning,' but also 'address.' It is clear that Mandel'shtam is talking about poetic speech as capable, not only of numerous metamorphoses and conversions, but also of invoking a broad series of addressees. I shall develop this aspect of Mandel'shtam's thought in the next chapter, in which I analyse the periodic structure of the changing landscape.

Finally, it is now possible to draw a meaningful comparison between Mandel'shtam's description of poetic discourse as home in the 1920s and his development of this image in the 1930s. He asserts that the power of poetic speech, like that of familiar speech, draws unconditionally; home remains the image of unconditional recognition. In the 1930s the notion of home undergoes considerable revision, or rather expansion. The plant that grows in response to the invitation of the air is 'akin [*srodni*] in equal measure to stone and lightning' (II, 154; 359). When we read, we 'marvel at our generic attributes' [*rodovye svoistva*], while we find ourselves belonging to the stages of a pattern that is constantly changing (III, 166; 394). Reading, therefore, is an acknowledgment that we are at home in our varied universe, and our response to this kindredness or kinship, often tragic and always dramatic in its essence, constitutes the emotional colorations of the *Inferno* (kinship with matter), the *Purgatorio* (kinship with nature), and the *Paradiso* (kinship with light).

5

Periodization in the Transmutation of the Poetic Landscape. Metamorphosis of the Addressee in the 1930s

1 The Hybrid Nature of Poetic Discourse

Mandel'shtam's writings of the 1930s – *Journey to Armenia,* 'Around the Naturalists,' and particularly *Conversation about Dante*[1] – confront the reader with brilliant, highly original, and undeniably ambitious attempts to identify the widest range of characteristics of poetic communication. These are principally the description of periodization and the specific qualities of the series of conversions and reconstitutions of what Mandel'shtam begins to term *poetic materia.* While scornfully dismissing all scholastic interpretations of the *Divina commedia,*[2] Mandel'shtam nevertheless closely approaches the pagan and Christian roots of Dante's philosophical thought. Mandel'shtam's depiction of the poetic texture is here reminiscent of the substantial 'forming' *logos,* the poetic impulse or shaping force entering matter, descending into its unformed, unstructured, purely quantitative dimension. Poetry is an imprint of the creative *logos* shaping matter in all its quantitative dimensions, and a living diary of the differentiated patterns of its vertical descent.

It is probable that Mandel'shtam's fascination with twentieth-century theoretical physics suggested the basic framework for this approach. If one substitutes the journey of the wave (in its transmutation from light into sound and thence into magnetic waves according to the stages of its descent) for the poetic *logos* entering into matter, one can still understand the basic landscape of Mandel'shtam's universe. Yet his own system is hardly this basic, and both the *Conversation about Dante* and *Journey to Armenia* call for an examination of the philosophical antecedents of Mandel'shtam's theory.[3] However, these philosophical precursors are

The Transmutation of the Poetic Landscape 69

not the concern of this study and, hence, I shall lay aside for now the problem of whether Mandel'shtam indeed understood that in *Conversation about Dante* he was much closer to Dante's philosophical and spiritual roots than he wished openly to profess as a result of his focus on the *logos* that comes into matter, then shapes it, inseminates it, dies in it, and yet also escapes it.[4] Whatever the reasons why this substantial-form or *logos* theory was never directly acknowledged by Mandel'shtam, there is no doubt that such a philosophical context was dangerous political and ideological territory. Therefore, while this context is implicit in the very way that Mandel'shtam develops his ideas, it was certainly politically prudent for him to belittle or ignore the excessively scholastic followers of Thomas Aquinas, who had perhaps lost the dynamic vision of their precursors. Whatever the case might be, Mandel'shtam certainly acknowledges and adopts the spirit of Dante.

In the 1930s, therefore, Mandel'shtam finds a new theoretical formulation for the hybrid process that he had always believed operative in poetry.[5] As we know, he was never interested in poetry as statement, message, or even coded image. Instead, he most valued poetry's capacity to transmit a hidden impulse and to initiate a multifaceted change. In the 1930s Mandel'shtam finally finds a formulation that gives this capacity for change full prominence. The definition is, for once, explicitly stated, and given added weight by being centrally positioned at the opening of the *Conversation about Dante*, although this is not to say that it is by any means easily understood. *One side of the process* he calls 'impulse' (an imprecise translation of the Russian *poryv* [thrust, breath], in Greek *pneuma*), which is described as the vibration of a wave, a change, a modulation, inaudible on its own, understood only in its effect upon something, which effect is *the second side of the process*, and which can be described as an aggregate of quantities, in itself formless and uninspired. In language we sense both: one is an instinct for change or an imprint of change; the other is the labour of a discourse as yet virginal, uninspired, and unimpregnated (the sexual metaphor is later developed into the image of mother, woman, *materia*, matter). Mandel'shtam's definition is so important that it will be helpful to quote it in full:

> Poetic discourse is a hybrid process, one which crosses two sound modes: the first of these is the change [*izmenenie*] we hear and sense of the armaments [instruments, *orudiia*[6]] of the poetic speech, appearing in its spontaneous flow [literally in motion or walking in its thrust: *na khodu v ejo*

poryve]; the second is the speech itself [*sobstvenno rech'*] or rather intonational and phonological labour, executed by the above-mentioned armaments ... It is only with the severest qualifications that the poetic discourse or thought may be referred to as "sounding," for we hear in it only the crossing of two lines, one of which, taken by itself, is completely mute, while the other, abstracted from armamental transmutation, is totally devoid of significance and interest and renders itself to paraphrase, which, to my mind, is surely a sign of non-poetry. For where there is amenability to paraphrase, there the sheets have never been rumpled, there poetry, so to speak, has never spent the night. (II, 363; 397, translation altered)

Thus, in poetry we sense and hear the modulation or change, inaudible on its own; and since this change remains the central characteristic of poetry, the poetic text confronts consciousness as a series of imperceptible, quickly vanishing changes, initiating in turn transmutations in the awareness of the reader, an awareness that the poetry has awoken. This double-edged definition can be understood only through a series of changing patterns, not merely as two prevailing qualities. In other words, because of the nature of the two principles that intertwine in poetic discourse, that is, the unceasing impulse of change inaudible on its own, and the quantitative *materia* through which we sense this change, in reading we confront the changing landscape of the continuous nature of this interaction.[7] Moreover, we can follow this transmutation, so to speak, up or down the ladder of the characteristics of their qualitative interpenetration: either into the depth of the matter, where the *logos* is finally encompassed, or towards its manifestation as pure differentiation – that is, Dante's unity in multiplicity in the *Paradiso*. This principle, therefore, does not limit the field of enquiry to two opposing poles; rather, it provides a possibility of charting the multiple levels and their specific characteristics along the vertical axis of these changing landscapes.

Mandel'shtam's ambition was not merely to present a series of changing stages, however, but to locate them within a framework that reinforces their validity. He coordinates the changing landscapes of interaction between *logos* and matter with the historical development of the natural sciences, that is, with the living chronology of humanity's insight into the secrets of nature. As always in Mandel'shtam, this attempt – the coordination of the stages of awareness, evoked by the poetic text, with the historical patterns of scientific investigation – is not made explicit (the reasons for his dislike of explicit statement capable of paraphrase can be understood in the context of the definition of poetry cited above; these will be examined below). In the absence of any explicit statement that such a coordination is being carried out, it is again left to the reader to infer this similarity, first, in the striking recurrence of similar images relating to poetic discourse in the *Conversation about Dante*, then from Mandel'shtam's treatment of the 'naturalists' in the *Journey to Armenia*, and finally from his essay on Charles Darwin. I shall attempt to show that each stage of ascent or descent along the axis of Dante's universe possesses for Mandel'shtam scientific patterns of an approach to organic life,[8] by following for the most part the patterns of the presentation in the *Conversation about Dante*. Each changing stage uncovers its own addressee and awakens a particular response from the reader, be it instinctual, intellectual, analytical, or visual. In the examination of these changing patterns I shall attempt above all to outline Mandel'shtam's view both of reception and of the changing stages of visualization in the addressee.

It must also be pointed out that throughout his prose of the 1930s Mandel'shtam employs the term *oboroty*, which can mean either 'turns' or 'turns of phrase' and 'turns of meaning.'[9] In Russian the words are indistinguishable in their natural conversational usage, yet the usage in the *Conversation about Dante* is unique. For Mandel'shtam the multiple transmutations of poetic discourse appear in their most minute unveiling. The turns of phrase are a part of these transmutations; they [*oboroty*] themselves literally turn. Thus, they are a performance of the poetic nature in its most immediate and natural imprints. I shall indicate wherever possible this double entendre: that is 'turn of phrase' as in ordinary conversational usage, and the intentional use of the word 'turn' to indicate the convertible, changeable nature of poetry.

In the first part of the *Conversation about Dante* we have already witnessed the origin of poetic discourse. As with every element in poetry,[10] this starts from the intersection of two different natures. Once discourse has been initiated, it cannot cease because it is moved by the energy that it continues to create. As Mandel'shtam observes in the *Conversation about Dante*, the direction of the poetic journey not only measures but also creates its surrounding energy: 'Here the trembling hand of the compass not only indulges the magnetic storm, but makes it itself' (II, 369–70; 403). Poetic discourse, then, is an initiation of movement that transfixes the poet and awakens the reader: 'Have you ever noticed that in Dante's *Commedia* it is quite impossible for the author to act, that he is doomed only to walk, to enter in, and to ask or answer questions' (III,

189; 451, translation altered). The journey starts as a movement into the depth of matter, literally into the depth of organic descent, that is, into the depth of rock itself. My goal is to outline the major steps of Mandel'shtam's journey along the vertical axis of Dante's universe (which Mandel'shtam reads as an accurate presentation of the transmutations of poetry) and to indicate the precise nature of the communicative strategies at each stage of the changing landscape. In order to make the complexity of Mandel'shtam's approach more accessible, a simplified diagrammatic presentation of the argument in sections 2 to 6 below will be found in the table entitled 'Changing Stages in the Apprehension of the Poetic Landscape' (pp. 108–9).

2 The Beginning of the Reading Process; Entrance into Matter. The Addressee as Completed Past

Chapter 2 of the *Conversation about Dante* depicts the communicative strategies at the beginning of the reading process. It is literally an infernal, hermetic process, since it is an unconscious first response to the text – a response, therefore, difficult to outline or analyse. However, a comparison of the striking images of this chapter with similar descriptions in *Journey to Armenia* suggests that Mandel'shtam is not being merely impressionistic, but is thoroughly consistent, and intent upon identifying the characteristics of this first interaction as a pattern whose delineations can be isolated and understood. Moreover, the characteristics of this first stage of interaction find their counterpart in the first steps of the development of European biology (according to Mandel'shtam, Dante's *Inferno* shares certain characteristics with the evolutionary understanding of nature developed by Jean-Baptiste de Lamarck (1744–1829), according to which specific instinctual needs created by the environment cause organisms to develop into higher evolutionary forms). It is my thesis that Mandel'shtam's thought can once again be understood only by means of careful attention to his imagery, and that this imagery, recurrent throughout his writings of the 1930s, provides the major key to his poetics. In other words, in order to grasp the principal characteristics of this poetics, it becomes necessary to develop a vocabulary, as it were, of the images used. The result of this approach will be to provide a new map of the characteristics of each stage and their ordering, or periodization, within the communicative process itself. Once the characteristics of each stage have been isolated, we shall, in fact, discover a systematic poetics of striking and brilliant consistency.

Our goal in subsequent sections of this chapter, therefore, will be, first, to isolate these characteristics in what appears at the outset to be a highly impressionistic if not impenetrable text, and then by means of this analysis to point out the principal patterns of the communicative strategies that, according to Mandel'shtam, unite reader and text in a process of changes so immediate, momentary, even unconscious, that they seem simultaneous and imperceptible.

The progression of images at the first stage of the reading process will be presented in the following order:

2.1 The beginning of the process: movement initiated near the tangible remnants of 'intelligible life'
2.2 The crack [proval]
2.3 Death as the result of entrance
2.4 Reading as awareness of intertextuality
2.5 The reversal of time
2.6 The construction of the organ of transmission and reception
2.7 Language as command
2.8 The ghost of the past as addressee

2.1 The beginning of the process: movement initiated near the tangible remnants of 'intelligible life'
The initial stage of the reading process follows closely upon the 1920s image of light that is unable to penetrate the levels of the earth, or the solidity of masses (see chapter 3). For Mandel'shtam the fundamental question is presented simultaneously within several universes of discourse: How can the black letters on the page be the beginning of an unceasing journey? How can light penetrate stone? How can one descend the organic ladder? Conversely, is it possible that the most immediate and tangible traces of the living universe carry the imprint of immaterial and intangible forces? In *Journey to Armenia* the question is repeated constantly with growing pathos: Are the black letters on the page the only vestige of the intelligible universe, or are they like insects surrounding a body that lies in the earth? Above all, can the path to intelligible reality be found in these traces? The passage cited below displays Mandel'shtam's multidimensional approach: the insects are equivalent to letters on the page, to the decaying body, to the degradation of life in the decay of material reality,[11] and all of these elements constitute the landscape of the *Inferno* (note the mention of the devil in the quoted passage):

> And somehow I saw the dance of death, the nuptial dance of the phosphorescent insects ... The Devil only knows where the wind carried them!
>
> Upon closer inspection, I noticed some insane electrified ephemera winking, twitching, making fine tracings, and then devouring the black reading-matter [*chernoe chtivo*] of the present moment.
>
> Our heavy fleshly body decays in precisely the same way, and our activity will be transformed into the similarly alarming pandemonium if we do not leave behind us substantial proof of our existence. (II, 158; 362)

Yet even in this depiction of the decay of life, there are vestiges of light, energy, change: the insects are phosphorescent, they are twitching, winking; even in the lowest levels of matter the imprint of change cannot cease.[12] But how can the journey up the organic ladder be initiated?

2.2 The crack [proval]

Mandel'shtam's answer is never stated directly. However, through a careful examination of the language he employs and his imagery the text becomes much clearer. More important still, we shall find that Mandel'shtam's position is remarkably consistent in all the passages where similar infernal imagery is introduced. Since the journey begins near the solidity of impenetrable matter, the way up is the way down *through* the solidity itself. Here invariably Mandel'shtam introduces the concept of the gap or crack [*proval*]. Several passages that would otherwise be bewildering employ this image: the impulse penetrates through a crack in the rock. Furthermore, the notion of the crack appears in every single context descriptive of the descent into the mystery of organic life. So too does the notion of the *trope*, which is a linguistic pun upon the idea of the narrow path [*tropa*] within the opened rock.

In the drafts of the *Journey to Armenia* the book is described as entering our consciousness through the gaps [*provaly*] and narrow paths [*tropy*] of our experience and memory, or as a crack [*razlom*] in the solidity of our biography:

> While not yet a product of the reader's energy, a book is already a crack [*razlom*] in the reader's biography; while not yet a find, it is already an extraction [*dobycha*]. A piece of streaked feldspar.
>
> Our memory, our experience with its gaps [*provaly*], the tropes [*tropy*] and metaphors of our sense perception, all fall into the book's rapacious and uncontrolled possession. (III, 165; 393)

In chapter 2 of the *Conversation about Dante* Mandel'shtam's journey with Dante begins exactly at the point where the image of the crack becomes explicit: Dante and Virgil invite the reader to follow them through the narrow opening of the rock into the dark solidity of the earth:[13] 'The beginning of Canto X of the *Inferno*. Dante urges us into the inner blindness of the compositional thickness [*vnutrenniaia slepota komposicionnogo sgustka*]: "Now we climbed up the narrow path [*uzkaia tropa*] between the wall of the rock and the tormented creatures – my teacher and I at his back"' (II, 369; 402).

Moreover, this proximity to the tormented creatures is not merely a metaphoric image but one that has poignant personal overtones. The beginning of poetry is also initiated by the 'crack' of the poet's inner balance, a balance further dismantled by one's apparent inability to be fully realized or fulfilled in a purely social life. Personal suffering then (or a lack of balance) becomes a fertile ground through which the impulse enters. Thus, the psychological state of a poet who can no longer fit contemporary discourses becomes transformed in the *Conversation about Dante* into an image of the ground accessible to the impulse of poetry, an impulse which then transfixes verbal *materia* and starts the process of differentiation and transformation. In other words, in describing Dante's 'wandering exile' Mandel'shtam also draws an unforgettable autobiographical picture of his own social decline in the 1930s and of his need for Dante, analogous to Dante's own semidesperate choice of Virgil as a guide to help him survive his chosen narrow path:

> His lapidary quality is no more than a product of the enormous inner imbalance which expressed itself in dream executions, in imagined encounters, in elegant retorts prepared in advance and fostered on bile, aimed at destroying his enemy once and for all and invoking the final triumph.
>
> How often did [Virgil] the kindest of fathers, the preceptor, reasonable man, and guardian correct the internal *raznochinets* of the XIV century who found it such agony to be a part of the social hierarchy, while Boccaccio, practically his contemporary, delighted in the same social system, plunged into it, gamboled about in it? (II, 373; 406, translation altered)

The beginning of the communicative process, then, is presented as a crack, a narrow *trope*, into a territory hitherto uncharted and blindingly dark, where the possibility for an investigation of the process is severely restricted. In *Journey to Armenia* Lamarck is Dante's scientific counterpart along the pattern of descent: 'In Lamarck's reversed, descending movement down the ladder of living creatures resides the greatness of Dante. The lower forms of organic existence are humanity's *Inferno*' (II, 164; 367). Lamarck is described as descending into the organic world through its gaps and cracks; he enters a universe where the possibility for scientific investigation is limited because of the absence (that is, another gap) of supporting data or material:[14] 'Lamarck feels the rifts [*provaly*] between classes. <These are the intervals of the evolutionary series. Empty spaces gape open [*zijajut*]>. He hears the pauses and syncopes in the evolutionary line. He instinctually feels the truth and chokes from the absence of supporting facts and materials' (III, 161; 390, translation altered; passages enclosed by angle brackets are from the drafts). We might also note that the first character introduced to us in *Journey to Armenia*, Professor Khachaturian, is 'an archaeologist as well as a teacher by calling' (II, 139; 345), that is, someone who literally cracks the earth in order to uncover the deposits of meaning within it. The passage in question ends, in fact, with Mandel'shtam presiding over an excavation site.

2.3 Death as the result of entrance
What is the result of this entrance into matter, this descent of the organic ladder, this loss of psychological balance and this crack in the reader's biography initiated by the book? All these phrases stress that there are limited possibilities on this level for any scientific analysis. The excavation site, which more or less opens the *Journey to Armenia*, uncovers 'some clay shards, and human bones,' plus a mysterious knife handle with the trademark N.N. Mandel'shtam also 'respectfully wraps up in his handkerchief the porous calcified piece of someone's skull' (II, 139; 345). Death and degeneration are the results of this entrance. Lamarck loses his eyesight, Beethoven his hearing, as they enter into the secrets of organic life: 'Lamarck cried his eyes out over his magnifying glass. His blindness is equal to Beethoven's deafness' (III, 161; 390). Dante, too, 'uses up all his material' (II, 378; 410). Furthermore, there are many indications in chapter 2 that Dante could never on his own have accomplished this descent, where 'all our efforts are directed against the density and darkness of the place' (II, 369; 402).

Dante's descent is portrayed as an eventual death, and yet this death is also an indication of the poet's willingness to become a part of the earth, his willing transformation into a seed. Once the book cracks the reader's biography, the poetic voice willingly dies within, that is, it falls as a seed 'into the window of hearing.' Thus, the entrance into matter is a personal death; the word is buried in the opening of the ear, and the delineations of personhood are in process of being lost: 'Meanwhile, instead of raising his sculpture on the pedestal as Hugo, for instance, might have done, Dante envelopes it in a sordino [a mute or damper], wraps it round with grey twilight, and conceals it at the very bottom of the sack of mute sounds. It is presented in the diminuendo stop, it falls into the window of hearing. In other words, its phonetic light is turned off' (II, 373–4; 406–7). The psychological imbalance of the listener has not been corrected: 'The grey shadows have blended' (II, 374; 407).

2.4 Reading as awareness of intertextuality
The personal death of the poet's voice within the infernal landscape of poetry (or within the chaotic psychological state of the reader) is also described as an entrance into the world of the past, and this involves a reversal of time, since the past becomes more powerful than the present.[15] One's death therein is unavoidable, because the past possesses only the traces of one's personhood.[16] This explains why the infernal landscape of poetry is described as the celebration of the endless subtextual referentiality of the text, an awareness not so much of the text as of its sources. The fragmentation into intertextual echoes affects *both* the text that is being apprehended *and* the inner world of the reader who begins to process the text: both the text and the reader are broken into segments of memory. The text at this level is not something spoken by a single voice (since the voice has been concealed 'at the very bottom of the sack of mute sounds'). It can be perceived only as a chorus of quotations, the echoes of antecedents therein understood as the only reality. Mandel'shtam always depicts the entrance into matter as an entrance into an infinitely divisible world: matter split into atoms; the linear evolutionary series opened to Lamarck; 'a piece of streaked feldspar' unearthed by the book's intrusion. All of these descriptions are presented in chapter 2 of the *Conversation about Dante* in an orgy of quotations that become audible and visible when we become a part of the infernal landscape:

> Here the Arab Averroes accompanies the Greek Aristotle. They are both components of the same drawing. They can both find room on a membrane of a single wing ...
> A keyboard stroll around the entire horizon of Antiquity. Some Chopin

78 Mandel'shtam's Poetics

polonaise in which an armed Caesar with a gryphon's eyes dances alongside Democritus, who had just finished splitting matter into atoms.

A quotation is not an excerpt. A quotation is a cicada. Its natural state is that of unceasing sound. (II, 368; 401)

2.5 The reversal of time
Thus, the entrance into matter is portrayed as an entrance into one's own poetic and cultural origins.[17] As a result Mandel'shtam is able to develop further characteristics of the infernal landscape. First, if the entrance into matter is the beginning of a reversal of time,[18] Mandel'shtam can present this first stage of the communicative process as a time of apprenticeship: that is, a reversal of time, where the teacher is faster, quicker, and younger than his student.[19] Therefore, every line can be heard as a referential echo, or as an awareness of the awakened past that constitutes the essence of education:

> Education is schooling in the swiftest possible associations. You grasp them in flight, you are sensitive to allusions – therein lies Dante's favorite form of praise.
> The way Dante understands it, the teacher is younger than the pupil, for 'he runs faster.'
> ... The metaphor's rejuvenating power brings the educated old man, Brunetto Latini in the guise of a youthful victor at a Veronese track meet. (II, 361; 400–1).

2.6 The construction of the organ of transmission and reception
The descent into matter is, indeed, a time of apprenticeship, but it cannot be accomplished without some artificial means. We have seen Lamarck descending into the gaps of the evolutionary series with the microscope.[20] The excavation site uncovers a knife handle, part of an instrument without which excavation is impossible. We read that the entrance into matter was for Dante a construction of the organ, that is, a time for education and the discovery of a vehicle to execute the journey[21] (the sexual overtones are implicit in the first quotation below, and the pun upon the word 'organ' is to be found in both passages):

> Dante never enters into a single combat with matter without having first prepared an organ to seize it, without having armed himself with some instrument for measuring concrete time as it drips and melts ... (II, 369; 403)

> Long before Bach and at a time when large monumental organs were not yet being built ... Alighieri constructed in verbal space an infinitely powerful organ and already delighted in all its conceivable stops, inflated its bellows, and roared and cooed through all its pipes. (II, 373; 406)

The characteristics of the infernal landscape are worked out with striking consistency. The infernal landscape constitutes that dimension where the personal voice of the poet cannot be heard, where it is concealed or has found its death.[22] Yet it is the level most rich in its intertextual referentiality, for here we approach the poet's origin, that is, his education by other poetic voices, which constitute at this point the only textual reality. The entrance into this level cannot be accomplished without some artificial means: a microscope for Lamarck, a methodology for a critic, art (an organ) for Dante. The artificial constructions allow one to discern what is otherwise indiscernible. Furthermore, the fact that a mediating organ is necessary for detecting the characteristics of this landscape explains why the language of this descent is always that of command. The construction of an artificial organ, necessitated by the impenetrability of matter, points to the absence of equality between observer and observed, subject and object, speaker and addressee, teacher and student.

2.7 Language as command.
The emphasis on command appears in every context where this descent is portrayed. Lamarck is consistently described as ordering and dictating the rules of nature: 'Lamarck was above all a legislator. He speaks like a French National Convention. He combines in himself both Saint-Just and Robespierre. He does not so much prove what nature is, as decree it' (II, 161; 390). In the *Conversation about Dante*, as Dante enters into the opening of the rock, the obligatory tonality of his writing is immediately pointed out: 'And, thus, we can see that the dialogue of Canto x of the *Inferno* is magnetized by the forms of verb tenses: the perfective and imperfective past, even the present and the future are all presented in the tenth canto authoritatively, categorically, obligatorily' (II, 370; 403, translation altered). The intrusion of the book into the gaps of our experience and memory, an intrusion that is a crack in the reader's biography, is presented not only in implicitly sexual terms but also as a categorical imperative: the book's power is that of 'rapacious and uncontrolled possession.' Moreover, 'the wiles of its proprietary powers are as varied as military subterfuges' (III, 165; 393). At this level, then,

the performative nature of poetic discourse reflects in a much more nuanced and polyvalent context the obligatory subjunctives of Mandel'shtam's treatment of Catullus earlier (II, 224; 114; see chapter 3 above).

2.8 The ghost of the past as addressee
If the address is that of command, who is the addressee of this verbal attack? Lamarck decrees *nature*. As Dante descends, 'A voice floats forward; it remains unclear to whom it belongs. It becomes more and more difficult for the reader to conduct the expanding canto. This voice – the first theme of Farinata – is the minor Dantean arioso of the suppliant type, extremely typical of the *Inferno*' (II, 371; 405). The image of the exiled beggar who meets Dante, the minor 'arioso of the suppliant type,' is a brilliant interpretation of the traditional Platonic image for matter.[23] Indeed, this identification is consistent with the notion of entry into the infernal landscape as an entry into the solidity of matter, a movement towards death. In Mandel'shtam's description the voice that meets Dante here does not belong to the reader (the reader does not descend so low as to be a conscious subject, for he conducts the canto); it belongs to the typical inhabitant of the *Inferno*, and the desire to see this inhabitant opens the chapter's action: 'First thrust: ... "May I be permitted to see those people laid in open graves"'? (II, 370; 403). The addressee here is the ghost of the past which, as the descent continues, grows to more and more real proportions, bringing the poet even further back to the reality of his forefathers.

> I fixed my eyes on him
> And he drew himself up to his full height
> 'Who were your forefathers?'   (II, 371; 403–4)

The first address of poetic discourse, therefore, is the awakening of the echoes of the past both in the text's referential landscape and in the reader's half-forgotten personal history.

The exiled beggar, the ghost of the completed past, slowly grows in power, 'draws himself to his full height,' while the poet's voice descends the self-effacing staircase. His words are lost amid the growing noise of intertextual quotations in a landscape where all communication is a command or decree. The poet's voice, in fact, also becomes a part of matter: it is a prefiguration of death, when the living essence becomes a willing seed falling as through a crack 'into the window of hearing' (II,

373–4; 407), willingly accepting an apparent death or seizure by matter. The desire to enter, however, brings with it its own rewards, namely, the construction of the organ, or artificial means, or in this case the construction of art itself, in order to discern the hidden levels of an otherwise impenetrable reality.

3 Expression as an Instinctual Escape from the Inferno. The Addressee as Instinctual Response

The second stage of the communicative process follows upon the entrance into matter and the apparent death therein. This new process reverses the direction of descent, yet it remains purely instinctual. Mandel'shtam compares it with impregnation and the subsequent growth of the embryo into space and human geography. The order of images studied in this new stage will be as follows:

3.1 Impregnation of the rock
3.2 Literal expression
3.3 Expression as a form of hidden structure
3.4 Metamorphoses of instinctual formations
3.5 The instinctual self as addressee

3.1 Impregnation of the rock

As we have seen, the entrance into matter invariably possesses sexual overtones. Two notions predominate within this context of the descent: 1 / the idea of the lengthening of the 'valve' [*udlinenie ventilja*] (II, 370; 404) – a musical-sexual pun developed within the image of the construction of the organ 'for the combat with matter';[24] and 2 / the image of expression in its literal sense, that is, writing as a 'squeezing out' [*vyzhymka*].

In chapter 2 of the *Conversation about Dante* the notion of death in matter is accompanied by a parallel image of the impregnation of matter. The lengthening of the organ accompanies images of death. Thus, the passage that describes 'the turning-off of the phonetic lights' is followed by a passage that subtextually introduces the images of intercourse, impregnation, and birth: 'The *Divina Commedia* does not so much take away the reader's time as augment [...] it. Lengthening, the poem moves away from its finish, and its finish comes unexpectedly and sounds as a beginning' (II, 374; 407). Moreover, the metaphors which describe the impregnation of the rock follow immediately upon the description of death. The structure of the poetic text is depicted as a stop in the organ and the subsequent intrusion of a foreign admixture into the opening (crack) of the rock: 'The structure of the Dantean monologue, built like the stop mechanism of an organ, can be well understood by making use of the analogy of rock strata *whose purity has been destroyed by the intrusion of foreign bodies*' (II, 374; 407, emphasis added). In other words, the idea of death in the rock is transformed into the image of the impregnation of rock and the beginning of a new life therein.

3.2 Literal expression

This transformation of death into a new beginning is developed in chapter 3 in terms of a geological image. The rock so invaded has expressed itself as the body of the text.[25] Mandel'shtam is here describing, among other things, Dante's *Purgatorio* and its formation: after Lucifer had fallen into the earth and 'cracked' it, the earth shifted and 'expressed' a great purgatorial mountain on the other side of its globe. Thus, entrance into the lowest forms of organic matter has resulted in the *expression* of this lowest form:

> Granular admixture and veins of lava indicate a single shift[26] or catastrophe as the common source of formation. Dante's poetry is formed and colored in precisely this geological manner. Its material structure is infinitely more significant than its celebrated structural quality. Imagine a monument of granite or marble whose symbolic function is intended not to represent a horse or a rider, but to reveal the inner structure of the marble or granite itself. In other words, imagine a granite monument erected in honor of granite as if to reveal its very idea. (II, 374; 407)

Descent and death are simultaneously presented as an ascent – not as a mere statement of the Heraclitean paradox that the 'way up' is the 'way down,' but as an introduction to the notion of the very transmutability of poetic matter and an interpretive development of the formation of the purgatorial mount in Dante.

3.3 Expression as a form of hidden structure

The poetic entrance into matter teaches us the first lesson of its 'turning,' its first metamorphosis. One cannot squeeze a form out of matter unless there is a form there in the first place. A poetic form cannot descend into unformed matter; the entrance into matter uncovers only its preformed status.[27] The structure of poetic discourse, therefore, is the display of the invisible structure of the matter that encompasses and arrests the descent (that is, the birth of *Purgatory* as a disclosure of earth formation, or Lamarck's discovery of the microscopic formations of the object under examination). Thus, the result of the entrance into matter, or the entrance of the text into the gaps of memory (the crack of biography), manifests itself as the discovery of the subterranean continuation of existence itself. Our tangible evidence of the text in its 'turn' is no longer its referentiality but its unity, its solidity, and yet also its growth. At its lowest tangible transformation the text presents itself as a body – as yet indivisible, or an embryo as yet undifferentiated, a monstrously exact formation: chapter 3 of the *Conversation about Dante* opens with the following depiction:[28] 'Examining the structure of the *Divina Commedia* as best I can, I come to the conclusion that the entire poem is but one single unified and indivisible stanza. Rather, it is not a stanza, but a crystallographic figure, that is, a body. Some incessant craving for the creation of form penetrates the entire poem ... It is inconceivable that anyone could grasp with the eye alone or even visually imagine to oneself this form of thirteen thousand facets, so monstrous in its exactitude' (II, 376; 409).

The landscape has clearly changed. We are no longer in the interstices of matter; rather, we are attempting to grasp its outer contours, the structure of its expression (that is, the crystallogical purgatorial mountain). We find that we are no longer dealing merely with rock, not even with impregnated rock, but with rock as living body, united through *instinct*. Thus, paradoxically perhaps, in our descent we are already in fact ascending the chain of being.

3.4 Metamorphoses of instinctual formations

Given this initial understanding of unceasing transformation, Mandel'shtam's thought becomes surprisingly consistent. The first expression is that of stone, yet it is living stone, a formation of crystallological growth directed by instinct.[29] In turn, the growing body creates space; the monstrous crystal becomes a brilliant stereometric instinct. The descent through the organic ladder which has ended in the arrest in matter ('the analogy of the rock strata whose purity has been destroyed by the intrusion of foreign bodies,' II, 347; 407) is reversed, and the process of apprehending the reality of the text is described as an opposing movement out of the stone towards the first stage of instinctual life, here represented by insects (bees):

> Only through metaphor is it possible to find a concrete sign to represent the instinct for form creation by which Dante accumulated and poured forth his *terza rima*.
>
> We must try to imagine, therefore, how bees might have worked at the creation of this thirteen-thousand-faceted form, bees endowed with the brilliant stereometric instinct, who attracted bees in greater and greater numbers as they were required. The work of these bees, constantly keeping their eye on the whole, is of varying difficulty at different stages of the process. Their cooperation expands and grows more complicated as they participate in the process of forming the combs, by means of which space virtually emerges out of itself.
>
> The bee analogy is suggested, by the way, by Dante himself. (II, 377; 409)

In other words, there is a reorientation that takes place both in the process of the poem's origin and in that of its reception. It cannot be given a strictly analytic explanation (see Mandel'shtam's 'only through metaphor' at the beginning of the passage cited above); its landscape cannot be properly drawn or analytically examined. As in the initial stages of any growth process, its delineations are purely instinctual – a state that by its very nature escapes delineation. It is life as a process of instinctual attraction [*tiaga*] and 'there is not and cannot be any meaningful [*smyslovaja*] orientation in embryology' (drafts of the *Journey to Armenia*, III, 162; 390). As such, it is still a part of inanimate nature: a rock turned into crystal, an instinct for growth in a crystal, serviced by the instinctual movements of bees, the flights of birds, the speed and power of rivers. Soon it becomes a *human* instinct for civilization, culture, politics, and freedom. Like the human embryo, the poetic embryo also possesses a variety of informed and informing instinctual activities. Yet it remains a metamorphosis, since here the lowest stage of organic matter wakes up into life and growth and into the further desire for movement: 'Dante's comparisons are never descriptive, that is purely representational. They always pursue the concrete task of presenting the inner form of the poem's structure or driving force [*tiaga*]. Let us take the very large group of 'bird' similes ... this entire group of extended similes always corresponds to the instinct for the pilgrimage, the journey, colonization, migration' (II, 377; 410).

What is represented in chapter 3 of the *Conversation about Dante*, therefore, is the state of inanimate matter in the process of becoming an embryo directed by the instinct for growth. The dead seed which had fallen 'through the window of the hearing' (II, 373; 406) becomes a stereometric body, and then a collection of growing powerful instincts, one of which is already the human instinct for freedom: 'The force of Dantean simile, strange as it may seem, operates in direct proportion to our ability to do without it. It is never dictated by some beggarly logical necessity' (II, 378; 410). As the crystallogical body gives birth to space created by the multiplicity of bees ('by means of which space virtually emerges out of itself'), so space immediately acquires human geography, discovered here not through reason but through the instinct for form creation. Not only do bird similes provide an insight into the powerful 'instinct for pilgrimage and migration,' but even the similes of rivers are 'distinguished by their extraordinary breadth and their gradual descent from tercet to tercet, always leading to the complex of culture, homeland, and settled civilization' (II, 377; 410).

3.5 The instinctual self as addressee
The stage that succeeds the descent into matter (that is, seizure by the material over which one has ceased to have power; or seizure by the book through the gaps of memory) is the apprehension and disclosure of matter's structure and geography, which is also a construction of the living, narrative universe, not identical with the structure of ordinary, physical reality. Yet the apprehension of this new constructed reality is still directed by the living instinctual response. The exact pattern of this reconstitution of the new poetical landscape (from its infernal stage to its rapid growth from embryo into landscape, space, and geography) is impossible to outline, for the process is instinctual. It is addressed to, understood, and carried out by our instinctual selves. This explains the significance of the image of bees central to this third chapter of the *Conversation about Dante* ('The work of these bees, constantly keeping their eye on the whole, is of varying difficulty at different stages of the process. Their cooperation expands and grows more complicated as they participate in the process of forming the combs,' II, 377; 409). The image of bees, in fact, invariably reappears in all of Mandel'shtam's descriptions of the instinctual response. In this context bees represent the new addressee of the reconstituted poetic landscape – our instinctual selves.

The significance of the bee image explains several striking passages in *Journey to Armenia*, where bees are depicted as the addressees of artistic creation. Of the poet Firdusi Mandel'shtam writes: 'Yesterday I was reading Firdusi and I felt as if a bumble bee were on the book sucking it' (II,

167; 370). The same thought is stated even more clearly in the drafts of the *Journey to Armenia*, where impressionist painting is described as the transformation of rock into colour and life. The addressee of this stage is the instinctual self, again best represented by the bee. Mandel'shtam describes in the drafts the lilacs of Claude Monet as a rock beginning to breathe (a porous sponge), beginning to acquire colour (lilac, a shade deeper than stone-grey), and attracting only our instinctual sensuousness or, rather, simply the sensuousness of bees: 'Luxurious thick lilacs of the Ile-de-France, their tiny stars flattened into a porous, cement-like sponge, formed a menacing mass of petals; wondrous bee lilacs which exclude <all feelings from universal citizenship> everything on earth except the wild impenetrable perceptions of the bumblebee, burned on the wall like the burning bush <and were more sensual, more crafty and more dangerous than impassioned women>, more complicated and sensual than women' (III, 160; 389, translation altered).

4 The Living Geography of the Text; Impression as Coloration of the Parts. The Reader as Addressee

Once the text is grasped instinctually as a living universe, the next stage, according to Mandel'shtam in chapter 4 of the *Conversation about Dante*, is the understanding of the text not as a whole but rather in its parts. Again, this shift is never explicitly identified as a further stage in the process of communication (unless a new chapter heading indicates that this may be the case) but is instead displayed through a series of highly impressionistic connections. These connections, however, are given a manifest logic when the new metaphoric pattern is compared with several important passages in the *Journey to Armenia*. This new stage again exhibits its own vocabulary – a specific interconnection of imagery which characterizes the communicative patterns within another newly reconstituted landscape. We shall discuss these characteristics in the following order:

4.1 Acquaintance with the parts
4.2 Colour as expression or squeezing of the vegetable dyes
4.3 Colour as speed, and thus apprehension of further movement or transformation
4.4 Coloration of the poetic text as imagination and its limitations
4.5 The reader as addressee

The Transmutation of the Poetic Landscape 87

4.1 Acquaintance with the parts
The examination of the details of the text in their immediate proximity is one of the most pleasurable aspects of reading. For Mandel'shtam this stage is not merely a fantasy or impression; it is simultaneously a training of the reader's perception. We must, so to speak, apprehend the surface of the individual images, and the first prerequisite is the observation of colour. In his writings of the 1930s the apprehension of particular objects in their proximity is invariably presented within the following configuration of images: colour, proximity of the object, attention to the parts rather than to the whole, and the art of the miniature (as a careful reconstruction of minor details). For example, chapter 4 of the *Conversation about Dante* opens with a discussion of the history of the illustrations for Dante's *Commedia* as a series of multicoloured miniatures. There is an obvious intercommunication between images: illustration as a *proximate* guide to the text, colour as an impression generated by the text, miniature as a detailed portrayal of the parts, and the history of illustration as a display of the series of impressions. Moreover, Mandel'shtam is careful not to lose the thread of the previous chapter, where the impregnated rock was transformed into living geography. While discussing one of the miniatures he depicts the further awakening of the granite not merely into an instinctual unity but into a multiplicity of colours: 'In other words, we see here bright-azure and rosy admixtures [*krapy*] into the smoky-grey nature' (II, 380; 412, translation altered). The notion of colour, therefore, is the central characteristic of this new landscape, and Mandel'shtam states that his goal is nothing less than irrefutable proof that the life of imagination starts with colour: 'With all my might I would like to refute that loathsome legend which depicts Dante's colouring as either indisputably dull or of an infamous Spenglerian brownish hue' (II, 379; 411).

4.2 Colour as expression or squeezing of the vegetable dyes
Mandel'shtam's intention to perceive the text as a training of perception can also be observed in his descriptions in the *Journey to Armenia* of three great naturalists: Carolus Linnaeus, 1707–78, a Swedish botanist and founder of the modern system of plant classification; Compte Georges Louis Leclerc de Buffon, 1707–88, a French naturalist who suggested that climactic conditions were important for the development of organisms; and Peter Simon Pallas, 1741–1811, a German naturalist – all Lamarck's forerunners in the examination of nature. Their activity displays patterns whose similarity with the images employed in chapter 4 of

the *Conversation about Dante* is impossible to ignore.[30] Linnaeus and Lamarck, in particular, are praised for their ability not to descend into nature's cracks, but to perceive the objects of nature in close proximity without microscope or binoculars, to express nature's reality, and thus to apprehend colour. Here again Mandel'shtam plays with the notion of expression as squeezing: to express natural objects is literally to express colour, to squeeze out vegetable dyes.[31] It is clear, of course, that neither Linnaeus nor Pallas squeezed dyes or painted miniatures. It is their approach to nature which is described by Mandel'shtam as yet another stage of natural science itself and simultaneously a principle of another landscape in the transmutation of the apprehension of poetic discourse.[32] Close proximity to detail literally squeezes out colour; this manner of apprehension produces colour as a result of the close scrutiny of surrounding objects:

> In the work of Pallas the noble subtlety and sensitivity of the eye, the attention to detail, and the sheer virtuosity of description attained their utmost limits, reached the heights of the miniature painting. ('Darwin's Literary Style,' III, 174; 339)

> Linnaeus, Buffon, and Pallas have colored my mature years ... (II, 163; 366)

> Linnaeus painted his monkeys in the tenderest colonial colors. Dipping his brush in Chinese lacquers, he would paint with brown and red pepper, with saffron, olive oil and cherry juice. (II, 166–7; 369)

> Pallas knows and likes only the *proximate*. He ties proximity to proximity with his ornate ligatured script ... (II, 163; 392)

> He paints and tans and distills nature out of red sandalwood. He makes extractions out of steep slopes and pine forests ... He distills dyes out of a mixture of birch leaves and alum for the Nankeen cloth used by Nizhegorod peasant women and for the blueprints of the heavens. (III, 163–4; 392)

> For the Linnaean naturalist attention is but on a single phenomenon. Description. The Picturesque. The 'miniatures of Buffon and Pallas ...' ('Darwin's Literary Style,' III, 170; 336)

4.3 Colour as speed, and thus apprehension of further movement or transformation

Journey to Armenia presents the perception of colour as more than a result of the proximate investigation of detailed phenomena. Mandel'shtam consistently emphasizes that colour, once perceived, communicates the impulse of each description as *speed*. Since the transfixing modulation caught in the object as colour can never assume a static quality without destroying the essence of the poetic process, this perceptive penetration results in a continuous movement: 'Only then did I begin to understand the obligatory force of color – and to realize that color is none else than the sense of the start of a race, tinged by distance and contained as dimension' (II, 159; 363). This transfixing impulse understood as speed continues the radical metamorphosis in the text and in the observer, transmitting further the desire to move in an increasingly dynamic manner,[33] and to change one's perception from instinctual response to intelligible participation. This is precisely how Mandel'shtam describes his own reaction to the impressionists, and particularly to Signac's theory of pointillism, which sets out 'the law of optical blending.' The metamorphosis of the foot-gear is clearly intended to emphasize the change in the transmitted impulse to move:

> At the first sounds of his triumphant theory, my nerves grew taut. I felt a shiver of novelty, as if someone had summoned me by name ...
> I seemed to have exchanged my heavy, dust-laden urban foot-gear for a pair of light Moslem slippers.
> I have been blind as a silkworm all my life. (II, 145; 351)

In the *Conversation about Dante* there is a restatement of this imagery. The close proximity to nature, which results in well-coloured miniatures/descriptions executed by Linnaean naturalists, is repeated early in chapter 4 in the description of the miniatures and their colouration as an illustration of Dante's text. Yet here Mandel'shtam is dealing not merely with impressions but with a training of the reader's perception. Thus, the chapter opens with a brief history of Dante's readers. Then Mandel'stam states that colour is an inescapable quality of Dante's text, and we are invited to examine in close proximity this 'textile brilliance.' Here, as in the *Journey to Armenia*, closeness presupposes not only impression as colouration, but also a necessary concentration upon a particularized object – here represented by the brightly coloured skin of

Geryon, a skin that is a flying carpet cutting through space.[34] Moreover, Mandel'shtam does not merely allude to the flying of Geryon in Dante's *Commedia*; he also unfolds the notion of flight from the impulse transmitted by the multicoloured surface itself. As we move from one part to another, and then from colour to colour, accommodating the eye to a rapidly changing perspective, we are learning about speed (expressed here as flight), a speed which has already been described in the *Journey to Armenia* as the essence of colour. The multicoloured skin of Geryon, therefore, teaches us the planning of a speedy flight:[35] 'The craving to fly tormented and exhausted the men of Dante's era no less than alchemy. A hunger after pierced space. All sense of direction vanished. Nothing was visible. Only the Tatar's back in front of the eyes – that terrifying dressing gown of Geryon's skin. Speed and direction can be judged only by the air whipping across the face. The flying machine was not yet invented, Leonardo's plans did not yet exist, but a problem of gliding to a safe landing was already resolved' (II, 381; 413).[35] Moreover, Geryon himself, a monster with three bodies and three heads in Greek mythology, is a symbol of the transmutation of the insect into a form that is almost human (a counterpart to the change of the silkworm in the *Journey to Armenia*). Geryon is only, of course, a half-accomplished metamorphosis: head of a man, body of a lion, tail of a scorpion. Thus, colour is a characteristic of transmutation, and not a primary quality in its own right, and the transmutation is presented in this landscape also as the proximity of objects, the speed of movement, and the human intellect arising out of the uncharted instinctual response.

In chapter 4, therefore, colour is the result of a further stage of the transmutation of the poetic *materia*. Here we have come to one of those significant uses of the word 'turn' [*oborot*] – the turns of poetry, turns of phrase as speech construction, turns of the ornament on Geryon's skin, turns as changes of speed, and finally the turns of Geryon's flight ('descend in broad, flowing circles'). Mandel'shtam goes further and attributes to Dante an intentional allusion to usurers in Geryon's canto as the display of one more example of these turns: this time the usurers' preoccupation with interest is nothing but a banking turn [*bankovskij oborot*].[36]

4.4 Coloration of the poetic text as imagination and its limitations

It is clear that the coloration of the poetic universe, as well as colour as such, is also an allegory for imagination or fantasy, a response awakened by poetic discourse. Geryon is the fantastic animal par excellence: his skin is compared to 'the Arabic fairy-tale with its technique of flying carpet' (II, 383; 415). The same image appears in *Journey to Armenia*, transposed into those light Moslem slippers which Mandel'shtam wears after reading Signac's theory of colour (II, 145; 351); this is clearly a reference to the relationship between colour and the life of the imagination, here represented by the imagination's most immediate signifier: fairy-tale material (that is, flying slippers).[37]

The reader's imagination, therefore, meets the text, not as a finished product, but in the space where the text is still in the process of its making – on the level of fantasy – in the writer's laboratory, in his studio.[38] However, this meeting with the text as an unfinished product that the reader is to colour together with the writer is as much a fact as an illusion, and by no means the only goal of poetic transmutation. The impressionistic response of the reader (a highly subjective coloration of multiple, minute aspects) is a stage as important as it is finally treacherous. Geryon himself is a symbol of fraud in Dante, a fact that Mandel'shtam does not emphasize but obviously implies as he describes the 'terrifying dressing gown' of 'the Tatar's back in front of the eyes.'[39] Chapter 4 concludes with an allusion to Dante's 'mocking his slow-witted reader' as the Italian poet 'brings Geryon back to earth and equips him for a new journey' (II, 383; 415).

This impression once created, the 'thinking in images' (II, 382; 414)[40] that the chapter displays is pleasant and exciting but ultimately unsatisfactory, except in so far as it trains the reader's perception prior to the understanding of the next stage of this transmutable landscape. This interpretation (that is, the use of colour as a necessary but limited understanding of objects) is consistent with the description of the Linnaean school in the *Journey to Armenia*. While praising the biologists' ability to 'straighten' the reader's eye, to distil natural colour, and to move from proximate to proximate in picturesque miniature descriptions, Mandel'shtam invariably stresses that this approach is ultimately destined for failure:

> The naturalist pursues the magical pictorial effect. <He fails to mention the anatomical structure of the insect.>
> About the time of Darwin's emergence on the scene, the art of the miniaturists, of the aristocracy of the natural sciences, was experiencing the final stages of collapse. (III, 174; 340)

4.5 The reader as addressee

As unsatisfactory as this stage is, it is nevertheless the beginning of the direct address to the reader, an involvement of the living audience, or a personal rather than instinctual summons. The description of different miniature illustrations that opens chapter 4 is a living history of actual if somewhat naive readings. Moreover, Mandel'shtam's description of Signac's pointillist theory reinforces the sense of both broad popular address and yet personal invitation that this theory – the theory of colour, miniature, proximity, training of perception – holds:

> Time and again, he referred to his *Journey to Morocco*, as if leafing through a codex of visual training intended as obligatory reading for each thinking European.
> Signac was trumpeting on his chivalric horn the last ripe gathering of the Impressionists ...
> At the first sounds of his triumphant theory, my nerves grew taut. I felt a shiver of novelty, as if someone had summoned me by name ... (II, 145; 351)

This stage, therefore, recaptures something of Mandel'shtam's 1920s conception of Rozanov's philology, both in its unsatisfactory side ('the philology of the *holy fools*') and in its unconditional personal address, with its inclusion into literature as into a family (see 'ripe gathering,' 'summoned me by name' in the passage quoted above, or the invitation to the writer's studio in the *Conversation about Dante*).[41] Personal inclusion within the poetic text begins as we examine its parts and as we come into close proximity with its details. The apprehension of colour in these objects is characteristic of the transfixing impulse caught at this level of proximity, and since the impulse never stops, and its nature is that of unceasing transmission of energy, the reader's coloration of these objects is actually creative. Yet if the absorbing creativity of imagination becomes the only goal of poetic communication, then this stage does not escape Dante's circle of fraud. Therefore, the transmutation of the poetic text is incorrectly understood as an exclusive invitation to creative involvement on the part of the imaginative reader, whereas the invitation is, instead, to journey further.

5 From Colour to Wave-Impulse as a Common Textual Characteristic. The Addressee as Co-traveller or Co-inventor

The stage that follows upon the reader's recognition of textual imagery

The Transmutation of the Poetic Landscape 93

in its proximity is the identification of the characteristics common to these images and, thus, an arrival at the text as a whole, which can now be comprehended through the knowledge of the qualities operating in the entire text. As in the previous chapters of the *Conversation about Dante*, Mandel'shtam develops a network of interconnected images that play out every aspect of this new stage of poetic transmutation, a stage easy to understand once we again examine the associated imagery involved. Here we shall proceed in the following order:

> 5.1 *Identification of the common characteristics: the shift from the notion of colour to the traces of light*
> 5.2 *The image of sailing*
> 5.3 *The self-erasing surface*
> 5.4 *The limits of language*
> 5.5 *The co-discoverer as addressee*

5.1 Identification of the common characteristics: the shift from the notion of colour to the traces of light

The notion of colour gives way to the image of 'a scattered alphabet, in the form of leaping, sparkling, well-splashed letters,' whose role is to present 'the very elements which, in accord with the laws of the transformability of poetic material, will be united into formulas of meaning' (II, 387; 418).[42] In this new metaphoric development Mandel'shtam achieves several goals which, though never stated explicitly, constitute the background to a network of images presented as a description of the newly unveiled landscape. Since in our subsequent analysis of the imagery this background will be discussed only in connection with the images, it is helpful to present a basic outline of the poet's argument:

1 By concentrating upon the impulse of light, which has earlier been interpreted as colour, the poet uncovers a more deeply rooted landscape of poetry where the elements can be grasped in their likeness, according to the traces of light in each image rather than in their differentiation as multicoloured texture.
2 This, in turn, permits Mandel'shtam to move towards the notion of the text in its totality (since he now observes the principles common to all aspects of the text) and also towards the process of reading as a quest that reaches the furthest limits of the landscape made available

to the observer through these recognizably common traits herein identified as the traces of light.
3 This poetic inquiry, which embraces the whole of the text, can now be juxtaposed to Darwin's all-inclusive classification of natural species.
4 Furthermore, since the notion of light corresponds to the notion of the impulse, the surface of the text becomes an illumined display of the impulses which have gone into its creation, and thus a performance of the numerous rough drafts, which have not been forgotten or discarded, but which become the impulses constituting the final text.[43]
5 All of the above, therefore, permit Mandel'shtam to dramatize Dante's landscape in the *Purgatorio*, where the souls are already present for eternity (by the very fact of their presence in the *Purgatorio* they are not lost souls).

It is clear, as it has been all along, that in discussing Dante as the master of transmutable poetic *materia*, Mandel'shtam is also describing his own ability to develop images within a series of related transformations in order to display a whole framework of related insights. In this context it is also understandable why, for this new landscape of poetry, Mandel'shtam chooses Odysseus's speech in the *Inferno* as the centre of the discussion. It is not the infernal setting that attracts him but Dante's canvas of the images of twinkling lights from which the different voices tell their story, and specifically Odysseus's story of the quest – the longest journey towards the limit of the human landscape:[44] 'Two basic parts are clearly distinguishable in this canto: the luminous impressionistic preparatory background [*svetovaja, impressionisticheskaja podgotovka*] and the well-balanced, dramatic tale, in which Odysseus tells ... about his journey into the deeps of the Atlantic' (II, 387; 418). Dante's framework here becomes for Mandel'shtam the best possible description of the qualities of the landscape: the tongues of light, the quest, the farthest reaches of the globe, and, finally, the radical transformation of the participants in the quest.

5.2 *The image of sailing*

The wavelike surface that has been uncovered in the text (three moments of the development of this image are in the process of being played out: the luminous twitching of the lights – light waves – waves) is also introduced as the desire of the artist to avoid direct answers or statements. The artistic impulse has to outmanoeuvre all possible impediments:[45] the poem is a survival of impulses which, like sailboats, must arrive without harm:[46]

> Dante is by his very nature one who shakes up meaning and destroys the self identification [*celostnost'*] of the image. The composition of his cantos resembles an airline net of connections or the indefatigable flights of carrier pigeons ...
>
> Let us remember that Dante Alighieri lived during the heyday of sailing ships and that sailing was a highly developed art. Let us not reject out of hand the fact that he contemplated models of tacking and the maneuvering of sailing vessels. He was a student of this most evasive and plastic sport known to man since his earliest days.
>
> Here I would like to point out one of the very remarkable peculiarities of Dante's psyche: he was terrified of the direct answers, perhaps conditioned by the political situation in that extremely dangerous, enigmatic and criminal century. (II, 385; 416)

The images chosen for this stage of poetic transmutation correspond to Mandel'shtam's examination of Darwin's insight into nature, and this juxtaposition allows us to have a clearer insight into the argument behind the immediate images in these texts. Darwin,[47] a scientist who breaks out of the school of Linnaean colourful descriptions, is presented invariably as a seafarer,[48] a voyager whose scientific work is an inseparable aspect of his travelling. He is indeed the scientific counterpart of the adventurer Odysseus: 'An around-the-world cruise on a frigate was incorporated into the educational plans of every young man with a serious future. Innumerable artists, scholars, and poets participated in this around-the-world pedagogy. That is why in Darwin's scientific writings we come across elements of geographer's prose, rudiments of a colonial tale, a seafarer's adventure story' (III, 175; 340). The notion of the seafarer, however, is authenticated not merely by the fashionableness of sea travel as an educational activity in Darwin's own time;[49] the pulsating wavelike surface of the sea journey itself is characteristic of Darwin's very wavelike approach to nature: 'The energy of the argument is discharged in "quanta,"' in batches. Accumulation and release, inhalation and exhalation, ebb and flow' (III, 176; 341). What Mandel'shtam emphasizes here is Darwin's ability to organize a vast amount of biological material into a heterogenous series, and thus to travel metaphorically through the entire organic world whose life he approaches as waves of similarities, each in turn succeeding the other (see his description of Dante's text as 'an airline net of connections or the indefatigable flights of carrier pigeons,' quoted above):[50]

> Here the demands of science happily correspond to one of the most fundamental aesthetic laws. I have in mind the law of heterogeneity which encourages the artist to seek to unite in one form the greatest number of different sounds, concepts of various origin, and even antithetical images.
> In Darwin's field of vision the entire organic world always appeared as a unified whole. He dealt with the most varied kinds of living creatures with astonishing freedom and ease. (III, 176–7; 341–2)

The description of Darwin as a seafarer, therefore, goes hand in hand with his work as a scientist who has achieved a more profound presentation of the pulsating world of nature.[51]

The poetic landscape that opens up to the reader once the impressionistic coloration has been left behind is, therefore, a universe similar to the panoramic vision of Darwin: the reader in this universe is a mature Odysseus, an aged man who has seen all: 'Old age, in Dante's conception of the term, means, above all, breadth of vision, heightened capacity, and universal interests. In Odysseus's canto the earth is already round' (II, 388; 419).

5.3 The self-erasing surface

The juxtaposition of Mandel'shtam's description of Darwin with the poetic landscape of chapter 5 makes it possible to pinpoint both the differences and the similarities between the scientific empirical approach to nature, on the one hand, and another stage in the apprehension of poetic material, on the other. Darwin concentrates upon facts and anatomic structures; he presents his arguments in 'sculpted constellations' (III, 176; 343): 'Darwin never described anything, he only characterized it ... He used nature as one would use an enormous, highly systematized card catalog' (III, 138; 333–4).

Poetry, however, characterizes only in passing; it demonstrates and enacts, rather than producing a stable product: 'Dante is able to describe a phenomenon so that not the slightest trace of it remains. To do this he uses a device which I would like to call the Heraclitean metaphor; it so strongly emphasizes the fluidity of the phenomenon and cancels it out with such a flourish, that direct contemplation, after the metaphor has completed its work, is left essentially with nothing to sustain it' (II, 386; 417). Poetry, in this sense, supersedes Darwin. While his 'book seethes with natural phenomena,' Darwin proposes ultimately limited and particularized readings, where the images turn immediately with the appropriate side; they play an active role in the argument and then yield their place to their successors' (III, 177; 342, translation altered). In poetry and its heterogenic rows there is no 'appropriate side.' Poetic material is all fluidity; it is an impulse that transfixes the reader, but over which the reader himself has no power. Thus, Mandel'shtam distrusts the possibility of scientific categorization on this level of the poetic texture; the impulses of light move through the images and through the hand that tries to grasp them.[52] This explains why Odysseus, in contrast to Darwin, does not achieve victory in his quest; the objects over which he thought he had control have literally overtaken *him*: 'The metabolism of the planet itself takes place in the blood, and the Atlantic sucks in Odysseus, swallowing up his wooden ship' (II, 388–9; 420).

At this stage the text, after promising the possibility of organization or categorization, still outmanoeuvres the reader. What had been within the reader's grasp moves on, leaving perhaps only a trace of its substance. Dante's text has preserved itself by leaving its readers with only an illusion of possession:

> If you give a child a thousand rubles and then suggest that he make a choice of keeping either the coins or the banknotes, he will of course choose the coins, and in this way you can retrieve the entire sum by giving him some small change. Exactly the same experience has befallen European literary criticism which nailed Dante to the landscape of Hell familiar from the engravings ...
>
> Dante has images of parting and farewell. It is most difficult to descend through the steps of his much farewell-bidding verse ...   (II, 387–8; 419, translation altered)

Mandel'shtam, therefore, clearly prefigures the future development of literary theory (from its basic empirical approach to its deconstruction of reading and structured unity) by insisting that poetry qua poetry always outwits or outmanoeuvres its addressee in its movement towards a landscape that is atemporal, ahierarchical, and ahistorical.[53]

5.4 The limits of language

The ability of poetry to outmanoeuvre the reader is extended further, in so far as it comes to include the range of language itself at this stage of the transmutation of poetic discourse. Mandel'shtam is intentionally ambiguous, dramatizing the essence of language as a departure and separation from both reader and writer alike. He describes the moment of parting, for example, in terms of a personal abandonment: poetic language has outdistanced the reader and bidden him farewell as it progresses on its momentous journey. Or has poetry left language behind in this self-erasing landscape and progressed as a wave, an all-transfixing impulse? At the end of chapter 5 Mandel'shtam speaks about the 'yielding pliability' of language [*ustupchivost'*], obviously playing upon the uncertainty thus created about whether language has yielded in order to give the right of way or whether it has yielded in order to outmanoeuvre our grasp:

> It is difficult for us foreigners to penetrate the ultimate secret of foreign poetry. We cannot be judges, we cannot have the last word. But it seems to me that it is precisely here that we find the enchanting yielding quality of the Italian language which only the ear of the native Italian can perceive completely.
> Here I am quoting Marina Tsvetaeva, who once mentioned the 'yielding pliability' of the Russian language.   (II, 390; 421)

Since chapter 6 of the *Conversation about Dante* is dedicated to music, it is quite appropriate that language, as a particularized national phenomenon, here undergoes a genuine and radical metamorphosis. This explains why chapter 5 closes with a glimpse of the reciter, who reads as if 'giving lessons to the deaf and mute'; in other words, the reciter in this context becomes a part of the impulse that (without sound as such) transfixes every movement of his face. Earlier in the chapter Mandel'shtam also described Dante's momentary loss of Italian and his secret enjoyment of Greek:[54] thus in Dante's tale of Odysseus, 'if you listen more attentively, you will see that the poet is improvising inwardly in his beloved [*zavetnyj*], secret Greek, using only the phonetics and the fabric of his native Italian idiom to carry out his purpose' (II, 387; 419).

Although the process in which language itself bids farewell is described in an intentionally ambiguous manner, the goal of the poet is to point towards a radical metamorphosis of language itself. Mandel'shtam's dramatization of the pliability of language forecasts another landscape of poetry where impulse operates before and after the appearance of verbal language, and this for Mandel'shtam is above all the landscape of music. Chapter 5, however, concentrates upon the distance to be travelled *before* one reaches these limits of verbal language.

5.5 The co-discoverer as addressee

In his treatment of Darwin Mandel'shtam frequently points out that the English scientist knew his addressee very well. Darwin wrote simultaneously for the educated public and for the specialist, but his appeal was to the average reader. While his 'desire was for widespread cooperation with the international scientific forces of the bourgeoisie,' Darwin invariably spoke 'directly to the broad reading public over the heads of the scholarly caste': 'We should also mention Darwin's appeal to the average reader, his great desire to be understood by the bourgeoisie with a secondary school education, by the average gentleman as he considered himself ... It was important to him to relate directly to this public. And the public did understand Darwin far better than the scholar-pedants. He brought his readers something actual, strikingly in tune with their sense of well-being; he answered a social demand' (III, 176; 341). There is an unmistakable air of poignancy in Mandel'shtam's wistful description of a relationship with the reading public that he himself was destined never to have: that is, the sense of well-being that is reflected in Darwin and his readers, and even in the timbre of the scientific text.[55] It is also clear that Mandel'shtam's description of the pulsating, wavelike unfoldings of Darwin's scientific arguments (which extend through their examples 'in length, width and depth') is intended to reflect Darwin's relationship with his reading public: his across-the-globe 'reporting to countless addressees around the world engaged in similar work' (III, 138; 334).[56]

The wavelike landscape of Dante's imagery which unfolds in chapter 5 of the *Conversation with Dante* is equally reflected in Dante's relationship with his addressee at this particular stage of the poetic landscape. However, the impulse that transfixes the poetic texture cannot be extended as a handshake to the average reader. The impulse outperforms, outruns, or outmanoeuvres the reader: 'If your head is not spinning from this miraculous ascent, worthy of Sebastian Bach's organ music, then try to indicate where the first and second members of the comparison are to be found, what is compared with what, and where the primary and secondary explanatory elements are located' (II, 387–8; 418–19). Writing determines its own reader. Like Darwin's addressee, the reader is a collaborator in the process. Yet if Darwin's reader exudes a sense of the well-being of the nineteenth-century bourgeoisie, Dante's addressee is the one who, in following the quick-yielding impulse, outruns his own era and, from what appears to be an ahistorical dimension of time, grasps the elusive content of the unfolding metamorphosis. The present level of the poetic landscape demands that Dante's addressee, in contrast to Darwin's average reader, must discard mediocrity:

> For Dante time is the content of history understood as a simple synchronic act; and vice-versa: the contents of history are the joint containing of time by its associates, competitors, and co-discoverers.
>
> Dante is an anti-modernist. His contemporaneity is continuous, incalculable and inexhaustible. (II, 389; 420)

The addressees in this self-effacing poetic landscape are co-travellers,[57] co-inventors, co-seekers, who hold together the vast sea of time; they are co-equals caught in the process of 'the close listening to sound and light waves found in all our theory of sound and light, in all our scientific study of matter, in all our poetry and music' (II, 390; 421). Yet the landscape is to change again, for chapter 5 serves as an introduction to our arrival upon the purgatorial slopes of the Dantean world,[58] slopes where the signs of previous existence are slowly being effaced, yet where the survival of souls is an integral part of the landscape. Darwin dealt, as we know, with the survival of the fittest. In chapter 5 of the *Conversation about Dante* we witness a state of poetry in which everything survives, but only by means of yet another transmutation of the wave-impulse.

6 Music as Verification of the Final Direction of the Poetic Impulse. The Addressee as a Figure of Authority within a Concert-like Setting

In chapter 6, Mandel'shtam presents the next stage in the unveiling of the poetic *materia* in the context of the final cantos of Dante's *Purgatorio*. The implicit pictorial background is the top of the purgatorial mountain (still a physical formation) surrounded on all sides by a new audience (namely, the open air of the *Paradiso*). According to the devel-

The Transmutation of the Poetic Landscape 101

opment of Mandel'shtam's argument, this landscape is perhaps the last stage of the physical ascent: that is, the last poetic territory susceptible of examination by the instruments of intellectual or scientific reasoning. The characteristics here are still open to human experience and scholarly experimentation, but a new perspective already prevails. We shall examine the imagery of this stage of the interrelation of impulse and quantitative characteristics in the following order:

6.1 *The progression from reason to faith*
6.2 *Music and chemistry*
6.3 *The conductor's baton*
6.4 *A further addressee: the concert-like circumstance of the presence of authority*

6.1 The progression from reason to faith
At no point in the *Conversation about Dante* does Mandel'shtam assert that poetry is the beginning of a transcendental metaphysical experience. But he does insist that the 'untameable' impulse of poetic discourse does not so much result in faith as uncover the metaphorical framework that is analogous to a progression from reason to faith. Chapter 6 of the *Conversation about Dante* deals precisely with the importance of this analogy.

For Dante, Mandel'shtam emphasizes, sacred theology is the meeting place of divine wisdom and human experience, the intersection point of the revelation of God and the revelation of the world. Here we come closest to the origin of the poetic impulse or *logos*: the *logos* cannot come simply from faith since it is dialogical in its nature. Rather, it springs from the genuine intersection of two universes (which are in Dante, as in the philosophical and spiritual tradition that informs the *Commedia*, the universes of nature and grace). Mandel'shtam alludes to this intersection in the first steps of chapter 6 when he isolates two forms of intersecting experience, Aristotle's physics and what he calls biblical genetics: in other words, generation from below and generation from above, or what were for the Middle Ages two sources of knowledge, physics and sacred scripture.[59]

This progression can be restated in somewhat different terms. The highest aspirations of early western culture were invariably directed towards the scientific verification of faith. Dante's *Commedia* is above all directed by the same powerful intellectual desire to unite the two disparate worlds, and the desire itself is already a poetic impulse: 'When the need for the empirical verification of Biblical tradition first dawned on Dante, when he first indicated a taste for what I propose to call a "sacred induction," the conception of the *Divina Commedia* had already taken shape, and its success was virtually assured' (II, 393; 424). The poetic impulse, therefore, is unceasingly caught in experimentation, continuously moving from faith to factual verification: 'The major antinomy of Dante's experience is to be found in his rushing back and forth between the example and experiment' (II, 392; 423). Poetic discourse on this level of its unveiling is both a locus for, and the principal agent of, this movement,[60] a constant wavelike action between two seemingly disjointed principles ('These two poorly matched things did not want to merge,' II, 391; 422); yet this very disjointedness of the two approaches is a most exact presentation of the dialogical origin of poetic formation, and the experimentation caught between the two is *poiesis* or 'making' as such:

> The position of the experimenter with respect to factology, insofar as he aspires towards a trusting union with it, is by nature unstable, agitated and off balance. It brings to mind the above-mentioned figure of the waltz, because after each half-turn on the toes, in coming together the dancer's heels always meet on a new square of the parquetry and in a qualitatively different way. The dizzying Mephisto Waltz of experimentation originated in the Trecento, or perhaps even long before that; furthermore, it originated in the process of poetic formation, in the undulations of formulating procedure in the transformability of poetic matter, the most precise, prophetic and indomitable of all matter. (II, 392; 423)

This unveiled stage of poetic discourse fills (at least as the territory or locus of its operation) one of the most obvious lacunae of human experience. It surpasses prose, since, according to Mandel'shtam, prose lacks the instruments of poetic discourse and will always appear only as the disjointed sign of the continuum of the reality in question.[61] Poetry however, fills this gap by the very nature of its 'undulation of formulating procedure in the transformability of poetic matter,' by being a wave from its origin,[62] and by being born out of a dizzying melody, 'the dizzying Mephisto Waltz.'

The argument here has five stages: 1 / the disjointedness between reason and faith; 2 / Dante's decision to verify the principles of faith through experimentation; 3 / the waltzlike movement between example (biblical stories) and experiment; 4 / poetry as the locus, instrument, and verifier of the experimentation in question; and 5 / the wavelike pattern of the experiment as the language of poetry, its 'dizzying Mephisto Waltz,' and its musical essence.

6.2 Music and chemistry

How precisely is the verification effected? In Mandel'shtam two new directions of thought-image resurface immediately: music and chemistry. As earlier, in the parallels from Lamarck, Pallas, and Darwin, chemistry is an organic counterpart to the new stage of the unveiling poetic texture, which is no longer language but music.[63] Music and chemistry become intertwined in order to accommodate the concertlike circumstances of the landscape. Furthermore, music forms or articulates, as it were, the experimentation in question, since it arranges the pattern of the argument: 'Music here is not merely a guest invited to step indoors, but a full participant in the argument; or to be more precise, it promotes the exchange of opinions, coordinates it, and encourages syllogistic digestion, stretches premises and compresses conclusions. Its role is both absorptive and resorptive: it is a purely chemical role' (II, 394; 425). What Mandel'shtam indicates here is that music obscures the statement of the conclusions as pure statement (that is, prose), and absorbs them into itself. Thus, the musical quality of poetic verse becomes the ultimate verifier, which draws the conclusion away from a statement and into its melodic essence.[64] Music and chemistry, therefore, do not so much instruct as 'encourage syllogistic digestion,' in other words, prepare the organs for reception and experimentation: 'but I must not fail to mention the preparation of the eye for the apperception of new things' (II, 394; 425).[65]

6.3 The conductor's baton

The musical analogy allows Mandel'shtam to develop the central motif of chapter 6: namely, the birth of a new dimension that comes as a result of the experimentation here described. Again, the concert-like circumstances of the chapter (the audience-*Paradiso* surrounding the top of the purgatorial mountain) reinforce the thought: music introduces the image of the orchestra and its collective performance, but a new element emerges from the equation – the conductor's baton. This new element is necessitated by the sheer multitude of the impulses of poetic discourse and the landscapes of their unveiling, all of which are preserved (even if in an altered form) in this new performance of the text:

> When you read Dante with all your powers and with complete conviction, when you transplant yourself completely to the field of action of the poetic *materia*, when you join in and coordinate your own intonations with the echoes of the orchestral and thematic groups continually arising on the pocked and undulating semantic surface ... then the purely vocal, intonational, and rhythmical work is replaced by a more powerful coordinating force – by the conductor's function – and the hegemony of the conductor's baton comes into its own ... projecting from the voice like some more complex mathematical measure out of a three-dimensional state. (II, 394–5; 425)

Thus, the birth of the conductor's baton plays a role of the utmost importance, which relates directly to the opening argument of the chapter – the relationship between the two disjointed universes, reason and faith. The birth of a new element, unanticipated prior to the equations of experimentation, clearly indicates the result of the experimentation in question – the emergence of a new level, and a new dimension. Furthermore, the new-born element is a conducting, and thus a dictating, factor.

At this point Mandel'shtam moves into the actual history of the appearance of the conductor's baton from 1732 (the tempo formerly tapped out with the foot, now usually with the hand) to 1810 ('a baton made of rolled-up paper without the least noise'). Mandel'shtam's depiction is subtle but concentrated and powerful: the conductor's baton slowly raises the instinctual (from the foot to the hand to the baton of rolled-up paper) into a new intelligible form of activity. What is clearly implied is the vertical succession of poetic landscapes, where the controlling presence is first indistinguishable, then instinctual, and finally central, pointing to a new orientation and a new dimension. What is last in the order of discovery becomes first in the order of apprehending the creative impulse.

In this sense poetry is literally a realization and meeting point of two apparently contradictory movements: what has been seen as development from the substratum up is now realized as substantial creativity from the top down. The conductor's baton is not merely an adjunct, a side effect or by-product: it contains and directs all the preceding levels; it is even perhaps their essence (chemistry is a natural metaphor, well suited to this context, which serves to emphasize that this new realization lies outside sense perception, yet informs the world of the senses): 'This baton ... is no less than a dancing chemical formula which integrates reaction perceptible to the ear ... . In a certain sense this invulnerable baton qualitatively contains in itself all the elements in the orchestra. But how does it contain them? It gives off no smell of them, nor can it. It does not smell of chlorine, as the formula of ammonium chloride or ammonia does not smell of ammonium chloride or of ammonia' (II, 396; 426). The conductor's baton, therefore, clearly indicates the central, and directing, role of an element or dimension that was earlier thought to be unnecessary or irrelevant. Does Mandel'shtam give any indication of his own view about the relationship between faith and reason, or grace and nature? As always in the theoretical works, there are only the dancing elements of the argument, ready, as it were, to be united into formulas of meaningful answers. Politically, historically, temperamentally, and above all artistically, Mandel'shtam cannot and does not want to add any further statement.

6.4 A further addressee: the concert-like circumstance of the presence of authority

The conductor's baton helps us to understand the figure of authority introduced in this chapter as a new listener-addressee. The baton serves to pinpoint the central question of the chapter: 'Which comes first, listening or conducting?' (II, 395; 425), which is, of course, a new form of the question: authority or experience? The audience, which is addressed directly by the poetic text, that is, the audience which listens to the text's performance, has a predominant role at this level, and is therefore a performer in its own right. In Dante this state is depicted metaphysically as occurring on the highest slopes of the purgatorial mountain where the pageant in the forest addresses its heavenly audience. Mandel'shtam renders this state as follows: 'The poem when most densely covered with foliage[66] is addressed towards authority; its sound is fullest; it is most concert-like especially where it is caressed by dogma, by canon, by firm gold-mouthed word' (II, 393; 424, translation altered). The address 'towards authority' here is met with a response (caressing 'gold-mouthed word'), and both are active participants in the dialogue thereby generated.

The addressee now appears with new and striking characteristics, for it represents authority as dogma or reception (that is, the Greek *dogma*, from the verb *dechesthai*, to receive). There is also an implicit ambiguity as to who is the real performer in this landscape, for the sense of joy at this meeting is mutual and common to both interlocutors; the concert-like setting is emphasized in every metaphor associated with the descriptions of the mutual address so disclosed. Each of the characteristics in this highly concentrated depiction is further played out and echoed in all the other images of chapter 6.

Moreover, the characterization of anonymous, invisible authority as dogma or pure reception is developed in the role of the baton as 'the most powerful chemical conductor of the poetic composition.' Authority here clearly represents a dimension of experience whose importance and even primacy were not, and could not have been, realized within the patterns that constituted the changing poetic landscapes prior to this new concert-like landscape. Moreover, the figure of authority reflects the cooperation between verification and experimentation in this particular landscape: just as textual experimentation verifies faith, faith verifies textual experimentation within an eternally recreated space: ('the dancer's heels always meet on a new square of the parquetry and in a qualitatively different way,' II, 392; 423). Mandel'shtam's joy at the very existence of this authority is noteworthy. His argument is at its most subtle here: he places the notions of authority and of spiritual dogma (notions perhaps alien to the twentieth-century reader) into the context of the artistic desire for a listener of impeccable judgment and taste. Mandel'shtam's joy is a celebration of the performer's natural anxiety in the presence of a much admired authority viewing the performance: the natural excitement consists in the fact that one is finally judged by a highly respected and even feared audience. The expectation of this audience is so much an aspect of the writing process that Mandel'shtam stresses its privileged status while at the same time emphasizing that no purely human authority can take upon itself the role in question. The desire to be verified is a characteristic of poetry,[67] and it is in this context that Mandel'shtam presents Dante's entrance into the *Paradiso*: 'But therein lies the problem: in authority, or to be more exact in authoritativeness, we can see only insurance against error, and we are not at all equipped to understand that grandiose music of faith, of trustfulness, to make out those nuances of demonstration and the beginning of faith as slender as an Alpine rainbow, which Dante has under his control' (II, 393–4; 424, translation altered). Equally important here is the notion of music: authority does not judge what is being said (that is, there is no Soviet-like political scrutiny of the text), but rather receives the nuances of the intonation, the musical essence of the poetic texture, and poetry's rootedness in achieved verification. In other words, this new landscape of poetry, which is uncovered after yet another stage of radical metamorphosis, provides a sense of verification, which is experienced not as verification of poetry as statement but as the spontaneous correctness of the musical structure of the poetic phrase, of its rhythm, and of its thoroughly satisfying articulation.

The concert-like circumstances of the setting are also of major consequence in this visualization of the addressee. The dialogical impulse of poetry outgrows itself here and becomes an orchestral celebration,[68] while still remaining a dialogue, and a meeting ground between faith and experimentation. Here we get a glimpse of the text as a concert-like polyphony of address where each word speaks to its neighbour – a stage that is displayed on the metaphoric level as a celebration that unites authority, author, musical instruments, conductor, and audience in the as yet unheard musical intonation of the text.

7 Preliminary Conclusions

As we have seen above, Mandel'shtam describes the unveiling of the stages implicit in the apprehension of poetry as a journey along the axis of at least five successively changing landscapes: 1 / the infernal; 2 / the instinctual; 3 / the impressionistic, or the landscape of colour; 4 / the structural (which displays the common traces of the text's essential characteristics); and 5 / the musical. Each new landscape emerges when the previous landscape has become too kinetically charged or too densely rich to sustain its own interplay of reversals and transmissions. Mandel'shtam considers the modulation or change that characterizes these inevitable metamorphoses to be the primary characteristic of the poetic impulse, an impulse inaudible on its own and yet generating an unceasing series of cooperations and transmutations by means of its transfixing action. As we follow the impulse along these Dantean landscapes, we ourselves participate in the metamorphoses of the poetic *materia* and witness the generation of the poetic universe, experiencing it as both descent and ascent, or generation from above and from below. However, once this universe is formed from below and its transmutation reaches the final stages of its physical formation, that is, its purely musical modulation in the open air of a complete universe, so to speak, we witness a movement in the opposite direction, namely, generation from above or spontaneous dictation.

Changing Stages in the Apprehension of the Poetic Landscape: Communication as Simultaneous Performance of Differentiated Strategies

	Stage of reception in reading/writing	Metaphoric formulation of each stage in *Conversation about Dante*	Scientific apprehension. Succession of sciences as counterparts to stages within poetic apprehension	Pattern of apprehension
1	Beginning of reading/writing process. Awareness of subtextual referential echoes and rediscovery of personal semiforgotten history	Descent into matter [Chapter 3]	Examination of nature under microscope. Descent of the organic ladder. Lamarckian biology	Apprehension of the text as chorus of intertextual quotations. Text as awakening of personal semiforgotten observations
2	Awareness of text as a unified whole, a living body	Creation as birth. Expression both literal and physical [Chapter 3]	Close examination of the details of the natural landscape. Proximate observation as awareness of colour, as imaginative response. Biology of Linnaeus and Pallas	Instinctual redirection of enquiry from the infinitely divisible past into the apprehension of one single growing text
3	Particularization of focus. Perception of text as unfolding of minute parts	Expression of nature resulting in colour. Text as multicoloured miniature [Chapter 4]	Embryology	Close scrutiny of the parts of the text. Awakening of fantasy likened to reading as colouring of miniature painting
4	Awareness of structural design, systematic organization	Apprehension through colour. Disclosed landscape of lightwaves crisscrossing the text as a tightly structured network [Chapter 5]	Nature as organization of species. Darwinian evolution as systematic dictionary of nature	Text disclosed as a structured unity that is both synchronic and diachronic. Survival of earlier drafts in the final version
5	Fusion of two axes: empirical knowledge and sacred revelation	Emergence into music. Universe as concert [Chapter 6]	Chemistry. Quantum physics	Apprehension of musical intonation as direction of language

The Transmutation of the Poetic Landscape 109

Time/space	Accompanying set of metaphors	Addressee within each stage	Counterpart in Dante's universe
Growing power of the past. Infinitely divisible space of the minute	Entrance through a crack in the rock. Gap. Trope as narrow path. Sexual intercourse. Reversal of time. Death. Impregnation	Ghost of the past	Inferno
Instinctual moment with no delineation. Body acquiring its own geography	Birth of text as crystallogical body. Growing crystal slowly becoming expanding space. Insects (bees)	Instinctual self. The bee	Birth of Purgatory. The expression of the earth
Unit – space. Inner dimensions within a miniature universe. Particularization	Geryon (change from insect to human and vice versa). Multi-coloured objects. Fairy-tale imagery. Expression as squeezing of colour from natural world. Vegetable dyes	Imaginative but naive reader	Double movement: apparent flight upwards which may also be descent. Geryon as illusion
Expanding space as disclosure of unknown landscape. Time as universal duration seen as single movement	Colour apprehended as light-waves. Wave-like surface of the poetic text. Sailing. Seafaring	Courageous co-discoverer, co-traveller	Ascent of Purgatory. Restoration of souls, none of which are to be lost
Time and space as functions of creative experimentation	Orchestral music giving birth to the conductor's baton, which preceded it	Figure of authority. Poet himself	Top of Purgatory. Heavenly pageant

It is clear that this insight into the hybrid nature of the generation of a poetic universe cannot be limited exclusively to poetic discourse. For Mandel'shtam poetry is one of the most complex and intense of human activities, and thus it is a part of all human actions, for it comprehends life and is, therefore, also a part of life and all its aspects. Once the poetic landscapes have been identified and the status of the addressee in each established, the *Conversation about Dante* examines the delineations of the poetic impulse in human life – a subject hardly alien to poetry even when the characteristics common to poetic formation and the formation of human experience are not the writer's primary interest.

Thus, the second part of the *Conversation about Dante* focuses on the hybrid transmutation of the impulse found outside the poetic texture as such. It deals directly with the different forms of human experience, and their infernal, purgatorial, and paradisal delineations, as it were, which are different by nature from the characteristics of poetic discourses. Since Mandel'shtam's primary focus in the last six chapters is beyond the immediate concern of this work, which is poetics, I shall refer to those chapters only in so far as they permit us to elucidate Mandel'shtam's thought on poetry as 'a reflexology of speech' or refer to the common characteristics of the reading and writing processes.

6

Conclusion: The Theoretical Implications of Mandel'shtam's Poetics

The object of this concluding chapter is to determine the theoretical implications of Mandel'shtam's poetics and to place them, however tentatively, against the background of literary theory. One word of caution needs to be given at the outset: the history of literary theory in the twentieth century has been enormously fertile and multifaceted, but this study must be limited to a finite number of theoretical questions; otherwise any conclusion will be impossible to draw.

This book remains primarily and emphatically a textual work, which argues throughout that one cannot get close to Mandel'shtam's thought about poetry from a single work or a single image, however memorable and striking a particular definition or thought may appear. Precisely because Mandel'shtam thinks and discourses through images, their configurations remain impressionistic and fleeting unless one traces the chronological shift of recurrent and new images, a shift that is not merely a change in impression but a shift in thought. Herein lies the difference between this study and much of what has recently been published on Mandel'shtam's views on art. In contrast to works such as those of Pollak (1995) and Clare Cavanagh (1995), I argue that only in the chronology of differences within a pattern of similar configurations can one find the key to Mandel'shtam's poetics, that is, the key to a pattern of thought enacted and discovered only as change, movement, and journey.

Mandel'shtam's temperament, at least in this regard, curiously reflects the character of his age, as he celebrates the capacity of images to outmanoeuvre their reader. In fact, Mandel'shtam's own reluctance, or inability, to state things directly becomes an insight not only into Dante but more generally into the ability of poetry itself to evade the destructiveness of finality in thought:

> he [Dante] contemplated models of tacking and the manoeuvring of sailing vessels. He was a student of this most evasive and plastic sport known to man since his earliest days.
>   Here I would like to point out one of the remarkable pecularities of Dante's psyche: he was terrified of a direct answer, perhaps conditioned by the political situation in that extremely dangerous, enigmatic and criminal century. (II, 424; 416)

This study attempts to trace at least some of 'the evasive and plastic sport' of Mandel'shtam's thought, in order to determine what he has contributed to modern-day poetics.

My investigation reveals, not the brilliant but erratic Charlie Chaplin figure of Russian poetry or a 'jester of many colours' (Freidin 1987), but rather a highly original, masterful, and tenacious thinker, whose ability to transform thoughts and images is often too fast and unexpected for a reader seeking the logical development of thought only on one level of discourse. The tenor of Mandel'shtam's writing is, perhaps, the best illustration of his recurrent pronouncement in the 1930s that poetic discourse resembles the fluid surface of swift underground streams, traversing several layers simultaneously and breaking out into quickly vanishing wave-explosions. My objective is to isolate, within the broader concerns of contemporary poetics, the underlying clusters of theoretical presuppositions that consciously or unconsciously direct the metaphorical dramatization of these different wave explosions, or rather of the different poetic landscapes unveiled in Mandel'shtam's work.

1 A Few Preliminary Observations on the Problem of Contextualizing Mandel'shtam

When Mandel'shtam speaks of poetic texture caught in transformation and escape, he also describes his own temperament, evident not only in his writings but also in the recollections of his contemporaries. In the rough drafts of the *Conversation about Dante*, Mandel'shtam describes Dante's help in elucidating a certain concept in the *Commedia*: 'We can comprehend this concept with Dante's help. However, Dante has already turned and vanished' (III, 181; 444). Dante's disappearance echoes, among other things, Mandel'shtam's elusiveness. Tsvetaeva, who spent several days in 1916 vacationing with the young poet, writes:

> – Let us go home!
> It must be said that Mandel'shtam – from the cemetery, and from a walk, and from the fair, always from everywhere – always wanted to go home. And always earlier than the others (even I)! And from home – without exception or delay – out. (Tsvetaeva 1979, I, 354; my translation)

Tsvetaeva's description, here, as is so often customary with her, captures more than an everyday, minor, even somewhat annoying characteristic; it is also an introduction to the expectation of speed, chase, dash in Mandel'shtam's work. In other words, when Mandel'shtam speaks of an intrinsically receptive nature of poetry that transmutes, so to speak, at the very moment of reception, he also dramatizes a particular feature of his own character, common to his life and writing, that is, an urge never to belong or to be consumed. His only sense of belonging, namely his loyalty to the acmeists, is extremely telling. The memoirs of Nadezhda Mandel'shtam are helpful, even in the wistfulness of her intonation, as she sifts through what was (for both) their beloved past:

> Three poets – Akhmatova, Gumilev, and Mandel'shtam – referred to themselves as Acmeists to the very end of their lives. I have often asked what it was that united three such different poets, so unlike each other, each with a different understanding of poetry, and why the bond was so strong ... Mandel'shtam invariably dismissed the question with a joke. Akhmatova, though she was always talking about Acmeism – particularly in her old age – was never able to give me an answer ...
>
> Whatever their failings or virtues, the three poets who revolted against Symbolism did not detach themselves from the mainstream out of pique ... but solely because they had come to recognize the basic difference between their understanding of life and that of their late mentors. (N. Mandel'shtam 1974, 38, 42)

The personal character of the memoirs points to something that critics and theoreticians have not given the attention it deserves, namely, the lack of a definitive artistic program binding for this group of poets. Instead, one senses a meeting of poets who refused to give words single directions of meaning, thereby adopting not so much a philosophical stance as an ethical *Weltanschauung* that subsequently came to define their fate.[1] In fact, acmeism (and this is rarely stressed), in contrast to symbolism and futurism, is an intellectually amorphous movement, and its emphasis on the material essence of the word does not amount to an artistic program because the materiality of the word is more complex and indefinite than the symbolist direction towards an immaterial transsense. This is not to say that the acmeist movement lacked a program or philosophical grounding, but rather to suggest that its program was motivated by a desire to escape the tyranny of a clearly defined and definitive intellectual position.[2]

Indeed, poststructuralist readings of modernism seem to have identified at least one thread of this desire for freedom of association. In a recent study Cavanagh emphasizes not so much the moral as the mythmaking freedom that characterizes Gumilev's and especially Mandel'shtam's acmeism: 'No matter what challenges Symbolists or Futurists may contrive for them, the Acmeists, by virtue of their superior mythmaking, retain poetic priority as practitioners of the first truly human creation' (1995, 63). Generally, Cavanagh argues that Mandel'shtam's acmeism places or finds him in the position of any true modernist poet, that is, of 'a pastist who had no past he could legitimately call his own' (1995, 7). Comparing him in this to T.S. Eliot and Ezra Pound, she defines Mandel'shtam's work within the tradition he chooses to belong to as a true work of fantasy, something that is as much 'a remembrance as invention' (1995, 26). Thus, acmeism becomes not so much a movement with a program as an escape into atemporality, a determination 'to overcome the constraints of time and space through a modern creation of tradition' (1995, 28).

However, if read in this way, Cavanagh's evaluation of the acmeists' ideological ambivalence uses a very limited model in its emphasis upon myth making and world creation as the only noteworthy characteristics of art. Any other explanation of attachment is disregarded in the postmodern penchant for the individualistic assertion of freedom. However, the choice of those whom the poet desires to address and call his tradition (be they his contemporaries or voices from the past) can be guided by moral, aesthetic, philosophical, ethical, and even emotional or temperamental principles or desires. The impulse for freedom in creation may not be directed only by myth making; it may already be an inner choice of direction, one whose full dangers will not become clear for at least a decade.

It is important, therefore, to define more precisely what is taken to be the postmodern character of Mandel'shtam's writings. In so far as acmeism proclaims the dynamism and existence of the image, the movement is not merely an artistic modernism par excellence, but also the

Theoretical Implications of Mandel'shtam's Poetics 115

first amorphous (but rather Russian) poststructuralism. Mandel'shtam's acmeism is striking for its poststructuralist foreshadowings. The nostalgia for world culture characteristic of Mandel'shtam's acmeism gives a new taste to the reading of the poetic line as 'an orgy of quotations,' a 'keyboard of references' (II, 368; 401). There is more than a passing similarity between Mandel'shtam's sense of the poetic word and the poststructuralist decentred sense of language. Let us, then, compare two classic (even in our postmodernist age) definitions of the word, one offered by Mandel'shtam in 1933, and the other by Barthes:

> Any given word is a bundle, and meaning sticks out of it in various directions, not aspiring to any official point. (II, 374; 407)

> We now know that a text is not a line of words releasing a single 'theological meaning' (the 'message' of an Author-God) but a multi-dimensional space in which a variety of writings, none of them original, blend and clash. (Barthes 1977, 146)

This sense of a decentred, multifaceted meaning is not an accidental coincidence, nor will it be helpful to look for the historical transmutation of influence, although it does exist, of course, in Jakobson and particularly Bakhtin, whom Barthes and Julia Kristeva read admiringly.[3] A more obvious explanation of the coincidence is the intense multilayered intellectual atmosphere pervading the aesthetic and artistic schools of the first quarter of the twentieth century in Russia (all eventually closed or exterminated in the rapid progression of ensuing historical developments).

Who can deny that, under the great pressure of monumental historical change, the cultural scene in Russia at the beginning of the century played out the theoretical debates and often opposing presuppositions of what has eventually grown in the West into the multinomial but emotionally restricted poststructuralist scene? With the rapidity of hothouse organisms formalists and semioticians, marxists and neo-marxists, idealist-theists and positivists, structuralists and anarchists emerged from their initially embryonic states into the maturity of an argumentation still prevalent in what Cavanagh refers to as our invented homeless and modernist culture.

The timbre of the argument, Mandel'shtam would say, identifies its essence (see chapter 5 above). If Barthes in the 1970s can welcome a field of autonomous citations ('the modern scriptor is born simultaneously with the text; is in no way equipped with a being preceding or exceeding the writing,' Lodge 1988, 170), Mandel'shtam in the 1930s is deeply unsettled, even terrorized, by the violent implications of the image of the future extermination of authorial voices, seeing in it 'the Trecento toss[ing] men in prison with astonishing unconcern' (*Conversation about Dante*, II, 437; 428). In the *Conversation about Dante*, the multiplicity of autonomous citations within a poetic line threatens to intimate to Mandel'shtam's 'external ear' the pleading voices of those chosen for extermination, 'the impulses and solo parts, that is, the arias and ariosos, peculiar self-avowals, self-flagellations or autobiographies, sometimes brief and capable of fitting into the palm of the hand, sometimes lapidary, like a tombstone inscription, ... sometimes well developed, articulated, and capable of achieving a dramatic, operatic fullness" (II, 436; 427). Moreover, the close proximity and intensity of meanings and citations 'resembling diffusion, mutual infiltration' give rise not only to the image of prison but also to the image of a chemical reaction, of experimentation within a tightly contained locality, 'a glass retort [*stekliannaia kolba*] ... accessible and comprehensible' (II, 437; 428), which eventually results in the tragic dénouement of a progressing chemical explosion, threatening even the spectators and burning the surrounding space: 'The ballad-retort with its familiar motif is smashed to smithereens. Chemistry with its architectonic drama takes over' (II, 438; 428).

This striking similarity between Mandel'shtam's view and the post-structuralist view of the text ('a multi-dimensional space in which a variety of writings, none of them original, blend and clash,' Barthes 1977, 146) must be accompanied by a caveat, that is, by a recognition that Mandel'shtam is not emotionally indifferent to the political and social implications of his own theoretical postulates. Rather, the sociopolitical realities of his time considerably affected and nuanced not only his life but also his poetics. Mandel'shtam believes that a poetics cannot exist in a neutral, scientifically protected, or objective space. The age, he claims, demands a more profound thought from art. This depth of thought, however, even if it uncovers scientific laws, cannot protect the experimenter and the experiment from the truth thus uncovered. In analysing poetry, as in analysing history, one analyses oneself:

> ... he plays on his unhappiness like a virtuoso, and draws out of his misfortune a timbre completely unheard of before and unknown even to himself.
> We must remember that *timbre* is a structural principle much like the

alkalinity or acidity of some chemical compound. However, the chemical retort is not the space in which the chemical reaction takes place. That would be too simple. (II, 437; 428)

Protection for the speaker who discovers the formula guiding the chemical reactions of one's own misfortune cannot be granted. This thought is stated with a Mandel'shtamian, but perhaps peculiarly Russian, emotional coloration, and separates Mandel'shtam from much of what has been written by the literary theoreticians of this century, who have tended to claim scientific immunity from the repercussions of their theories. Any approach to the text has, in Mandel'shtam's view, political overtones, and terrifying ones at that. An objective examiner of speech may become an executioner of the infernal landscape:

After all, isn't a murderer something of an anatomist?
Didn't an executioner in the Middle Ages slightly resemble a scientific worker?
The art of war and the art of execution remind you a bit of the threshold of a dissecting room. (II, 441; 432)

All this, in turn, places the reader in a theoretical dilemma. Mandel'shtam does not want to be contextualized and treated like an anonymous citation or even like an objective illustration of an anaesthetized, anatomized poetic law. With all the polysemantic transformations of the text under his control, Mandel'shtam warns the reader that such a context has already been found for him, so much so in fact that no temperamental desire to escape could have made a bit of difference. A mad dash to escape death from hunger in prison would not succeed:

The following elements of the ballad are to be found ... the prison situation, that is, counting the dripping of the water as a measure of time which brings the father and his three sons closer to the mathematically conceivable threshold of death by starvation no matter how impossible it may seem to the father's consciousness. The same rhythm of mad dash emerges here in disguise, in the mute wailing of the cello, which strives with all its might to break out of the situation and gives a sound situation of a still more terrifying, slow chase, breaking speed down into the most delicate fibers. (II, 438–9; 429)

If we are to insist upon Mandel'shtam's foreshadowing the development of formalist-structuralism into the poststructuralist field, the latest turn of metaphor characteristic of the *Conversation about Dante* (chapters 7–9) reaches an almost Foucauldian rhetoric, given Michel Foucault's insistence on the corridors of power in academe, and academic patterns of research. All in all, it is clear that Mandel'shtam not only wants the reader as a co-traveller within the polemical layers of a transforming field of references; he also wants a human reader who will not deny the poet's life and name: 'Moreover, the compassionate one is invited to enter as a new partner, and we already hear his quavering voice from the distant future' (II, 438; 429).

2 The Polemical Focus of Mandel'shtam's Mature Poetics: The Hybrid Nature of Poetry as a Reinterpretation of the Aristotelian Concepts of Form and Matter

The central polemical issue of Mandel'shtam's poetics is his postulation of the hybrid nature of poetic discourse as forming impulse [*poryv*] and receptive *materia*. Poetry, as we have seen, is a continuous unveiling of the interpenetration of these two principles. Moreover, poetry in this context constitutes a diary of natural phenomena, for it is an uncovering of the essential reality of the two principles, which operate not only in language but also in the physical universe.

However attractive Mandel'shtam's observation that he incorporates into his poetics the development of twentieth-century physics (that is, 'the help of quantum theory' (II, 183; 446), this hardly obscures the fact that he restates the central principles of the Aristotelian and neo-Aristotelian tradition (which tradition is, of course, the foundation of Dante's thought), namely the principles of form and matter.

Aristotle applies these two principles in order to explain the whole range of substantial and accidental change throughout nature (*Physics* 1–2; *De generatione et corruptione* 1–2):

> Since 'nature' has two senses, the form and the matter, we must investigate its objects. That is, such things are neither independent of matter nor can be defined in terms of matter only. Here too indeed one might raise a difficulty. Since there are two natures, with which is the physical concerned? Or should he investigate the combination of the two? But if the combination of the two, then also each severally. Does it belong then to the same or to different sciences to know each severally?
>
> ... If we look at the ancients, physics would seem to be concerned with

the matter. (It was only very slightly that Empedocles and Democritus touched on the forms and the essence.)

... But if on the other hand art imitates nature, and it is the part of the same discipline to know the form and the matter up to a point (e.g. the doctor has a knowledge of health and also of bile and phlegm, in which health is realized, and the builder both of the form of the house and of the matter, namely that it is bricks and beams, and so forth): if this is so, it would be the part of physics also to know nature in both its senses.

... Again, 'that for the sake of which,' or the end, belongs to the same department of knowledge as the means. But the nature is the end or 'that for the sake of which.' For if a thing undergoes a continuous change and there is a stage which is last, this stage is the end of 'that for the sake of which.' (Aristotle [ed. McKeon] 1941, *Physics* 2.2.194a.12ff)

For Aristotle soul is the form or actuality [*entelecheia*], that is, the active meaning or functioning of the body in the hierarchy of life (1941, *De anima* 2.1: 'soul must be a substance in the sense of the form of a natural body having life potentially within it'). This is to say that it is form that makes body what it really is, and although in one sense the form of anything is visible in it, still most of the content of the form is not visible at any given moment in the course of organic development: 'Since in every class of things, as in nature as a whole, we find two factors involved, (1) a matter which is potentially all the particulars included in the class, (2) a cause which is productive in the sense that it makes them all (the latter standing to the former, as e.g. an art to its material), these distinct elements must likewise be found within the soul' (1941, *De anima* 3.5.430a.11ff). By means of a complex tradition filtered through the Stoic and Neoplatonic positions – from which the *logos* doctrine primarily comes, and in which Aristotle's notion of mind as the ultimate productive form (*De anima* 3.4–5) unmixed with any visible material quality becomes highly developed – this Aristotelian view is ultimately transformed to a new Christian purpose: first, in Aquinas (among others), for whom the 'intellectual soul' is now the 'substantial form' [*forma substantialis*] of body (*Summa theologica* 1. questions 75–6); and later in Dante, who again distinguishes the *forma sostanziale* from the *forma accidentale* (for example, *Purgatorio* XVIII.49) as the creative basis for matter's transformation into new forms. The basis is ultimately a spiritual form rooted in the divine idea, which shines in the universe (*Paradiso* I.104; XXXIII.91), but which in the human being is imperfect in its realization according to the lack of capacity in the matter that helps to actualize it (*Il Convivio* 3.6.5–6). Dante finally celebrates this form by gazing at it in *Paradiso* XXXIII at the close of his journey:[4] 'In its depth I saw ingathered, bound by love in one single volume, that which is dispersed in leaves throughout the universe: substances and accidents and their relations, as though fused together in such a way that what I tell is but a simple light. The universal form [*la forma universale*] of this knot I believe that I saw, because, in telling this, I feel my joy increase' (Dante [trans. Sinclair] 1961, *Paradiso* XXXIII.85–93). Mandel'shtam's 'crossing of two lines' in poetic discourse, 'one of which taken by itself is completely mute, while the other, abstracted from its prosodic transformation, is totally devoid of significance and interest' (II, 364; 397), has a complex traditional philosophical flavour, all the more so because, starting from Aristotle, form is also identified as *energeia* [energy or act] and *ergon* [function], which awaken even in the basic elements of rudimentary organisms the impulse or instinct for development, as well as other desires, even the desire for understanding (see Lear 1988).

The 'impulse,' which Mandel'shtam terms the 'mute' line, cannot be isolated, investigated, or scrutinized, but without it 'poetic material ... is devoid of form as it is devoid of content for the simple reason that it exists only in performance' (II, 452; 442). Poetic speech outside the impulse 'is susceptible of paraphrasing, which ... is surely a sign of nonpoetry. For where there is amenability to paraphrase, there the sheets have not been rumpled, there poetry, so to speak has never spent the night' (II, 364; 397). What confronts modern poetics, therefore, is the question of the applicability of this traditional framework in its new metaphorical dramatization of form as imperceptible impulse rather than simple meaning, or message, or content: 'In talking about Dante it is more appropriate to bear in mind the creation of impulses than the creation of meaning [*poryvoobrazovanie a ne smysloobrazovanie*] (II, 452; 442, translation altered).[5] The impulse, therefore, is never equivalent to an articulate discourse, but lives in a discourse as modulation or change.

Even more foreign for Mandel'shtam is to speak of impulse as *power* or *force* [in Russian *sila*], which Mandel'shtam never uses, but which could be one of the meanings for Aristotle's form as *dynamis* or *energeia*. In this context the notion of the hybrid nature of poetry becomes even more challenging given Mandel'shtam's insistence that the questions posed herein are not ancient but decidedly contemporary.

3 The Hybridization of Impulse and *Materia* as an Implicit Debate with the Russian Formalists

In his postulation of the impulse, imperceptible and mute, except in performance, as the only real distinguishing characteristic of poetic speech or material, Mandel'shtam had, of course, also a contemporary interlocutor or co-traveller – the Russian formalist school with its aim of finding the scientific principle that separates poetry from standard speech.

A certain irony of terminology is hard to overlook. The *form* of the Aristotelian tradition, with its undeniably Platonic roots, became for the formalists the thingness or matter of literary construction, and the search for the specific *literariness* of art, although never identified with content or image, became focused upon a study of art as material or device. The specific, emphatically technical focus of the formalists (see Shklovsky's search for the 'how' of artistic expression) was still not sufficiently materialist in the new postrevolutionary state, and the formalists could not separate their movement from the idealistic premise implicit in the term 'formalist,' a premise that they themselves eschewed, but one which nonetheless made them ideologically vulnerable. Eikhenbaum tried (in vain) to persuade his attackers, led by Trotsky, that the concept of form was used in its material, and invariably specific, meaning:

> ... the basic efforts of the Formalists were directed neither toward the study of so-called 'form' nor toward the construction of a special 'method,' but toward substantiating the claim that verbal art must be studied in its specific features ... As for 'form,' all that concerned the Formalists was to shift the meaning of that badly confused term in such a way as to obviate its persistent association with the concept of 'content,' a term even more badly confused than form and totally unscientific. It was important to do away with the traditional correlation and by so doing to enrich the concept of form with new meanings. As matters further evolved, it was the concept of "device" that had a far greater significance ... (1978, 14)

Eikhenbaum here summarizes the very foundation of formalism hoping that this can defend him: for the formalist there are no formal methods, only formal principles upholding the status of literary and poetic texts as specific data, capable of being elucidated through scientific investigation.

Mandel'shtam, it seems, agreed with the formalists that poetic speech possesses its own unique characteristics different from those of non-poetic expression, but he came to reject their view that these characteristics could be isolated or specified within a limited or determinate field of quantities and qualities. For Mandel'shtam impulse cannot be isolated: it enters into new combinations because of the energy or modulation it carries. Thus, while the formalists seek to isolate the poetical principle, either in the transrational substance of language (Kruchenykh's *zaum*), or in the deautomatization of perception (Shklovsky), or in the 'rhythmical impulse' (Osip Brik), or even in the correlation between sound and meaning (Tynianov, Eikhenbaum), Mandel'shtam suggests by contrast that the impulse enters into combination with all these aspects of poetic *materia*, and deautomatizes our perception of them at every level of reception. Thus, the quality of the textual construction being informed by the impulse is already pervaded by communicative and receptive patterns. In other words, Mandel'shtam shifts the focus from one particular combination, or from the series of isolated combinations analysed by the formalists, to the existence of a principle with no tangible characteristics except that of a modulation which operates as a changing and transformable quality within the widest dimensions of the poetic field. Moreover, Mandel'shtam asserts that the same principle operates within the scientific investigation of nature and in nature itself.

There is one further consequence worth noting that flows from Mandel'shtam's position. By refusing to accept the limitations imposed upon the field of poetic enquiry, that is, by rejecting the singular dominant concern or methodological demand of the formalists – the need to define 'the specificity of one's area of enquiry,' if 'formalism is to be worthy of the title of "science"' – Mandel'shtam also escapes the need to speak of each poem as a complete and finalized product whose communicative ability has to be explained by another separate enquiry. In other words, Mandel'shtam's thought – which refuses to grant poetry the finalized, completed status of a literary construction and which views it rather as a performance of rough drafts caught at different levels of their reception (and at different intensities) by poet and reader alike (that is, as the performance of an impulse) – manages to avoid, curious as this may seem, the central impasse of formalism, namely the inability to elucidate the communicative patterns of poetic speech.

The legacies of Ferdinand de Saussure and Karl Bühler in particular affected Russian formalism in at least two ways: poetic language as an *expression* possessing qualities not found in 'practical speech' was a prime focus of *Opoiaz* [Society for the Study of Poetic Language, later known as the Formalist School] (Jakubinskij, 1916, v, 1), whereas the examination of the *effective character* of poetry, shared by the poet and the reader, was at best a secondary issue. In other words, the Russian formalists were primarily concerned with the characteristics of literary construction [*literaturnaia konstrukciia*], rather than communication. The possibility of approaching these structural characteristics as communicative strategies was not investigated except in a cursory fashion, even when literary construction had been replaced by the literary system [*systema*], or when interest had shifted to a wider investigation of models for the evolution of literary forms 'characterizing the succession of entire cultural epochs' (Davydov 1985, 98–9). Only Shklovsky's defamiliarization or deautomatization seems to deal with communication rather than construction, but the notion was not developed with a view to poetic texts. The transformation of defamiliarization into deviation, so characteristic for the development of formalism, again underscored the primary emphasis upon the construction of the text rather than its communicative strategies. In other words, the development of formalism demonstrated that from the beginning of the century the theories of *language system* and of *language communication* developed in parallel, if not mutually exclusive fashions. Mandel'shtam's performance of poetic speech, by contrast, seems to avoid this opposition altogether.

It is instructive to observe that in his famous address 'Linguistics and Poetics,' Jakobson searches for a solution to bridge the gap between the two modes of language study (language both as system *and* as communication). Jakobson's famous postulation that every linguistic communication follows a basic model – 'The ADDRESSER sends a MESSAGE to the ADDRESSEE' – accords poetry the status of 'the set towards the MESSAGE as such, the focus on the message for its own sake' (Jakobson 1960, 356). In other words, while poetic speech participates in communication, poetry foregrounds itself as expression and construction. On the surface, therefore, Jakobson offers a brilliant solution to the dilemma of the specific nature of poetic language and of its belonging, nevertheless, within the general pattern of all communicative speech. In reality, however, he avoids speaking about the precise nature of communication *in* poetry, since he situates poetry as one form of a more general communicative strategy. The American theoretician Jonathan Culler makes this critical point succinctly when he asserts that Jakobson does not solve but rather avoids the problem of what the implications of linguistic patterns are for the understanding of the effect these patterns transmit: 'Poetic effects constitute the data to be explained. Jakobson has made an important contribution to literary studies in drawing attention to the varieties of the grammatical figures and their potential functions, but his own analyses are vitiated by the belief that linguistics provides an automatic discovery procedure for poetic patterns and by his failure to perceive that the central task is to explain how poetic structures emerge from the multiplicity of potential linguistic structures' (Culler 1975, 74). It would appear, therefore, that Jakobson fails to resolve one of the most serious challenges that confronts poetics, namely, the challenge to relate genuine discoveries in the area of the *construction* of poetic speech to poetry's ability to *transmit* and *communicate*. Jakobson's system overlooks the real paradox confronting poetics in this area. What he proposes to be a mode of speech apparently concerned exclusively with self-expression (in Jakobson's terminology, poetic function as 'the set towards the MESSAGE as such, the focus on the message for its own sake' [Jakobson 1960, 356], which is clearly a reapplication of Shklovsky's defamiliarization) is simultaneously the triumph of communication and effective speech which his system cannot explain.[6] Any advertisement, according to this view, might be taken as a 'set towards the addressee,' but it would still lose its contest with poetry, which outperforms, in longevity and constancy of effect, patterns of speech concerned solely with the manipulation of their listeners. Thus, formalism seems to be extremely far removed from Mandel'shtam's characterization of poetry as a transmuting and transmutable *[obratimaia i obrashchaiushchaiasia] materia*.

This does not mean that Mandel'shtam learned nothing essential from the formalists and owed them no debt. Along with his obvious indebtedness to Shklovsky's defamiliarization, Mandel'shtam was also influenced to a great degree by Tynianov's notion of the tightness of the poetic line, and even more by Tynianov's views of the 'tight neighbourhood' [*tesnota*] of words in the poetic series[7] and the resulting notion of the 'oscillation of meaning,' which Tynianov describes as follows:

> The unity of the work is not a closed, symmetrical intactness, but an unfolding, dynamic integrity. Between its elements is not the static sign of equality and addition, but the dynamic sign of correlation and integration.
>
> ...
>
> The form of the literary work must be recognized as a dynamic phenomenon.

...
> This dynamism reveals itself firstly in the concept of the constructive principle ... Here verse is revealed as a system of complex interaction, and not of combination. Metaphorically speaking, verse is revealed as a struggle of factors, rather than as a collaboration of factors. It becomes clear that the specific plus of poetry lies precisely in the area of this interaction, the foundation of which is the constructive significance of rhythm and its deforming role relative to factors of another order. (1981, 33, 40–1)

Thus, although Tynianov works with poetic construction here, the construction (that is, the tightness of the series) becomes the key to the dynamism of the poetic effect. Clearly, Mandel'shtam's vision of poetry as a dynamic oversaturation of meanings reflects Tynianov's notion of tightness, dynamism, complex interaction, manifested in 'the deforming role' of poetic rhythm, which manoeuvres the multivalency of meaning into a tightly held unity. Equally suggestive is Tynianov's belief that these factors result in the 'enlivening of the metaphor, conditioned by the unity of the verse series' (1981, 81). However, in order to resolve the dynamic intensity of complex interactions within the poetic line, Tynianov accepts and develops the notion of the dominant, the *one central factor*, characteristic of the more general development of formalist thought: 'Without this sensation of subordination and deformation of all factors *by the one factor* playing the constructive role, there is no fact of art ... If this sensation of the interaction of factors disappears (which assumes the compulsory presence of two features, the subordinating [the dominant] and the subordinated), the fact of art is obliterated. It becomes automatized' (1981, 33). In contrast, Mandel'shtam rejects the notion of the *dominant* within poetic language, and begins to move in a poststructuralist direction; instead of the dominant, he develops the landscape of the ever-new, pulsating, and disappearing foci of meanings.

In fact, one may well argue that Mandel'shtam both parodies and lovingly reconstructs Tynianov's notion of the subordination and rhythm of the poetic text as constructed by the dominant, not only when Mandel'shtam speaks of poetry, but when he describes the literary language of Darwin and emphasizes that therein 'the demands of science happily correspond to one of the most fundamental aesthetic laws,' that is, to 'the law of heterogeneity which encourages the artist to seek to unite in one form the greatest number of different sounds' (III, 176–7; 341). Indeed, the emphasis upon the *needed* side of the natural phenomena which Darwin accepts as the field of examination more than recalls

Tynianov's notion of the dominant around which the poetic text is organized in a hierarchical, rhythmical pattern:

> The energy of the argument [in Darwin] is discharged in quanta, in batches. Accumulation and release, inhalation and exhalation, ebb and flow ... In *On the Origin of Species* animals and plants are not described merely for the sake of description. The book seethes with natural phenomena, *but they turn to the reader only with the needed side*; they play an active role in the argument and then yield their place to their successors. Above all, Darwin prefers to use a serial unfolding of signs, and the collection of intersecting series. His gradual accumulation of essential signs gives rise to his crescending scale.   (III, 177; 342, translation altered, emphasis added)

The refusal to ascribe the dominant or the notion of hierarchy to the poetic text brings Mandel'shtam into proximity with poststructuralist thought, a similarity discussed in depth below. However, it is precisely here that Mandel'shtam's originality is situated. Instead of the decentred, endlessly self-renewing, ahierarchical poetic text, Mandel'shtam visualizes the movement of the 'mute' poetic impulse, which transforms a kinetically charged single layer of reading into the series, or layers, of apprehension or reception. In describing this series Mandel'shtam avoids the restriction of a polysemantic but still monodimensional approach to the text.

In other words, the waves of energy which characterize the poetic text unite into formulas of meaning at each stage of their differentiated interpenetration: meaning is not a prefabrication but an act, or rather acts, of a performance. Furthermore, in reading we follow almost unconsciously the living impulses of the textual surface, from landscape to landscape, and from stage to stage. Each stage of the landscape emerges from the previous level because that level has become too kinetically charged to contain a single interpretation or a single centre. Strictly speaking, this pursuit of the changing impulse cannot be simply message reception, because what one sees in the phenomenon communicated to the reader is the phenomenon's own nature as recipient. Every stage of the wavelike surface disperses in ever widening circles, yet it stretches and straightens the vision, heals the ear, and points to the next stage. Thus, we move through the layers of a changing landscape, anticipating a signifier which is always *about to emerge*. There is always an element to the message which, after the layers of its receptivity have been disclosed, remains as yet unsaid. Poetry, therefore, is not so much a dramatization of finalized and perfectly shaped thoughts and experiences as a disclosure of the layers of receptivity in creative experience and in the object in question.

Decisively, therefore, Mandel'shtam rejects the notion that a constructed literary text communicates a message (that is, what in time becomes Jakobson's model: 'The ADDRESSER sends a MESSAGE to the ADDRESSEE'). Instead, he upholds the concept of a mute poetic impulse as the only real distinctive characteristic of poetry which he sifts, as it were, through Tynianov's tight poetic row. In other words, Mandel'shtam's dominant is not a subordinating principle, or a tightness of enlivened metaphor, but a vibration of an impulse that has already escaped, just as it has finished forming or deforming the texture. Thus, Mandel'shtam insists that poetic communication is a training of receptivity in poet and reader alike, while he also creates a system of poetics that differs radically from Jakobson's development of the same concepts of Russian formalism into semiotics and the theory of communication.

4 An Assessment of the Theoretical Validity of Mandel'shtam's Impulse for Modern Poetics: Mukařovský and Pasternak

However striking and apparently unscientific Mandel'shtam's postulation of the impulse [*poryv*] may appear, he was not the only one who felt the need to add another line of enquiry to the formalists' understanding of the poetic text. Jan Mukařovský, one of the leading theoreticians of the Prague school, redefined the work of the Russian formalists within the much wider scope of Czech structuralism. In his work on poetry Mukařovský eventually came to the conclusion that a dual model had to be postulated in order to explain the operation of poetic speech. In his long essay 'On Poetic Language' he proposes, rather like Mandel'shtam, that in poetic speech we confront two parallel but far from identical semantic modes, one of which is a functional linguistic utterance concerned fundamentally with self-expression, the other a psychic phenomenon, which cannot be discerned through linguistic analysis. Mukařovský stops short of saying that the psychic semantic mode is *transposed into* language: 'We therefore believe that we are not too far from the truth if we characterize the interrelation of an utterance and the relevant psychic process as *the relation of two concurrent and correlated semantic series*. The difference between the two series is, of course, that only linguistic meaning is fully communicable, having at its disposal a system of sensory perceptible symbols, whereas *psychic meaning lacks such a possibility of systematic expression*' (1977, 59, emphasis added). Unfortunately, Mukařovský did not develop this further into an analysis of verbal communication but moved instead towards a semantics of gesture. Even there, however, Mukařovský's development runs parallel to what becomes in Mandel'shtam one of the stages of the impulse's progress, that is, gesture as a part of meaning. 'If you attentively watch the mouth of an accomplished poetry reader, it will seem as if he were giving a lesson to deaf-mutes, that is, he works with the aim of being understood even without sounds, articulating each vowel with pedagogical clarity. And thus it is enough to see how Canto XXVI sounds in order to hear it. I would say that in this canto the vowels are anxious and twitching' (II, 429; 421). Mukařovský emphasizes equally that gesture identifies a semantic level of meaning, which takes us beyond language and yet remains a part of language's meaning: 'Here we find ourselves on the border between language and psychic process; indeed, we even see the psychic process penetrating the utterance as one of its components. The direct participation of the psychic which obtains when the partner's psychic reaction becomes a reply can, of course, occur only under the condition that the psychic process becomes a *communicable* meaning without changing its essence' (1977, 58). It is also clear that in postulating 'two concurrent and correlated semantic series,' one of which lacks 'a system of sensory perceptible symbols' (Mukařovský 1977, 59), Mukařovský was aware that semantics as such becomes less and less materially grounded, for he emphasizes at the close of 'On Poetic Language' that the future of poetics is 'the discovery of semantic dynamics,' which goes beyond the study of the material substrate (materials) of what he calls 'semantic statics' (1977, 63). This movement, he asserts, is neither nebulous nor idealistic; it remains open to scientific investigation as a study of energy: 'meaning no longer appears as a mere illusive reflection of reality but as a source of energy, and thus we need not fear its confrontation with man's other life forces' (1977, 64).

One may, therefore, suggest on good grounds that Mandel'shtam's discovery of the hybrid nature of poetry departed from formalist theory in a manner similar to that of the work of Mukařovský. In developing formalism further both thinkers posited the presence of a mute partner, possessing no 'sensory perceptible symbols.' The difference between the two consists in the fact that Mandel'shtam visualized a much wider role for his mute impulse than the mute semantic series (or specific as yet undifferentiated source of energy) of Mukařovský's work.

It can be argued that Pasternak comes closest to the spirit of Mandel'shtam's insistence upon the central role of the imperceptible impulse, except that Pasternak returns to its traditional philosophical name of *form* [*forma*] in *Doctor Zhivago*, in what may well be his mature definition of his art: 'As he [Yuri] scribbled his odds and ends, he made a note reaffirming his belief that art always serves beauty, and beauty is the joy of possessing *form*, and *form is a key to organic life since no living thing can exist without it*, so that every work of art, including tragedy, witnesses to the joy of existence. And his own ideas and notes also brought him joy, a joy so tragic and filled with tears that it made his head ache and wore him out' (1966, 404, emphasis added). It is clear that Pasternak independently follows Mandel'shtam's direction of thought, even in placing the form of art within the context of natural and organic processes. Mandel'shtam the theoretician, therefore, finds powerful support in his contemporary compatriot for his reapplication and transformation of the traditional notion of form.

Mandel'shtam is also not alone in refusing to equate his *impulse* or *form* with power, order, or success (which might well be considered one medieval interpretation of the Aristotelian *form*). Like Pasternak, whose hero Yuri weeps when he realizes both the importance of form and yet its tragic impotence in its immediate surroundings, Mandel'shtam emphasizes the powerlessness of the impulse when it is confronted with the social manifestations of political ability or commanding presence: 'What for us appears as an irreproachable Capuchin and a so-called aquiline profile was, from within, an awkwardness surmounted by agony, a purely Pushkinian, *Kammerjunker* struggle for social dignity and a recognized social position for the poet. The shade which frightens children and old women took fright itself, and Alighieri suffered fever and chills: all the way from miraculous bouts of self-esteem to feelings of utter worthlessness' (II, 372; 405–6). A curious interplay exists between the political turbulence of a particular age and the anthropomorphic thematization that the notion of the substantial form undergoes. The medieval world-view had suffered much from the identification of substantial form with the duties and responsibilities of the monarch. Even Aquinas was not free from the political orientation of this important philosophical concept: 'Therefore, let the king recognize that such is the office he undertakes, namely, that he is in his kingdom what the soul is in the body, and what God is in the world.'[8]

In contrast, the Russian poets of the twentieth century display a tendency to associate substantial form with the endangered and suffering self. Mandel'shtam's impulse, therefore, is always fleeting and vulnerable, although it is hard to catch because of its capacity to outmanoeuvre its recipients. As a result, while disclosing the stages of hybridization, Mandel'shtam also drew upon the stages of his own life, with its intellectual breadth and freedom, as well as upon the surrounding pervasive menace of the suffocating social and political reality. The postulation of successive landscapes of poetry became the personal diary of an anxious and often overwhelmed poet who found in the 1930s that he was, after all, a wandering Jew, destined to become a political prisoner, and a Jew paradoxically in love with the medieval Christian Dante, another endangered outcast and wandering exile.

In Pasternak this state of vulnerability is often identified with the position of a woman, and as early as *A Safe Conduct* the word *form* operates in the text with a considerable semantic range: 'How the first sensation of woman was linked for me with the sense of a naked formation [*obnazhennyi stroi*], closed ranks of anguish ... How I became a slave of forms [*nevol'nik form*] earlier than I ought because, in them, I had seen too early the form of women-slaves [*formy nevol'nits*]' (Pasternak 1985, 66). In Mandel'shtam, however, the metaphor for the impulse is only too often the imbalanced, threatened poet, and thus even Dante becomes, as we have seen, 'the internal *raznochinetz* [commoner] of the fourteenth century who found it such agony to be a part of social hierarchy' (II, 412; 406).

Its vulnerability notwithstanding, Mandel'shtam's impulse enters into a 'trusting union ... unstable by its nature' (II, 431; 423) with different aspects of the quantitative nature of poetical material. And it is here, perhaps, that Mandel'shtam is most original as he insists that this swiftly vanishing diary of hybridizations and transmutations has an organic counterpart and can be explained by the scientist, preferably (or at least initially) the biologist. In short, Mandel'shtam's structure of the disappearing stages enacted in artistic comprehension must be understood, he claims, through 'the mysteries of organic life' (III, 161; 390).

5 The Continual Transformation of Poetic Communication and Its Organic Structure

It was Mandel'shtam himself who cautioned his readers in 'On the Nature of the Word' about the danger of biological analogy in poetics: 'Pure biology is inappropriate to the construction of a poetics. A biological analogy may be good and fruitful, but to apply it consistently would be to develop a biological canon, no less oppressive and intolerable

Theoretical Implications of Mandel'shtam's Poetics   131

than the canon of pseudo-Symbolism' (II, 259; 132; see also V.V. Ivanov 1991, 281). As we have seen in chapter 5, the biological analogies in Mandel'shtam's poetics appear only during the first stages of poetic transmutation. He discloses (at least) five different landscapes and communicative strategies involved in the unveiling of poetic texture. The characteristics of each landscape have much in common with Dante's *Inferno, Purgatorio,* and *Paradiso* and the transitional stages between these states, but they also correspond to the study of nature, for 'Dante's poetry partakes of all the forms of energy known to modern science' (II, 406; 400). What then are the theoretical roots and implications of such a position?

The landscapes and their communicative patterns may be characterized as follows: 1 / the infernal landscape; 2 / the instinctual; 3 / the imaginative; 4 / the structural, or a landscape that displays visible traces of a unifying impulse; and 5 / the musical. Biological counterparts occur in the first two landscapes and only partially in the third stage. That is why the biological, that is, infernal, imagery has terrifying political ramifications, which may appear also as euphemisms for Stalin's era (Isenberg 1987, 155ff). This 'expression of the general atmosphere of the time' (Ivanov 1991, 292) gives way to other sciences in the higher landscapes. Mandel'shtam's later works, therefore, express the conviction that the hierarchy and periodization thus discovered are not accidental; they are rooted in patterns of growth and in major changes of the organic world (see chapter 5 above). As we can see, Mandel'shtam borrows the division for his poetics from at least two sources: 1 / the structure of the universe of the *Commedia*, which presupposes the broadest philosophical and religious framework of its time as its informing source; and 2 / a historical account of the development of science – Lamarck, Linnaeus, Darwin, and ultimately the world of chemistry and twentieth-century physics. All of these have political counterparts: different stages of oppression, bourgeois well-being, and freedom.

How original is Mandel'shtam's thought in this regard? Ivanov, in attempting to answer precisely this question, emphasizes both Mandel'shtam's pioneering voice, that is, his 'remarkable intuition' (1991, 294), and his traditional sources. As far as tradition is concerned, Ivanov correctly stresses the poet's consistent love for the Middle Ages, which we have more precisely defined as his debt to the Aristotelian, Neo-Aristotelian, and Thomistic philosophical tradition. As early as 'François Villon' (see Ivanov 1991, 281) Mandel'shtam refers to this organic unity between philosophy and science as the 'physiologically brilliant Middle

Ages' and singles out 'the logical development of the concept of the organism – the Gothic cathedral' (II, 323; 63). As we know, the *Conversation about Dante* develops this thought in relation to the growth of the crystallographic theme (II, 376; 409), that is, in directions only vaguely sensed in the early Mandel'shtam.

The Middle Ages aside, it becomes harder to find the exact sources of Mandel'shtam's position. Striking parallels exist between him and Bergson (whom the poet names in the 1920s), as well as Baudelaire, Lamarck, and Queneau (Ivanov 1991). Pollak has noted the fascinating connections between the language of the *Journey to Armenia* and Goethe's Italian journal; she is undoubtedly right in claiming that Goethe's journal is a major source of influence on Mandel'shtam (1995, 15, 16ff).

On the whole, Mandel'shtam scholars agree that the question of influence cannot be resolved by studying his traditional roots. Of equal value is the transforming insight with which Mandel'shtam approached his discussions with Kuzin (Kuzin 1983; 1987), and also his insight into Alexander Gurwitsch's field theory, the importance of which is stressed both by Pollak (1995, 15) and Ivanov (1991, 294). The parallels between Mandel'shtam and these theorists point to areas for future investigation, as the revival of Gurwitsch's theory already indicates (Ivanov 1991, 294). Nevertheless, the differentiated stages of poetic apprehension, so crucial to understanding Mandel'shtam's poetics, find no clear parallel in any of the works cited above. Ivanov has strongly emphasized that Mandel'shtam's thought is, as yet, not properly understood: 'Mandel'shtam was ahead of his time. His mode of synthesis seems borrowed from a future age' (1991, 295). Mandel'shtam's view of communication in poetry almost certainly originated in philosophy, found its sources of contact and opposition in contemporary poetics, was strengthed by biology and a critical view of modern science, and still remains a challenge to poststructuralist poetics, particularly in its emphasis on the interplay between poet and reader, where Mandel'shtam may be said to strike familiar notes in what is perhaps an unfamiliar key.

6 The Difference Between Writing and Reading, Author and Addressee, within the Differentiated Levels of Poetry

There are, perhaps, no more divisive issues in contemporary theory than those relating to the implied or actual reader of the text and authorial control over textual meaning. 'The birth of the reader must be at the cost of the death of the author': this was the famous proclamation of Barthes in 1968 (1977, 148); and so the universe of the reader, 'the space in which all the quotations that make up a writing are inscribed without any of them being lost' (Barthes 1977, 148), came into the world of poetics, to be re-examined, of course, but ultimately to remain substantially unchallenged. Against the reader's unbroken, absolute power over the text stands Iser's view that the text directs and commands the reader even if the reader's individuality does colour his or her reading of it: 'I would say that the text constitutes the reader, because it gives him certain instructions which he has to fulfill; but it is, of course, beyond question that the chain of images produced in a continual process of ideation is *colored and permeated by highly individual associations*' (1980, 63, emphasis added). Iser's position does not, as we know, fare well in modern pluralistic criticism, and the argument of Norman N. Holland that every reader reads in his or her own manner still possesses major force: 'If we leave readers on their own, as one might read a novel or a book of poems in an armchair at home, we find little or no commonality in what literants report about their response to literature' (quoted in Iser 1980, 58).

The reader has power over the text, and over the author, unless as Stanley Fish (1981) and Jonathan Culler (1982) assert, it is not so much the text but the interpretative conventions of the community that in their turn overpower and guide the reader. All in all, however, if the reader is guided, it is not by the author; as Terry Eagleton humorously observes: 'The growth of the Reader's Liberation Movement (RLM) over the past few decades has struck a decisive blow for oppressed readers everywhere, brutally proletarianized as they have been by the authorial class' (1986, 181).

Even a casual overview of these debates awakens countless parallels and echoes in Mandel'shtam's writing, parallels which have not only a decidedly contemporary ring, but which also point in different, perhaps even contradictory, directions. In Mandel'shtam there is a whole range of patterns which he believes characterize the complex activity involved in artistic apprehension and which, one may also argue, appear on different sides of the contemporary debate. Mandel'shtam's major difference from other theoreticians resides in his denial of the communication model that underlies, either implicitly or explicitly, most, if not all, contemporary views: author/transmitter *versus* reader/addressee. In contrast to these views, Mandel'shtam's emphasis upon the dynamism of poetic processes results in his granting the status of addressee to poet, text, *and* reader. All foci or *loci* of destination in poetry are forms of transmission and address. Moreover, for Mandel'shtam the range of poetic addressee goes beyond that of the autonomous, self-aware subject to include simultaneously the ghost of the past, the instinctual self, the naive or imaginative reader, the reader as co-discoverer, and ultimately the poet, who begins to realize that he or she is in fact a recipient of the musicality of language and must therefore respond to the invisible baton of the conductor. Such a conception of poetic communication is difficult to grasp by its very nature. What seems to be the expresser is in fact that which is expressed; what appears as the addresser is also the addressee. Mandel'shtam calls this process 'the addressing and the addressed, transmutable and convertible' *materia* of poetry; he observes that what in poetry appears in the nominative case should in fact be in the dative case, thereby indicating that such subjects are not performers in themselves but recipients and reflectors of movements toward them: 'All nominative cases must be replaced by the case indicating direction, by the dative ... Here everything is turned inside out: the noun appears as the predicate and not the subject of the sentence' (II, 224; 442). Mandel'shtam also refers to this mutual address in poetry as the reflexology of speech. This is why he believes that it makes little sense to speak about poetic communication when the model one has in mind is that of the poet as sole transmitter and the reader as sole addressee. Nor does it make sense to speak of poetry as a form of non-communicative expression. Poetry communicates in its every form. However, the recipient of that communication is not a passive recipient, but an addressee developing into an active performer.

At the same time, in Mandel'shtam's poetics the author invariably stands outside the reader's grasp. This escape of the author is presented not so much as a Barthean authorial death but rather as an outmanoeuvring that lies at the foundation of poetic turns of speech. Because of the author's fusion with the received transmutable and convertible material at the musical stage, the author becomes a part of the structure of the text, which for Mandel'shtam is not a tangible pattern (in Mandel'shtam's view, this is where poetry goes beyond Darwin's analysis of nature), but rather the non-reified expression of waves of meaning, which, exactly after the manner of waves, elude the reader's grasp. As always, Mandel'shtam's presentation of this moment in poetry is not descriptive but metaphorical, because for him metaphor fills an obvious, but necessary, gap in descriptive language before other modes of investigation and description, theoretical and scientific among them, may begin to examine the blank in our manner of thought, a manner already landscaped by poetry.

Although some of the major issues of modern and contemporary debate appear in Mandel'shtam's poetics, they are from the beginning, as it were, already recast onto a very different plane. Reading for Mandel'shtam is training not in the construction of meaning but in the reception of meaning's extension along a whole range of functions, and at least in this regard he is an antimodernist. The emphasis upon the freedom and independence of interpretation has on the whole led contemporary poetics to undervalue the importance of receptivity as a desirable activity. Owen J. Miller, for example, in an analysis of American texts, observes that understanding and interpretation are equivalent: 'Only in an act of imaginative interpretation do the events take on some meaning. If this interpretation of the novel has some validity, the Faulkerian text is telling us that the process of reconstruction by the reader is an integrative holistic endeavour where to 'understand' is to interpret' (Miller 1978, 27). In contrast, Mandel'shtam's poetics is founded upon a space *between* understanding and interpretation, a space that Mandel'shtam himself regards as the initially unfilled interval. In this unfilled interval artistic apprehension begins, and it is there that the poetic text receives or takes the reader into its initial possession:

> There exists a middle activity between hearing and articulation. This activity is the closest to the performance [or fulfilling, *ispolnitel'stvo*] and contains, as it were, its very heart. Unfilled interval between listening and articulation is idiotic in its essence. (III, 182; 445, translation altered)

> A book in use, a book established on a reader's desk, is like a canvas stretched on its frame.
> While not yet a product of the reader's energy, a book is already a *crack* in the reader's biography; while not yet a find, it is already an extraction. A piece of streaked feldspar ...
> Our memory, our experience including its *gaps*, the tropes and metaphors of our sense perceptions and associations, all fall into the book's rapacious and uncontrolled possession. (III, 165; 393, emphasis added)

> What is important in poetry is only the understanding which brings it about – not at all the passive, reproducing, or paraphrasing understanding. (II, 403; 398)

The interval then trains receptivity, a 'middle activity between hearing and articulation.' There reception matures into performance, which becomes a transformation rather than the repetition of poetic *materia*. The interval, however, cannot be erased, although, until it matures, it has no characteristics ('not yet a find,' but 'already an extraction'). It is, I believe, Mandel'shtam's emphasis upon receptivity in the creative process that causes Pollak to equate the poet's writing with reading in *Mandelstam the Reader*, and to place this equation more generally within the context of the poet's continuing loyalty to his Judaic roots: 'Mandelstam's poet works on the word much as the rabbinic scholars did, making connections across time, receiving distant events as simultaneous. His poet is a reader in the Talmudic tradition' (Pollack 1995, 7). Pollack contrasts Mandel'shtam, with his loyalty to a traditional root [*rod*], to Pasternak, whom she views rather as a transgressor-poet than a reader. However, it is more plausible to argue that there are different stages of receptivity in Mandel'shtam's theoretical thinking, and that he himself *as a poet* articulated clearly only certain stages, being himself particularly sensitive to poetry's receptive capacity. Nor is it fair to say that Pasternak never understands the importance of receptivity. Like Mandel'shtam in the *Conversation about Dante*, Pasternak, as early as 1918 and as late as *Doctor Zhivago* (1957), emphasizes the receptive rather than the constructive role of the poet:

> Contemporary trends of thought imagine art is like a fountain, whereas it is a sponge.
>
> They have decided that art should gush forth, whereas it should absorb and become saturated.
>
> They think it can be broken down into the means of depiction, whereas it is composed of the organs of perception.
>
> Its proper task is to be always among the spectators and to look more purely, more receptively, more faithfully than any one else; but in our day it has come to know powder and the make-up room, and it displays itself from a stage. ('Neskol'ko polozhenij,' 1982, 110)

The relationship between the forces that govern creation stands, as it were, on its head. The primacy goes not to the man and the state of soul he is seeking expression for, but to the language with which he wants to express it. Language, the home and repository of beauty and meaning, itself begins to think and speak for the man, and becomes all music, in respect not of its external, audible sounds but of the headlong swiftness and power of its inner current. (*Doctor Zhivago* 1985, 245)

Given this striking emphasis upon receptivity in poetry, we may ask a further question: is there a difference between writing and reading in Mandel'shtam's poetics, a difference that Pollak prefers to erase in Mandel'shtam's case? Throughout the *Conversation about Dante*, Mandel'shtam depicts writing and reading as a series of actions played out on each level of the changing landscape. However, it is uncertain whether there is a qualitative difference in the activities of poet and reader at each stage of this periodization. Mandel'shtam seems to insist that in reading we repeat, consciously or unconsciously, the stages of the generation of the text. Thus, the 'infernal' stage awakens in the reader the subtextual awareness of the text's unending referentiality: for reader and poet alike it is 'a keyboard stroll around the entire horizon of Antiquity' (II, 368; 401). There is no qualitative difference in the power of the unceasing sound of half-forgotten phrases that overwhelms the consciousness of both reader and poet. Similarly, the instinctual stage, which directs the apprehension of the text as a single, indivisible, yet growing body, is equally characteristic of both reading and writing. Imaginative coloration (the third stage), which leads into the perception of common characteristics (the fourth stage), demands from the reader an ever-growing effort to develop a capacity for 'the close listening to sound and light waves' (II, 390; 421). Still, the activity of author and recipient is the same; writing and reading at this stage are 'the joint containing (co-holding) of time by its associates, competitors, co-discoverers' (II, 389; 420). Finally, the perception of the musical essence of poetry as the verification of poetic metaphor also presupposes an activity common to both poet and reader.

Where, then, is the difference between the two to be situated? Is it possible that poet and reader share similar stages of activity, but that the sole difference resides in the intensity of the poet's agency at each level? Does the difference, then, lie only in this intensity of act?

Mandel'shtam's answer is twofold. First, the difference is characterized by both intensity and speed. The difference between the poet and the reader is given at the infernal stage, where 'the teacher is younger than the student, for "he runs faster"' (II, 366; 400). The relationship with the author of one's favorite poetic line will invariably be characterized as a relationship with one who outruns you.[9] In the manuscripts of the *Conversation about Dante* we find a description (already cited above) of the momentary awareness of the author's presence and his availability to answer the reader's inquiry: 'We can comprehend this concept with Dante's help. However, Dante does not teach us ...: he has already turned and vanished' (III, 181; 444). The image of Dante, who evades or overtakes his readers at each turn, appears, perhaps in its most arresting form, at the close of the *Conversation about Dante*, where Mandel'shtam utilizes Dante's description of the lucky gambler in the *Purgatorio* to represent the poet's ability to outperform his readers. In this description there appears the figure of the man who has just won a game of dice and who rushes past a cheerful, noisy crowd: 'But fortune's favorite walks right on, listening to all alike, and with a handshake for each, he frees himself from his importunate followers' (II, 412; 441).

The relationship between author and reader, therefore, at every stage of the changing landscape is enacted in the reader's apprehension of the wave-impulses that interpenetrate and constitute the poetic texture. These impulses, which crisscross every aspect of the text, disappear just before their apprehension. The poet in the text actually becomes part of the work of these impulses.[10] Therefore, no matter how engrossed the reader may be in the text, the poet's embeddedness within it is always more immediate or more complete. Paradoxically, this embeddedness is characterized by the poet's disappearance: he vanishes just prior to the reader's actual apprehension of him, just prior to their potential unity, or interpenetration.

Thus, although the hybrid texture of poetry (forming impulse and receptive *materia*) prefigures the dialogical relationship between poet and reader, the status of the poet in the text is characterized by a stronger degree of unity with the text than that experienced by the reader. The poet is an inalienable part of the swiftly vanishing impulse, which the reader is destined to follow. The poet's role, therefore, consists in an accelerated intensity of activity which prefigures that repeated by the reader. For the reader, however, the poet will always be an integral aspect of the unveiling of the text, who disappears just prior to the reader's potential achievement of the status of coequality.

However, the difference between poet and reader is not located only in the different levels of intensity of their similar patterns of activity. According to Mandel'shtam, poetic activity has yet another stage to disclose, which is not shared by the reader, and which cannot be experienced as part of the textual strategy. That stage is writing as such, and paradoxically it is experienced not as accelerated activity but as intensified receptivity. The organs of reception have been stretched and prepared by the previous stages, and the process of writing itself is a performance of the ability to receive and hold:

> He is filled with a sense of the ineffable gratitude towards the copious riches falling into his hands. For he has no small task: space must be prepared for the influx, the cataract must be removed from the rigid vision, care must be taken that the bounty of poetic material pouring out of the cornucopia does not flow through the fingers, does not flow away through an empty sieve ... it is not enough to say 'copying,' for what we are involved in here is calligraphy in response to dictation by the most terrifying and impatient dictators. (II, 405–7; 435–6)

One should stress that at no point does Mandel'shtam insist that the experience of this periodization which prepares the organs of reception happens consecutively. While it is true that he holds to the periodization in question, nevertheless, along with the hierarchical changes of these landscapes, he develops the notion of the standing still of literary time. Every poetic metaphor, as a *turn* of phrase, presupposes the fleeting presence of the landscapes thus evoked as a synchronic experience of what is ultimately an alternating pattern of differing insights: 'But it seems to me that Dante's metaphor designates the standing-still of time. Its roots are not to be found in the little word "as," but in the word "when." His *quando* sounds like *come*' (II, 410; 439). In other words, the highest stage of receptivity – the process of writing – does not follow consecutively upon the accomplishment of the previous stages, yet the state of writing presupposes a developed and trained receptivity which the reader does not possess to the same degree.[11]

The hybrid nature of poetry prefigures the patterns of writing and reading, as well as that of the presence of poet and reader in the text. Like the receptive *materia* itself, the reader pursues the vanishing impulse within the poetic texture. Paradoxically, although the reader is a recipient, his role is also that of agent; he journeys after the vanishing impulse from landscape to landscape. The poet too is a part of that journey; he too has followed the impulse, yet the impulse has not escaped him, but has fallen into his hands, and the poet has been able to hold on to it. This is why the poet's experience of the journey has been more intense; he has become a part of the impulse because he has been able to receive it. As a part of the received impulse, the poet appears and disappears through the waves of the textual apprehension; that is why 'he has already turned and vanished' (III, 181; 444), and that is why 'he walks right on ... and ... frees himself from his importunate followers' (II, 412; 441). For Mandel'shtam writing, therefore, presupposes the fullest range of receptivity. Reading, by contrast, is an awakening into the receptivity that constitutes the work of art.

What are the implications of this view for present-day poetics? It is challenging to regard poetry as the training of receptivity simultaneously on several levels of consciousness. The message, so to speak, never arrives; poetry is a diary of awakened landscapes that come to be realized, while reception as such takes place only at the moment of writing. This is Mandel'shtam's final position. Modern-day poetics is not as yet ready either to validate or to reject this stance, for if the relation between author and reader is to be conceived only as that of message-transmission and control, Mandel'shtam's view of the author's role cannot be recovered or investigated.

7 Intertextuality and the Previous Poetic Tradition in the Context of Poststructuralist Poetics

Mandel'shtam's emphasis upon receptivity holds it axiomatic that writing poetry is impossible without a previous poetic culture. For the early Mandel'shtam, at the heart of poetry lies a hearth, a gathering place of several kindred poets coming from different historical eras; in poetry's external world there is an unending fight with inimical traditions, a battle with poet-foes (see chapter 2). In the 1930s this metaphorical depiction of duality and contrast, of literary love and strife, gives way to a multidimensional semantic structure of radically different, intertextual relations traversing the same text and capable of being unveiled as a sequential system in a quasisynchronic journey: infernal subtext, imaginative play, co-exploration, kindredness, and farewell. Intertextuality is thus presented as a pattern of relations in their difference and as literal 'differing,' and yet simultaneously intertextuality is always a personal awareness, a kindred recognition, which ranges from its first visualization as a father-son relationship among autonomous quotations on the infernal level, extends to the ironic player of the imaginative universe, and finally emerges as the figure of the powerful co-traveller in the levels of structural exploration. It is clear that this dramatization of intertextuality presents a clear challenge to other intertextual versions, particularly those that employ the transactive model (but one in a state of constant radical alteration) that is characteristic of the present

Theoretical Implications of Mandel'shtam's Poetics 141

theoretical scene, whose main proponents are Barthes, Kristeva, and Harold Bloom.

Barthes addresses directly the evasive nature of intertextuality by presenting the literary text as a 'mirage of citations,' suggesting a plurality of other already anonymous texts and lost codes (Barthes 1970, 16). The autonomous nature of Barthes' intertextual codes brings something of a shiver even to Culler, who has always courageously braced himself while confronting the death of the main 'speaking subject,' the author of the immediate text: 'Barthes's tautological naming of the intertextual as "déjà lu" is so anticlimatic as to preclude excited anticipations' (Culler 1981, 108). Nevertheless, 'a Barthesian space of infinite and anonymous citations' is a logical development of Jakobson's 'set towards the message as such, focus on the message for its own sake' (Jakobson 1960, 356). For Barthes this self-reflexivity of the text for its own sake or, as he names it, the 'intransitive' manner of writing automatically negates authorship and allows no text to bear a name: 'As soon as a fact is narrated no longer with a view to acting directly on reality but intransitively, that is to say, finally outside of any function other than that of the symbol itself, this disconnection occurs, the voice loses its origin, the author enters into his own death, writing begins' (Barthes 1988, 167).

Barthes intends this description to apply to every artistic text, but Kristeva recognizes in this space the universe of the European literary avant-garde and, as a result, unconsciously limits the power of this infinite anonymous field to a specific scene of radical political writing that constitutes for her the conscience of art. Hence, in Kristeva's version the liberated interpreter confronts a tradition finally defeated, processed, and discarded. Writing becomes a liberation threatened only by ghosts with no names or origin, a state described in a different and sinister context by Scott Fitzgerald: 'a new world, material without being real, where poor ghosts, breathing dreams like air, drifted fortuitously about' (Fitzgerald 1925, 162). Not all critics can be happy in this reinterpretation of the Barthean space of disconnection and lost origin, but in 1977 Kristeva accepted it as the deathbed of the past and welcomed it as the receptacle (that is, as the reformulated material principle of Plato's *Timaeus*) of new and uncontaminated signifying devices:

> Dans l'asphyxie économique et politique de la société capitaliste, les discours s'usent et s'effondrent avec une rapidité jamais atteinte. Les trouvailles philosophiques, les formalismes scientifiques ou esthétiques se suc-

cèdent, rivalisent, disparaissent, sans destinataires convaincus ni adeptes conséquents ... Un seul langage semble de plus en plus contemporain: celui qui serait, à plus de trente ans de distance, l'équivalent de *Finnegans Wake*.

C'est à dire que l'expérience de l'avant-garde littéraire est, par sa caractéristique même, vouée non seulement à devenir le laboratoire d'un discours (et d'un sujet) nouveau, effectuant ainsi une 'mutation aussi importante, peut-être, que celle qui a marqué, relativement au même problème, le passage du Moyen Age à la Renaissance' ([Barthes,] *Critique et Vérité* 48); mais qu'elle refuse les discours figés ou éclectiquement universitaires, s'approprie leur savoir quand elle ne le déclenche pas, et en invente un autre, inédit, mobile et transformateur.

...

Comment la littérature réalise-t-elle cette subversion positive du vieux monde? Comment s'effectue, à travers elle, cette négativité propre au sujet autant qu'à l'histoire, qui déblaie les idéologies et jusqu'aux langues 'naturelles' pour formuler les nouveaux dispositifs de la signifiance? Comment condense-t-elle aussi bien l'explosion du sujet que celle de la société dans une nouvelle distribution des rapports entre symbolique et réel, subjectif et objectif?   (Kristeva 1977, 23–4)

Kristeva's identification of Barthean space as an explicitly avant-garde writing, in which she also includes Barthes' own work, poses one of the central issues of recent theoretical debates: the possibility that the space so described reflects first of all the character of the literary and political space inhabited by the author or the authorial figures of his/her explorations. The unconscious or conscious reflection of one's literary space in this constructed literary scene, in fact, continues to live and reproduce itself in Kristeva's appropriation of the Barthean 'mirage of citations.' Exploring Barthes's space, Kristeva actually changes its sexual delineations, positing the scene as one colossal womb, a germination process, where writing is 'un "On" impersonnel dont la mère Oedipienne semble bien être le substrat' (1977, 36). Kristeva's introduction of the Oedipal mother as a substratum of the writing scene inadvertently remodels the Barthean space – further, perhaps, than either theoretician might have desired. Appropriating Barthes's universe of anonymous codes to a new sexual framework, Kristeva transforms it into a land of perpetual battle where intertextual voices are adopted only at the cost of the rejection of their history. These intertextual voices are recognizable only at the moment of their depersonalization, defeat, and

Theoretical Implications of Mandel'shtam's Poetics 143

death. Culler comments with insight upon this shift from the *anonymous* codes of Barthes to codes *negated* in Kristeva. Although Culler remains indifferent (or oblivious) to the sexual politics of this transition, he clearly identifies the inadvertent negation of the Barthean vision in the very moment of its acceptance in Kristeva's poetics; in other words, as Kristeva seeks to demonstrate the correctness of the Barthean insight into the anonymity of the intertextual voices, she traces the death of specific codes and in this very process identifies them and, thus, defeats the notion of anonymity: 'A criticism based on the contention that meaning is made possible by a general anonymous intertextuality tries to justify the claim by showing how in particular cases "a text works by absorbing and destroying at the same time the other texts of intertextual space" and is happiest or most triumphant when it can identify particular pretexts with the work the text is indubitably wrestling' (Culler 1981, 107, quoting Kristeva 1969, 146). To show how the author is depersonalized, one must describe the process and thereby identify the author or the text. The visualization of intertextual space, therefore, provides a rather uncomfortable view of the role adopted by the writer or theoretician: the anonymity of discernible codes does not ensure that the examined space is value free, but is rather an unconscious (or conscious) reconstruction of one's manner of reading and writing.

In contrast to the French poststructuralists, the American theoretician Harold Bloom, almost heroically, it seems, names these codes and transforms them from the French avant-garde space of anonymous citations to a battleground where the author defeats his great predecessor (Bloom 1973; 1975). The Oedipal framework that Bloom shares with Kristeva and the vigorous application of Freudian analogies, however, still remain a particularized vision: in fact, as he reconstructs the world of rebellion, Bloom himself emerges as a critic from the romantic tradition. One may well argue that Bloom presents precisely a universe of romantic intertextuality, that is, the relationship with a previous tradition as a battle. Moreover, Bloom himself relives this syndrome, embodying this process in his theoretical works and yet simultaneously announcing his victory over romanticism's encompassing boundaries.

As one compares the presentations of intertextuality in Barthes, Kristeva, and Bloom with that in Mandel'shtam, one must observe the indisputable fact that these viewpoints, however different and apparently mutually defeating, are not in reality mutually exclusive. In fact, such a comparison may support Mandel'shtam's assertion that his journey into the life of language uncovers layers of poetic density unattainable through any other linguistic craft. Barthes, Kristeva, and Bloom in describing language describe their own political space within language, a space responding to a very particular angle of inquiry. A comparison of the positions of what may be called professional theoreticians with those of Mandel'shtam makes it clear that these theoreticians create hypostases only within a very limited range of enquiry, an enquiry that is presented by Mandel'shtam in a much wider and significantly more differentiated context. Mandel'shtam is not perhaps as focused as they are, but what he loses in focus, he may well gain in breadth. The modern theoretical viewpoints outlined above correspond with surprising precision only to one stage of Mandel'shtam's description of intertextuality: the infernal stage. Mandel'shtam's infernal 'stroll along the keyboard of references' does not differ very much from either Barthes' 'mirage of citations' or Kristeva's genotext and its colossal germination process, whereas Bloom's fight with the father-figure closely parallels the unexpected and menacing, growing ghost figure that almost overcomes the poet in Mandel'shtam's otherwise infinitely divisible, infernal universe.

The decision that Mandel'shtam and these theoreticians are making is an aesthetic one, but aesthetic decisions also possess political and ideological dimensions, which mirror the writers' own attitudes to, and work within, a tradition. For all three theoreticians the process of writing is an escape from a decaying or tyrannic tradition, but for Mandel'shtam the escape is only the initial stage in a complex journey into the roots of a tradition that remains the foundation of language and culture, which are his poetic material. Obliteration, conflict, and rebellion are not the only characteristics of this journey. Attachment, admiration, attraction also play a formidable role.

Mandel'shtam is not the only Russian poet who, throughout his writing career, stresses the pivotal importance of love for intertextual quotations and echoes, a love that he attributes not just to himself but also to Dante: 'If Dante had been sent forth alone, without his *dolce padre*, without Virgil, scandal would have inevitably erupted at the very start' (II, 411; 405). Tsvetaeva is also well known for her passionate proclamation of love for poets: 'From then on, yes, from then on, since the time in Naumov's picture, when, before my very eyes, they killed Pushkin, and every day, every hour, unceasingly they kept killing my whole infancy, childhood, and youth, I have divided the world into the poet – and all of *them*; and I have chosen – the poet – have chosen the poet to be among those I defend: to defend the poet – from all of *them*, however they all are garbed, however they all are named' (*My Pushkin* 1980, 320). Nor is Pasternak less reticent than Tsvetaeva in his insistence that personal love for certain artists in the tradition constitutes the movement of artistic formation: 'Tradition has appeared to all of us; to all it has promised a face; to all, each in a different way, it has kept its promise. We have all become people in the measure in which we have loved people and had the opportunity to love' (*A Safe Conduct* 1985, 68). In *Doctor Zhivago* the same insistence upon love as a forming principle of art is restated with a more detached and careful precision when Pasternak compares poetry with science, which he believes develops through debate: 'A step forward in science is taken according to the law of repulsion, from refutation of prevalent errors and false theories ... A step forward in art is taken according to the law of attraction, from the desire to imitate, follow and worship well-loved precursors' (1985, 236).

Joseph Brodsky, a poet and theoretician who found himself in a strong position to compare the modern poststructuralist poles of these debates, both Russian and western, cast his vote in 1994 in favour of the Russian poets: 'The real poet never avoids influences and indebtednesses, but often nourishes and emphasizes them by all available means. There is nothing more physically (and even physiologically) pleasing than repeating in one's head or aloud (in full voice) someone else's lines. The fear of influence, the fear of dependence – this fear – and sickness – is characteristic of a wilderness inhabitant [*dikar'*] and not of culture, which is all – receptivity, all – echo. Let someone pass this on to Harold Bloom' (1996, 224–5, my translation). A relationship to tradition and culture, therefore, is capable of the widest differentiation, where danger, rebellion, and the death of the poetic voice constitute only a small fraction of what is necessarily internalized by the writer who needs to grow as an artist and not merely to repeat himself.

Mandel'shtam's complex relationship to tradition initiated a search for a theoretical framework that could offer both breadth and coherence of thought and insight. He did not choose Dante in the same way as the Pre-Raephelites or the Russian symbolists did; the kernel of his attraction was not towards a particular time-set or group of symbols powerfully contrasting with the rest of the tradition. For Mandel'shtam Dante represented the taproot of the whole western poetic tradition; he was an artist who brought within his purview the deepest levels of insight that had gone into the formation of European culture and who in turn remained its dynamic reflection and source. Thus, Mandel'shtam speaks of Dante's poetry as a prophetic, untameable unveiling of

146 Mandel'shtam's Poetics

a poetic *materia* covering in its extension the dimensions of *human* and *poetic* experience, which are broad indeed. What is particularly fascinating in Mandel'shtam's choice of Dante is that, surrounded by the building of a Soviet culture which defined itself in contradistinction to a traditional heritage and in explicit terms of present and future progress, Mandel'shtam chose Dante as an artist and found in him not only a school of poetry but an interlocutor-friend and a source for his theoretical, philosophical, and ethical journey of thought.

8 Poetry as Reflexology of Speech

We can now begin to see why Mandel'shtam speaks about Dante's writing as 'a bird's mating call,' a fife: 'The fife is nearly always sent forth to scout ahead' (II, 411; 441). Dante's poetry does not transmit a message; it awakens, stretches out, and develops a response. It is a generative principle of literature. Without ever accomplishing a full celebration of perfectly achieved communication, the poem awakens into writing a generation of writers to come. It precontains, as it were, its subsequent history: 'The miracle-ship left the shipyard with barnacles adhering to its hull' (II, 412; 441).

In this sense poetry is not speech as such: it is a performance of the reflexology of speech, a display of the most intense stimulation executed on different levels of the awakening desire to speak: 'Speech preparation is even more within his sphere than articulation, that is, than speech itself' (II, 405; 435). Poetry, therefore, is an awakening call to a performance as yet to come, to a full communication as yet to be accomplished. Simultaneously, poetry is the most precise diary of the awakened and swiftly vanishing responses to a message never fully given.

At the end of the *Conversation about Dante* Mandel'shtam, under the guise of discussing the future of Dantean criticism, foretells the future of poetics as he sees it: 'I should hope that in the future Dante scholarship will study the coordination of the impulse and the text' (II, 413; 442). Perhaps our investigation has thrown new light on this statement and disclosed some of its significance. For Mandel'shtam the next step of poetics is to approach poetry as the diary of the periodization of the reception of speech. Impulse transfixes linguistic *materia*, and the poetic text is the imprint of this interpenetration. At the same time, since the text is a diary of the impulse's reception of the impulse, it can be regarded as the performance of the reception of speech as such. Poetics is to be concerned, therefore, with the charting of the characteristics of each stage of speech reception. Here Mandel'shtam rearranges accepted approaches to the literary text. Literary devices are not emblems of poetic expression, but rather characteristics of a particular stage of reception and perhaps the only possible identifying marks of each stage. Poetry displays what is periodic as simultaneous. It is, therefore, up to poetics to discern the stages apparently erased therein.

Notes

Introduction

1 Pollak notes that there are few investigations of Mandel'shtam's late period, mentioning only the works of Jennifer Baines (1976) and Peter Zeeman (1988), which are dedicated to Mandel'shtam's late poetry (Pollak, 1995, 1).

Chapter 1

1 The argument of 'Pushkin and Skriabin' has always caused trouble. See, for example, the explication of Clarence Brown, who cites Nadezhda Mandel'shtam's testimony that Mandel'shtam 1 / saw the article as his personal credo, and 2 / later had some profound misgivings about it (1973, 23–231).
2 See, for example, Derrida's postulation of the trace as a reconciliation of grammatology and the philosophy of Heidegger: 'Reconciled here to Heideggerian intention ... this notion [of the trace] signifies, sometimes beyond Heideggerian discourse, the undermining of an anthology which, in its innermost course, has determined the meaning of being as presence and the meaning of language as the full continuity of speech' (1976, 70).
3 While Paul Ricoeur's work shows that 'the contextual effect of metaphor goes farther than mere actualization of the potential range of commonplaces or connotations' (1991, 319), the metaphor remains suspect. Thus, in Derrida's view, 'a metaphor would be forbidden. The presence/absence of the trace ... carries in itself the problems of the letter and the spirit' (1976, 71).
4 A letter to Tynianov, 21 January 1937, translated by Jane Harris (Mandel'shtam 1979, 563).

5 See, for example, Freidin's conclusion about Mandel'shtam's world-view in 1931: 'The ideological frame of reference that Mandel'shtam had absorbed in the course of his life left him and many of his contemporaries with a limited choice ... His inability to reject this procrustean dilemma altogether, to substitute for it another, more varied discourse, helps to explain why he found it necessary in 1931 to reaffirm his pledge ... to the fourth estate' (1987, 231). See also Pollack's treatment of stone as a metaphor that remains constant throughout Mandel'shtam's works, as well as her belief that the image of 'the message in the bottle' is applicable to the works of the 1930s (1987). Similarly Mandel'shtam's 'culturology' is assessed by Pollack as being constant in its dependence on 'deconcretization as a method which shows an object as if from a bird's flight' (1992, 9).
6 More than one critic has commented upon the difficulty of the thematic aspect of Mandel'shtam's poetry. For example, Marina Tsvetaeva observes that, outside the magic of Mandel'shtam's words, his thought is weak and even non-existent (1961, 329), and B. Bukhshtab's well-known essay argues that Mandel'shtam's view of poetry excludes the development of a theme because of the poet's singular attitude to words (1971, 270ff), while Jurii Lotman questions whether it is possible to explain Mandel'shtam's poetry at all (1984, 133–4).
7 Harris (in Mandel'shtam 1979, 583).
8 The notion of hypnotism in poetry is not, of course, Mandel'shtam's invention. In 1913 it was particularly popular among symbolists. Valeri Briusov, for example, stated that the goal of symbolism is to hypnotize the reader. Yet all critics agree that Mandel'shtam was particularly sensitive to the hypnotic power of poetry (e.g. Ronen 1983, 7–13; Freidin 1982, 419–20; Brown 1973, 129).
9 On the intentional ambivalence and contrariety in Mandel'shtam's poetic expression see Levin 1969, 106–69.
10 Here Mandel'shtam's idea is not original. R.D. Timenchik investigates the use of hiatus [*ziianie*] as a constructive principle in futurist and acmeist poetics (1977, 281ff).
11 Without overstating the point, it is still helpful to quote Nietzsche's well-known description of Dionysiac hypnotic rupture in 'The Birth of Tragedy from the Spirit of Music': 'If we add to this awe the glorious transport which arises in man, even from the very depths of nature, at the shattering of the *principium individuationis,* then we are in a position to apprehend the essence of Dionysiac rapture, whose closest analogy is furnished by physical intoxication. Dionysiac stirrings arise either through the influence of those narcotic potions of which all primitive races speak in their hymns, or through the

powerful approach of spring, which penetrates with joy the whole frame of nature' (Nietzsche [1872] 1992, 630).
12 See S.V. Poliakova's observation that Persephone is out of place in *Tristia* (1992, 81–2). See also Taranovsky 1971/3.
13 In Mandel'shtam's poetry a similar image appears: the necklace of dead bees in *Tristia* (I, 84). Much work has been done on the significance of the bees and their proximity to the kingdom of death as a source of poetic creativity. See Venclova 1985, 101, 109; Taranovsky 1976 83–114.
14 See Struve 1982, 107–10; Harris (in Mandel'shtam 1979, 592–6).
15 Harris (in Mandel'shtam 1979, 8).
16 On the different aspects of time in Mandel'shtam and the different scholarly interpretations see Terras 1966, 344–54; Segal 1973, 395–405; Brodsky 1985, 123–44; Laferriere 1977, 127; Freidin 1978, 421–37; Freidin 1980, 141–86; Ronen 1983, 1–363; Nilsson 1985, 283–5.
17 Mandel'shtam's alternation here between *phon* and *grunt* is singularly arresting. 'Canvas' [*phon*] in the 1915 version suggests the image of a unified structure surrounded by emptiness, whereas the idea of the preparatory foundation of painting [*grunt*] gives the image an added complexity (II, 286). It signifies the superficiality of the exclusive movement towards unity. See the editors' note to 'Peter Chaadaev' (II, 288).
18 The image of the Gothic cathedral appears in almost every one of Mandel'shtam's earlier essays. We see it in the essay on François Villon (II, 308–9), and particularly in 'The Morning of Acmeism' (II, 322–3).
19 The notion of the break or blank was also extremely popular in art, particularly among cubo-futurists. The group around Maiakovsky especially emphasized the importance of the explosion and break as a source of creativity. Fragmented presentation was very much in vogue; see Karabchievsky 1985, 108.
20 S.P. Kablukov states that Mandel'shtam saw sex as a dark force and yet welcomed it (1979, 153). The acceptance of a dark force as a creative principle is definitely in harmony with the main thrust of Mandel'shtam's prose.
21 V.V. Khlebnikov and Kruchenykh, two of the main futurist theoreticians, speculated that words are brought out of nothing; see Pomorska 1968, 94. Perhaps Mandel'shtam is aware of this when he entertains the idea that the blank is the origin and source of creativity.
22 N.I. Khardzhiev points out in a somewhat different context that for Mandel'shtam loss or lack is more important than progress (1974–5, 21).
23 See N. Mandel'shtam 1972, 120–1.
24 See n 18 above.
25 On Kablukov's influence on Mandel'shtam in his 'switch' from Rome

(which, I hold, is associated with the metaphor of stone) to Byzantium (Orthodoxy, but also Hellenism, most often associated in Mandel'shtam with the metaphors of fertility and depletion), see Struve 1982, 113–15.
26 On the influence of V.V. Gippius on Mandel'shtam in his concept of the 'mad Hellene' see Harris (in Mandel'shtam 1979, 600). The concept of the 'mad Hellene' also represents an ongoing polemic with the poet Viacheslav Ivanovich Ivanov (1907) 51–2.
27 Indeed, Mandel'shtam's theory of assertion and cancellation anticipates to a remarkable degree Iser's notion of the blank and its constructive role in the reader's perception of the text. However, Iser's theory undermines the notion of the text and inevitably leads to a position of radical subjectivism; see Iser 1971, 1–46; 1972, 279–99.
28 On the importance of the concepts of games and toys for Mandel'shtam's notion of art see Ronen 1983, xv–xvi. Similarly J.M. Meijer emphasizes the cult of childish playfulness in the symbolists and its influence on Mandel'shtam (1979, 528).
29 On the discussion of this concept of Christian art in Mandel'shtam see Brown 1973, 230–7, 244–5.
30 In 1922 in 'On the Nature of the Word' Mandel'shtam ascribes the statement-blank pattern exclusively to the development of western culture and proclaims Russia's independent cultural history based on the free incarnation of the Hellenic spirit in its language: 'If Western cultures and histories lock their language in from the outside, surround it with the walls of State and Church, and become completely permeated by it so as to decay slowly and blossom again in good season when it disintegrates, Russian culture and history are ever awash on all sides circumscribed only by the threatening and boundless elements of Russian language, which cannot be contained within any governmental or ecclesiastical form' (II, 245; 121).

Chapter 2

1 Mandel'shtam had written the essay also as a polemic against Kruchenykh's 'Deklaratsia slova kak takovogo' (1913); see Khardzhiev 1978, 255.
2 On the image of stone representing the notion of the word in Mandel'shtam see Ronen 1973, 369. On the importance of stone in Nicolai Gumilev and M.L. Lozinsky see Segal 1983, 362–7.
3 The relationship between Mandel'shtam and Fiodor Tiutchev and the centrality of the image of stone is discussed in Toddes 1974, 69–85.
4 See here the collection of different views in R.D.B. Thomson's discussion of

Mandel'shtam's transition from the notion of the seashell to that of the stone and its implications in his poetry (1991).
5 See ch 1, n 9 above.
6 On the importance of the organic theory in Russian criticism see Terras 1973, 35–53.
7 Raoul Eshelman notes that, as the destructive hunger surrounds the word, the objects that used to be positive become negative (1983, 163–80).
8 The comparison of poetry with the plough is now almost standard among critics discussing Mandel'shtam's definition of poetry, but they invariably overlook the fact that the comparison in this passage is preceded by another stone metaphor.
9 See a parallel investigation of this theme in Pollak's treatment of the poet's stone in 'Mandelstam's Mandel'shtein' (1995, 14ff).
10 Harris, for example, sees Mandel'shtam's attitude to Rozanov as purely positive, which makes it necessary for her to abbreviate the quotation before Mandel'shtam's criticism of the writer enters into the argument (in Mandel'shtam 1979, 14).
11 See Segal 1983, 362–7.
12 Mandel'shtam here actually argues with his own earlier position in 'Peter Chaadaev' (1914), in which he adopts Chaadaev's view of Russia as absolute emptiness.
13 See here Bukhshtab (1971, 271), who argues that for Mandel'shtam the word has never signified a thing but is always a 'psyche.' See also Terras (1973, 456), who takes this passage as the key to Mandel'shtam's view of the role of words in poetry.
14 Terras and many other critics believe that Mandel'shtam's theory of the word, which he proposes in 'The Word and Culture' (1921), 'remains with him until the end' (Terras 1973, 455). In this chapter I am arguing against this established view, for in the 1920s Mandel'shtam's position was undergoing serious revision.
15 Since for Mandel'shtam word always stands for literature, I believe that we see here an example of the influence of Tynianov upon Mandel'shtam, for it was Tynianov who spoke about the internal constructive function in the work of art, which consisted in the relationship between different elements and aspects of the literary work. Tynianov published his thoughts on internal function and relationship in literature in 1927, but this approach had coloured his attitude to literature for many years prior to the publication of this essay (1927, 50ff; see also Pomorska 1968, 40–1). However, as Ronen observes, it is always difficult to establish the direction of influence and feedback between Mandel'shtam and Tynianov (1983, 19).

154   Notes to pages 33–41

16 One of the best accounts of the relationship between acmeism and unamism, a movement dedicated to the finding of unity in the work of art, can be found in E. Rusinko (1982, 496–510). She also provides an important examination of the notion of unity in Bergson. See also Ronen 1983, 135.
17 On Mandel'shtam's originality in applying Bergson's fan to suit his own theoretical purpose see Struve 1982, 130–2.
18 Without attempting to diminish Mandel'shtam's originality, one must note that in the 1920s it was fashionable to apply physics to the laws of poetry. See Iu. Karabchievsky's account of Jakobson explaining the theory of relativity to Maiakovsky, who was overcome by its significance (Karabchievsky 1985, 201). Furthermore, the Russian futurists considered themselves to be a link in the scientific revolution; see Stepanov 1968, 41.
19 It is difficult to estimate how the idea of the word as inner space enters into Mandel'shtam's corpus. Timenchik speaks about the word as landscape in the acmeists and futurists (1977, 281–300).
20 Segal argues that it was Tynianov who influenced Mandel'shtam's conception of the unity, dynamism, and density of the word (Segal 1983, 332). On the dynamism of Tynianov's conception of the word see Pomorska 1968, 39.
21 On the interconnection between the intellectual and the physical in Mandel'shtam's poetry as inseparable aspects of the same act see Zholkovsky 1979, 74ff.

Chapter 3

1 Joseph Brodsky emphasizes this aspect of Mandel'shtam's credo when he comments that for Mandel'shtam poetry is acceleration (1985, 129–30).
2 A.A. Morozov observes in his commentaries on the *Conversation about Dante* that Mandel'shtam operates there with the notion of 'the dual existence of matter: in its material form and in the form of its emanation (the theory of the light-waves)' (1967, 75). We can trace the origin of this theory to the 1920s, when Bergson's fan (the movement of self-gathering and dispersion) is echoed in Mandel'shtam's view of poetry as an intensified condensation of energy.
3 This in turn explains a puzzling image in 'Badger's Hole' (1922), where Alexander Blok's poetry is compared to a process of unification or hybridization of a numberless row of strands (i.e. the image of the fan appears unexpectedly in a new formulation): 'indeed, Blok sensed the life and language of a literary form not as a break, not as destruction, but as hybridization, as the conjoining of different species or strains, or the grafting of various fruits onto one tree' (II, 270; 136).

4 Even in the 'Morning of Acmeism' Mandel'shtam, while proclaiming the principle of identity between words and things ('A = A: what a magnificent theme for poetry,' II, 324; 64), insists nevertheless on the essence of the word as act: 'Love the existence of the thing more than the thing itself and your own existence more than yourself: that is Acmeism's highest command' (II, 324; 64). Mandel'shtam's inherent awareness that the word is an event, not just a thing, could easily have been the reason for Gumilev's discarding the essay for its theoretical impurity. See Struve, Struve and Filippov in Mandel'shtam 1967–81 II, 647; or Gumilev 1962–8, IV, 598nn.

5 Mandel'shtam is both original and polemical here, for the symbolists considered the word to be a symbol and a sign, the formalists a sound or word identical to itself [*slovo kak takovoe*], and Gumilev saw the word as a thing. Mandel'shtam, perhaps considerably influenced by the notion of dynamism in Tynianov (see Segal 1968, 159–60; Segal 1973, 389–405; Ronen 1983, 19), considered the word to be an act, and this explains much of the critics' difficulty in explaining his poetry purely in terms of meaning (Lotman 1984, 133–4).

6 See ch 1, n 27 above.

7 Here again Mandel'shtam's idea may not be original. See Timenchik's investigation of hiatus [*ziianie*] as a constructive principle in acmeist and futurist poetics (1977, 281ff). Khardzhiev notes in a somewhat different context that for Mandel'shtam loss or lack is more important than progress (1974–5, 21).

8 The notion of hypnotism in poetry is not, of course, Mandel'shtam's invention. In 1913, it was particularly popular among symbolists. Briusov, for example, stated that the goal of symbolism is to hypnotize the reader. Yet all critics agree that Mandel'shtam was particularly sensitive to the hypnotic power of poetry (e.g., Ronen 1983, 7–13; Freidin 1982, 419–20; Brown 1973, 129).

9 In Mandel'shtam's poetry a similar image appears: the necklace of dead bees in *Tristia* (I. 84). See Venclova 1985, 101, 109; Taranovsky 1976, 83–114.

10 See ch 1, n 19. Mandel'shtam accepts the idea that blank is a source of creativity, but only temporarily.

11 Ronen argues conclusively, it seems, that 1923 was the year of the creative impasse (1983).

12 Although there have been many studies of Hellenism in Mandel'shtam, I have not found any explanation of this aspect of his thought. The examination of Hellenism in Mandel'shtam is usually concerned with imagery; see Terras 1966, 251–67; Levin 1975b, 5–31. In 'Zametki ...' Levin suggests that Mandel'shtam probably borrowed the idea that the Russian people belong to Hellenic culture from Viacheslav Ivanovich Ivanov; see also Mandel'shtam

1972, 449–58; V.I. Ivanov 1979, 62–77, 117–26. In the passage cited here Mandel'shtam evokes the notion of the creative *logos*, present in all incarnational experience but not exhausted or diminished thereby. This idea is, of course, fundamental to Stoicism and Neoplatonism, and also to early Jewish (Philo) and Christian thought.

13 Lotman observes that Mandel'shtam's theory provides a key to the reading of his poetry (1984, 140–1). This notion of the destiny and life of impulses in Mandel'shtam's poetry has been succinctly stated in one of the early essays of Segal: 'But his themes do not remain unchanged: they become interwoven with each other, they exchange their main attributes, they intermingle with the concrete sensual tangible features. These last ones jump [*skachut*] from one voice to another, return, intermingle' (Segal 1972). Furthermore, the notion of Dionysian frenzy as the essence of art was also much in vogue among symbolists and postsymbolists (Ronen 1983, 18–21).

14 Mandel'shtam could well have been influenced here by the symbolist view that silence and motionless tranquillity [*tishina*] characterize the surface of the poetic text; see Pomorska 1968, 68–70. See also Taranovsky's observation on how the notion of absence is developed as a principle of silence in Mandel'shtam's poetry in the 1920s (1972, 126–31).

15 About *zlost'* as a cultural position in Mandel'shtam see Segal 1975, 118–22; Ronen 1983, 189–91.

16 Here Mandel'shtam also clearly plays on the conditional quality of the subjunctive, that is, outside the regular passing of time.

17 It is difficult to establish Mandel'shtam's possible theoretical sources here, but in a general sense this insight opens up an unexpected view of the performative nature of art. In Greek drama, for example, the effect of tragedy is interwoven with the notion of recognition [*anagnoresis*], that is, the reminder of home, origin, face, or sign (Aristotle, *Poetics*); and one generally accepted traditional view of art considers it to be woven out of aspects that bring both surprise and recognition (Glazova 1988).

18 Mandel'shtam never directly discusses the work of Shklovsky but invariably speaks about him without irony, which in Mandel'shtam's case is tantamount to a resentful acceptance (see 'Literary Moscow,' II, 327; 146).

19 See Harris's discussion of the concept of philology in Mandel'shtam's treatment of Rozanov and Annensky (in Mandel'shtam 1979, 14–15).

20 See also the image of love as a mover that concludes Mandel'shtam's essay on Blok ('Badger Hole,' II, 275; 138). Also see N.A. Nillson on the notion of love in Mandel'shtam as a shaping power in poetry (1974/5, 133–58).

21 Here lies the originality of Mandel'shtam, for he equates the performative power of poetry with the notion of home, the beloved intonation of

the familiar scene. It is possible that it was Mikhail Kuzmin who emphasized the notion of home and home-ness [*domashnost'*] and in so doing influenced considerably the world of the acmeists (Pomorska 1968, 44). Yet this attitude, not as yet given much attention in the study of poetics, is of great longevity; it is very prominent in *Doctor Zhivago*, where Pasternak states that the emotion of homecoming is the essence of art (Pasternak 1959, 167–8).

22 The use of tone and half-tone as a major poetic principle in Mandel'shtam was first pointed out by Tynianov, who believed that Mandel'shtam's specific ability was in bringing out the nuances in the tone and meaning of words (1977 189ff).

23 The image of blood circulation – that is, the invisible, dynamic, and living source of culture – is particularly obvious in the following passage in 'On the Nature of the Word': 'Europe devoid of philology is not even America; it is a civilized Sahara desert, cursed by God, an abomination of desolation. As in the past, the European Kremlins and Acropolises, the Gothic cities, the cathedrals ... will continue to stand, but people will look upon them without comprehension, unable to understand what force may have erected them or what blood may flow in the veins of those powerful architectural monuments surrounding them' (II, 250–1; 125).

24 On the study of the Jewish theme in Mandel'shtam see Taranovsky 1976, 49–67, 145–55; see also Harris (in Mandel'shtam 1979, 27–9).

25 Another powerful image of the hypnotism at the centre of poetry depicts a family atmosphere and a pull towards the centre, underscored by the attraction of the trees towards the seminar inside the room: 'Literature is a lecture, the street; philology is a university seminar, the family. Yes, it is precisely that university seminar where five students, friends calling each other by name and patronymic, listen to their professor while branches of familiar trees of the university garden reach in [*lezut*] through the window' (II, 249; 123, translation altered).

26 Struve points out that in opposition to the symbolists' glorification of the eternal feminine, the acmeists, and Gumilev and Mandel'shtam in particular, were glorifying masculine courage and virility (Struve 1982, 26).

27 It is also possible that political considerations about the necessity for him to adapt in the new Soviet state guided Mandel'shtam's criticism of the Latin West in 1922.

28 The opposition between a single contest, a single voice, which acquires form on the outer boundary, and that of the multiple, dynamic, almost noisy exchanges 'inside' is also present in 'The Birth of Plot,' in which Mandel'shtam depicts the gathering of the multiple strands of folklore into the

singularity of the plot as the process by which the 'chirping of the grasshoppers is transformed into the melodic soprano of the skylark' (II, 338; 115). *The Noise of Time* (1925) even in its title addresses just this notion of the 'noisy' dynamic inner life. There the image of noise [*shum*] is described as a process of education for the poet, his growth through the sea of sound to the finding of a single poetic voice (II, 99).

29 Zholkovsky observes the importance of cold as a highly polyvalent 'external' characteristic (1979, 161). Also, Segal relates the notion of cold to that of anger [*zlost'*] (1975, 99ff).

30 There is a similar image in Eugenii Zamiatin, who writes about the Lednikovyi period as a return of the ice age.

31 Gumilev also employs the concept of catastrophe in his essay 'The Reader' ['Chitatel'], but for Gumilev it is only the sense of every poem being written as if it were the poet's last word (1962-8, IV, 178).

32 On the importance, and the difficulty, of the notion of catastrophe in Mandel'shtam see Fleishman 1982, 451-2.

33 This essay has been published in Fleishman 1982, 451-7. In his preface Fleishman discusses its importance for the whole range of images in Mandel'shtam's writings in the 1920s.

34 See the image of the earthquake in 'Human Grain,' also presented as the juxtaposition of stillness and hidden sound, the 'insistent hum': 'The political ranging of Europe ... can be understood as a continuation of a geological process, of its waving-gyration ... The soul of politics – its nature – is a catastrophe, an unexpected shift, an earthquake ... The earthquake is pleasant at a distance for then it is not terrifying. If there is no sound of the insistent hum of political events in Europe, which is political in its very understanding of the world, it is already an event ... that is, the mere absence of catastrophe was felt almost tangibly, as a certain slim ether of silence' (Fleishman 1982, 455, my translation).

35 See Ronen 1983, 298, n 105.

36 This view explains the bewildering, misquoted, and mistranslated passage in 'Some Notes on Poetry' about the positive and negative poles of poetic expression. Harris, for example, understands 'turbulent morphological flowering' to be poetry's positive pole, and 'the solidification of the morphological lava' to be its negative aspect (in Mandel'shtam 1979, 166), but for Mandel'shtam after 1923 an unsealed turbulence is a spilling of catastrophe into disaster. Poetry seals the living volcano, and this represents for him its positive role.

37 Many scholars have observed this abrupt change in Mandel'shtam's aesthetic principles around 1923 (see Ronen 1983, 1). Some of the most striking

examples of Mandel'shtam's changed attitude to the symbolists and his invariable depiction of them as masters of control are as follows:

> Blok, the most complex phenomenon of literary eclecticism, was a collector of Russian poetry, of all that was scattered and lost by the historically shattered nineteenth century. Blok's valuable work of collecting Russian poetry is still not evident to his contemporaries: they only sense it instinctively as a kind of melodic power. Blok's acquisitive nature, his striving to centralize poetry and language, brings to mind the political instinct of the historical leaders of Moscovy. ('Storm and Stress,' II, 347–8; 177)

> Briusov's best (non-urban) poems contain one feature ... which makes him the most consistent and skillful of the Russian Symbolists. This is his courageous approach to the theme, his perfect mastery over it, his capacity to exhaust the theme completely, to extract from it everything it can and must give, and then to find for it the most appropriate and capacious stanzaic vessel possible ... he offers models of capaciousness of his verse and of the astonishing arrangement of a semantically rich and varied lexicon within a frugal measured step. ('Storm and Stress,' II, 342–3; 173)

> When individually perfected poetic phenomena emerged from the womb of Symbolism ... everything was no longer covered by a tribal hat ... After ... the rich medley *crowned by a dense gospel* of Viacheslav Ivanov, the age of personality, of individuality dawned ... Oh acorns, acorns, who needs an oak when we have acorns? ('The Thrust,' II, 230; 203, emphasis added).

38 It is only in this context that the title and the long introduction of the critical essay 'Storm and Stress' (1923) come into clear focus. In this essay the birth of each literary school is depicted as an earthquake, or rather a volcanic eruption, at first overwhelmingly grandiose, but in time finding its proper space and flow within the movement-life of culture and language. The desire of the literary school to remain upon the crest of the unleashed wave is now ridiculed: 'Each new literary school – be it Romanticism, Symbolism or Futurism – emerges at first in an artificially inflated condition, exaggerating its unique qualities, ignoring its external historical limitations. It inevitably passes through a period of 'Storm and Stress.' Only later ... is their rightful place in literature established, their objective value clarified ... [Symbolism and Futurism] revealed a desire to remain at the crest of their respective waves, and both failed in their desire, for history was already preparing the crests of new waves, and at the appropriate time imperiously ordered them to recede, to return to the maternal bosom of literature, to the common elements of language and poetry' (II, 339–40; 170).

39 See Ronen's insightful treatment of Mandel'shtam's answer to Blok in

'Humanism and Modernity,' in which Mandel'shtam uses the same images of culture and revolution against the background of the catastrophic life of the earth (Ronen 1983, 105).

40 See, for example, the wave imagery in the passage quoted above (n 38) or in the description of Pasternak's poetry (II, 264; 168), or the appearance of these same images of 'clucking, crackling, rustling, sparkling, burning' in the presentation of the inner life of folklore: 'Listen closely to folklore and you will hear thematic life stirring in it, the plot breathing ... It sets everything in motion, it intrigues, it threatens. The brood hen sits on a heap of straw, cackling and clucking; likewise, a folklorist prose-writer cackles and clucks about something ... In actual fact, however, he is occupied with something more important – he is hatching a plot' (II, 336; 153).

41 Interestingly enough, we find a similar image of hidden explosions in Pasternak's *Doctor Zhivago*: 'Already from his years in the gymnasium, Yuri dreamt about prose, about a book of life-events, where in hidden explosive nests [*v vide skrytykh vzryvchatykh gnezd*] he would put the most striking aspects of what he had time to see and think' (Pasternak 1959, 65–6).

42 The translation of *poryv* as 'impulse' here is not entirely successful, but it is perhaps the best approximation to be found. *Poryv* is more physical than 'impulse'; it is more an impulse-thrust. The word is also associated with yearning, the thrust of the wind, breathing.

43 It is not usually accepted that Mandel'shtam's views in his theoretical writings of the 1920s and 1930s underwent major changes. Ronen habitually quotes *Conversation about Dante* (1933) to support his reading of Mandel'shtam's poetry in 1923–4 (Ronen 1983), and Terras states that Mandel'shtam did not alter the view he expressed in 'The Word and Culture' (Terras 1973, 455). Yet this is not so. Further, Struve observes that at least in poetry Mandel'shtam's views underwent drastic changes from one book of poetry to the next (1982, 152).

44 See Ronen's discussion of Mandel'shtam's concept of the magical powers of poetry (Ronen 1983).

45 Again I must refer to Zholkovsky's observation that Mandel'shtam invariably discusses both the physical and intellectual features of the creative work (1979, 173).

Chapter 4

1 I suggest that a very careful reading will readjust slightly the general critical consensus that Mandel'shtam starts to address the role of the reader directly in about 1925 (Harris, in Mandel'shtam 1979, 22).

2 Mandel'shtam may also be thinking about Gumilev's essay 'The Reader,' written near the end of his life (Gumilev 1962–8, IV, 159–89).
3 As in the similar descriptions of Khlebnikov and Iakhontov, Mandel'shtam notes that the inner hidden life of Nadson's poetry corresponds exactly to the consciousness of his readers, the aura of the times: 'How many times knowing already that Nadson was bad ... have I reread his book and ... tried to hear it as it sounded to his generation. How greatly was I aided in this by the diaries and letters of Nadson; the time itself, the continual literary drudgery, the candles, the applause, the burning faces; the tight ring of his generation and in the centre, the altar – the lecturer's table and glass of water' (II, 60; Brown 1965, 84).
4 The 'End of the Novel,' the essay Mandel'shtam places at the very centre of his book *On Poetry* (where the essays are intentionally not placed in chronological order), depicts the inevitable death of the individual voice as it descends into the dense chaotic nature of modern events (II, 269). No critic has so far been able to provide an exact date for the writing of this essay. It nevertheless undermines most of Mandel'shtam's work up to 1924. On this point see Harris (Mandel'shtam 1979), who holds the same opinion.
5 The following is the passage in question: 'There is the voice of the epochs requiring interpretation, and there are *oblique* speaking times [*kosnoiazychnye vremena*] devoid of voices. From *oblique* articulateness the most transparent voice is born. From transparent despair it is but one step to joy. To the future all the poetry of Sologub is addressed. He was born in timelessness and was slowly saturated with time; he learned how to breathe and taught us how to love. Our grandchildren and great-grandchildren will understand Sologub and will understand him in their own way, and for them *The Flaming Circle* will be a book which burns up melancholy, and transforms our *oblique-sluggish* nature [*kosnuiu prirodu*] into pure light ash' (II, 357; Brown 1965, 207).
6 The notion of obliqueness has a well-known echo in Gumilev's 'Kosnoiazychie,' which was an extremely positive quality for the symbolists (Moses and Paul being their classic example). Equally noteworthy is a much quoted line from Gumilev's 'Vos'mistishie': 'A high inarticulateness is granted to you, poet [*Vysokoe kosnoiazychie tebe daruetsja poet*]' (Gumilev 1962–8, 248).
7 There is also a direct parallelism, suggested by the double entendre of the word game, between the birth of the transparent voice and the burning of our sluggish nature. Thus: '*kosnoiazychie* [oblique speech] – produces – transparent voice; *kosnaia priroda* [sluggish nature] – turns into – pure light ash.' The images of burning and transparency imply the notion of poetry as light or fire, which on a material, particularized level becomes heat – hence, the image of burning, also authenticated by Sologub's title 'The Flaming Circle.'

8 Owen J. Miller, summarizing the present theoretical debate, argues that this blank does not exist, that understanding and reinterpretation are one and the same act (1976, 19–27).
9 On the popularity of the idea of generation out of nothing among the futurists see Pomorska 1968, 94. Perhaps Mandel'shtam has applied the notion of generation out of nothing to the reading process.
10 We can see how close Mandel'shtam is here to the formalists and the futurists. Mikhail Bakhtin observes that for both of these schools 'linguistic laws were purely physiological' (1982, 82, translation mine). Mandel'shtam clearly accepts this, but only as a stage in the unveiling poetic process.
11 Many friends and critics of Mandel'shtam have observed the importance of his friendship with the biologists, and particularly with B.S. Kuzin. See N. Mandel'shtam 1972, 608–10. She also describes the importance of zoology and biology for Mandel'shtam and his views on poetry (1972, 608–9).
12 Sidney Monas gives the following explanation of a termenvox: 'To my query, Clarence Brown responded: "The termenvox is the well-known musical instrument named after its inventor, the immortal Lev Termen (b. 1896) ... Roger Maren informs me that Lev Termen was known in the United States as Leon Theremin. The instrument was called Thereminvox, but is now referred to as the Theremin ... One plays it by moving the hands in the air in spatial relation to rods or 'wands' on the instrument that control some oscillators. The sound comes out of loudspeakers."' (Monas 1979, 76, n 11).
13 Here Mandel'shtam brilliantly develops the traditional notion of transformation as a metaphorical principle. Pomorska correctly points out that this was a principle that united symbolists and acmeists, a principle that the acmeists did not alter (1968, 82).
14 Ronen observes that for Mandel'shtam art is a network of horizontal parallelisms (1983, 50).
15 Further examination is necessary in order to explain why this process, the physiology of reading, is also called by the poet a 'reflexology of speech' (see ch 5). I can say in advance that, for Mandel'shtam, in reading we follow the impulse that has constituted the text in the first place: in this sense the act of reading is a reflection of the act of writing whose patterns are embedded in the text as imperceptible explosions or waves. That is why Mandel'shtam speaks of reading and writing at the same time and applies similar descriptions to each: the text literally reflects these processes.

Chapter 5

1 Emma Gershtein in her memoirs about Mandel'shtam (as well as in her edi-

tion of Rudakov's letters) stresses on several occasions that Mandel'shtam spoke about the *Conversation about Dante* as a key to his views on poetry (1986, 165ff).

2 Mandel'shtam stresses most emphatically that he chose Dante for his book not because of Dante's scholastic view of the universe but because he best understood the metamorphoses of poetic discourse and displayed its stages in their most striking form in his great work: 'Dante was chosen as the theme of this conversation not because I wanted to focus attention on him as a means to studying classics ... , but because he is the greatest, the unrivalled master of transmutable and convertible [*obratimaia i obrashchaiushchaiasia*] poetic material (II, 396; 427).

3 It is possible that the philosophical influence is more an influence of the Russian artistic *milieu* prior to 1917; for example, both Kuzmin and Viacheslav Ivanovich Ivanov were deeply knowledgeable in classics and classical philosophy. It would be difficult to discern a more specific philosophical direction, for, according to his widow, Mandel'shtam's philosophical interests were strictly limited (N. Mandel'shtam 1970, 253–61), and apart from her memoirs we have very little biographical evidence.

4 This succession of images clearly echoes a philosophical view that is found in the metaphors of light of Saint John, reaching back to the thought of Plato (especially the *Republic* and *Timaeus*), and also part of the complex heritage of the metaphysics of light of the medieval period (notably in Robert Grosseteste, Albert the Great, in Bonaventure, and Thomas Aquinas).

5 We have shown in previous chapters that in Mandel'shtam's earliest views on poetry (up to 1919) poetic discourse is regarded as a mingling of tangible reality and nothingness, a view that was superseded in the 1920s with another set of polar opposites – the inner and outer essence of poetry, each side exhibiting a particular effect on the reader.

6 The word 'armaments' [*orudiia*] in the poetic context is a reiteration of the acmeist vocabulary, particularly that of Gumilev (1962–8, IV, 177).

7 Here Mandel'shtam uses the image of Dante's wrestlers, who must wrestle throughout infinity; they 'tie themselves in a knot' (II, 363; 397; *Inferno* XVI. 22–4).

8 As Mandel'shtam says: 'To ignore the formal side of scientific writing is just as incorrect as ignoring the content of literary works, for the elements of art are present in both' (III, 139; 334–5). Thus, Mandel'shtam's work on the naturalists explains many of his positions in the *Conversation about Dante.*

9 Zholkovsky points out the importance of the notion of sudden turns [*vnezapnye povoroty*] in Mandel'shtam (1979, 174).

10 The elements of poetic language, such 'turns' of phrase as metaphor or

analogy, are emblematic of this beginning, for therein two realities are brought together. In his drafts of the *Conversation about Dante* Mandel'shtam even attempts to present the hybrid metaphoric yearning as the origin of at least the *Inferno*: 'We might substitute Rome for the Inferno and hardly recognize the difference. Indeed, perhaps, the comparative relationship 'Rome to Florence' served as a jerk [*tolchok*] to form creation which resulted in the *Inferno*' (III, 190; 451).

11 In the drafts of the essay's ending, where several textual versions operate simultaneously, Mandel'shtam states that the goal of his writing is an attempt to touch the bottom of the organic descent, where the work is inhabited by insects, and yet to find in this the way back: 'I want to get to know my bones, my lava, the very depth of my grave <how the life below begins to play with magnesium and phosphorus, how life below will smile at me: arthropodal, reproachful and droning life.> ... With all the fibres of my being I want to exert pressure against the impossibility of choice, against the total absence of freedom ... <Yet> If I accept as a deserved reward both the shadow of the oak tree and the shadow of the grove and the stony-solidity [*tverdokamennost'*] of speech articulation, *how shall I feel our present age?*' (III, 168; 395, translation altered, emphasis added).

12 Ronen holds that Mandel'shtam was much influenced by Viacheslav Ivanovich Ivanov's notion of poetic creation as a creative descent; see Ivanov 1974, 'O granitsakh iskusstva,' II, 627–51; Ronen 1983, 45.

13 In a different context Ronen comments on Belyi's influence on Mandel'shtam's taking the path of (and through) stone; see Ronen 1983, 96–7.

14 The notion of gaps, cracks, and gaping spaces [*ziianie*] is possibly a restatement of Mandel'shtam's image of absence or blank of 1914–20. Indeed, Mandel'shtam does transform his earlier images throughout his years of writing until he is finally satisfied with their interpretation. However, here the blanks are not a creative part of the process: they are the openings through which one can enter with the trope, that is, through a narrow path [*tropa*]. The image is also obviously sexual.

15 This, in turn, explains the description of the battle between past and present, and the verbal endings, the description of which dominates Mandel'shtam's discourse in chapter 2.

16 Mandel'shtam employs the well-known cliché that the end is also the beginning when he adds to the description of Dante's disappearance into the grey shadows the observation that, 'the very end approaches unexpectedly and sounds like the beginning' (II, 374; 407).

17 The critical works of Taranovsky and his followers approach Mandel'shtam's

text by finding intertextual references, or the referential subtext; see, for example, Taranovsky 1976; Ronen 1983. This awareness of subtextual quotation is, according to Mandel'shtam, a beginning of reading, the first step in entering the poetic text. However, this method on its own cannot be sufficient; it has to be transformed into a different approach and a new landscape.

18 Although this is not a part of my investigation, I must stress that Mandel'shtam develops a different concept of time along each successive stage of the journey. Numerous articles on the notion of time in Mandel'shtam point to his sensitivity to the phenomenon, yet the different concepts of time in each chapter of the *Conversation about Dante* have not as yet been discussed. On the different aspects of time in Mandel'shtam see Segal 1973, 395–405; Brodsky 1986, 123–44; Laferriere 1977, 127; Freidin 1978, 421–37; Freidin 1980, 141–86; Ronen 1983, 1–363; Nilsson 1985, 283–5.

19 In the description of Lamarck in the *Journey to Armenia* there is a similar portrayal; a descent down the organic ladder reverses time as Lamarck becomes progressively younger: 'See how this blushing, semi-respectable old man races down the staircase of living creatures as a young man favored by a government minister or made happy by his mistress ... I tip my head and let the teacher walk ahead of me: May the youthful thunder of his eloquence never be silent' (II, 164–5; 369).

20 Henry Gifford comments upon the significance of Lamarck's microscope as well as the binoculars of the archeologist Khachaturian: both are connected with seeing something previously invisible; thus, they are a symbol of clairvoyance (Gifford 1979, 28–9).

21 This is by now a familiar thought. The power of our past needs a mediating constructed presence to become real. We enter organic mysteries only through artificial means, which should be powerful enough to protect us from our own destruction. Yet the entrance into the secrets of matter is already a descent, an invitation to death (an unleashing of an atomic energy): 'Here the trembling hand of the compass not only indulges the magnetic storm, but itself creates it' (II, 369–70; 403).

22 In the drafts of the *Conversation about Dante* Mandel'shtam was attempting to point towards a *seeming* death of the voice, which in reality never enters the Inferno but only illuminates it in passing. The light *escapes* darkness because it never truly enters into it:

> But the compositional roots of the tenth Canto <of all the Cantos> of the Inferno lie in the gathering of the storm [*groza*] which matures like a meterological phenomenon, and all the questions and answers rotate about a single issue – did it thunder or not?

To be more exact, this is the gathering of a storm which *is bypassing us, taking a roundabout route.* (III, 189; 451, emphasis added)

However, this passage has not been included in the final version of the *Conversation about Dante.*

23 See, for example, *Penia* [Poverty] in Plato's *Symposium* (203b–e).
24 The sense of matter as a feminine principle is even more obvious in Russian where it is *materia*, mother.
25 In the drafts of *Journey to Armenia* there is a counterpart to this insistence on literal expression, so to speak. In a curiously negative-positive overview of his mental state Mandel'shtam describes his poetic activity in his unfortunate and painful state, in which the squeezing of the residue bursts for his wife (her only mention in his work):

> I am living poorly now. I am living without perfecting myself; rather I am squeezing out of myself last bits of residue, some remnants.
>
> This fortuitous sentence just burst out of me one evening after a dreadful, incoherent day instead of my so-called 'creative work.' For Nadia. (III, 152; 382)

26 Here it is possible that Mandel'shtam remembers Khlebnikov and his conception of shift [*sdvig*] as a necessary stage in art, a necessary deformation which opens up into a new dimension (Pomorska 1968, 100–5). See also the notion of catastrophe discussed in chapter 2 above.
27 Mandel'shtam here implicitly argues with Pasternak, who in one of his earlier poems announced that he could squeeze poetry from the sponge left overnight in the garden ('Vesna, I'). Mandel'shtam, however, insists that the act of squeezing is a discovery of matter's formation: 'But only a wet sponge or a rag can be squeezed out into whatever it may be. Try as we may to twist the conception even into a plait, we will never squeeze any form out of it unless it is already a form itself. In other words, any process involving the creation of form in poetry presupposes rows, periods, and cycles of sound-forms, as in the case of individually pronounced semantic units' (II, 375–6; 408).
28 There is another singular image of expression / squeezings [*vyzhimka*] in the drafts of *Journey to Armenia,* centred on a character whose creative life has been abruptly finished and 'whose lips are sewn with silk thread.' The infernal creative existence of Kakavadze, a radio-waves operator, is described as being dangerously close to the world of sickness and death, and yet this subterranean existence is a process of uncovering a secret form of energy. 'It seemed that <somewhere and at some time> he had an entire lemon grove squeezed out of him. Jaundice and malaria dragged after him. Even in his dreams he calculated his own personal fatigue. He struggled against it, however, and his health returned <as soon as people asked him> about some-

thing interesting. His fatigue was but a secret form of energy' (III, 158; 387). This description of Kakavadze is accompanied by the notion of a growing sign that Kakavadze finds in his unconscious state, in his 'subterranean' sleep: 'He had the sleepy expression of a mathematician who produced from memory, without a blackboard, multinomial [figure] ... (II, 158; 387). This multinomial discovery is reminiscent of the formation of the *Purgatorio*, the process of form-creation discussed in this section.

29 Here Mandel'shtam reintroduces the image of stone so central in his earlier work. As was the case with the blank, the stone also has been transformed into an image filled with new significance, and here it grows in front of our eyes, becomes a crystal, and then a living collection of insects.

30 For a different reading of the poet's treatment of the naturalists see Pollak 1995, 19ff.

31 Mandel'shtam continues the image of expression introduced in chapter 4. There the expression is the squeezing of an impenetrable solidity; the continuation of this expression as applied to geography produces colour, in the same way that vegetable dyes are produced by expression from particular plants and insects.

32 It is not accidental but highly relevant that the addressee of many passages of the *Journey to Armenia*, B.S. [Kuzin], Mandel'shtam's young biologist friend, is sent to Armenia 'to supervise the production of cochineal, an insect of which most people have never heard. A superb carmine dye is made from the cochineal once it's dried and pulverized' (II, 147–8; 353).

33 We have discussed in chapter 3 Mandel'shtam's conception of poetry as an intellectual movement developing into physical action. Here, in Mandel'shtam's discussion of the impulse or modulation understood as colour, there is a careful working out of the poetic transmission of impulse into the physical notion of speed, accelerated movement.

34 The notion of cutting through space finds its counterpart in Mandel'shtam's advice to his readers on how to look at impressionist paintings. In the description of the first stage of the visual accommodation to the painting there are all the familiar images: perception as movement, walking; an entrance of the eye into matter (new material ambiance; literal cutting through the waves; the eye as a crystal and an animal. The notion of cutting through space here represents an impulse of colour caught as speed:
Walk straight on, with the strides of a stroller along the boulevard.
Cut through the large heat waves of oil painting space.
Calmly, not impetuously ... dip your eye into the new material ambiance, however, always remember that the eye is a noble, but stubborn, animal. (II, 161; 365)

35 I shall overlook temporarily the negative aspects of this description.
36 Here is the passage in question:
   The textile brilliance of this comparison is blinding, but the commercial perspective of textiles revealed in it are completely unexpected.
   With respect to its theme, Canto XVII of the *Inferno*, devoted to usury, is very close both to commercial inventory and to the turnover of the banking system. Usury, which made up for a deficiency in the banking system ... was also a necessity which eased the flow of goods in the Mediterranean region. (II, 380; 412)
37 Mandel'shtam, in fact, presents this turn to fantasy as an inevitable turn of the poetic texture: 'Canto XVII of the *Inferno* is a brilliant confirmation of the transmutability of poetic material ... the craving for flight underscored by Eastern ornament, which turns [sic] the material towards the Arabic fairy tale' (II, 383; 415).
38 This explains why colour is suddenly presented not as coloration of the text but as the colours still on the artist's palette: 'The colours are listed with a kind of professional harshness. In other words, the colours are presented at that stage when they are still found on the artist's palette, in his studio' (II, 381; 413).
39 Numerous critics have commented on Mandel'shtam's use of eastern imagery (with the exception of Armenia) as invariably terrifying and negative; see Glazova 1984, 305–8.
40 Early in chapter 4 Mandel'shtam praises Dante's ability 'to think in images' [*obraznoe myshlenie*], obviously referring to the controversy that surrounded the notion in the early part of the century. Here Mandel'shtam argues for the traditional view of the art but is careful to put it into the context of the role of reading as impression. Also thinking in images was disdained among the futurists (see, for example, Pomorska 1968, 122; Toporov 1979, 249–326).
41 In the passage in which Mandel'shtam describes the apprehension of colour in the poetic text as the apprehension 'of the artist's palette, in his studio,' he develops this notion of the personal invitation even further when he underscores Dante's knowledge of colours as evidence of the latter's inclusion in the family of painters: 'And what is so astonishing about that? Dante felt right at home in the world of painting; he was a friend of Giotto' (II, 381; 413).
42 A similar image in *Journey to Armenia* is the multicoloured bouquet of flowers presented as a scattered alphabet, ready to be united into the formulas of meaning: 'And there on the table lies an elegant syntax of confused, grammatically incorrect field flowers, their names printed in a variety of

alphabets, as though all the pre-school forms of vegetative being were merging in a pliophonic [*polnoglasnyi*, 'full-vowelled] anthology poem' (II, 149; 354).

43 Mandel'shtam argues that the text is the survival of the rough drafts: 'Rough drafts are never destroyed. There are no ready made things in poetry, in the plastic arts or in arts in general ... Thus the safety of the rough draft is the law of energetics assuring preservation of the power behind the literary work. In order to arrive on target one has to accept and take into account winds blowing in a somewhat different direction. Exactly the same law applies in tacking a sailboat' (II, 384–5; 415–16).

44 Although the speech in question is that of the infernal hero, the goal of Odysseus's quest is identified by Dante himself as the location of Purgatorio.

45 Here Mandel'shtam takes up and develops his position of 1923–30 that the poetic voice must escape all attempts to grasp it (see chapter 3). There is, of course, a reference here to the political situation of the time.

46 It is within the context of the simultaneous release of many boats that Mandel'shtam demonstrates most fully the life of the poetic impulse: there is no final poetic text, only the racing of the multiple drafts, all brought to birth and transfixed by the impulse whose wavelike nature dictates rewriting and, thus, the simultaneous survival of multiple final texts.

47 Charles Robert Darwin (1809–82), was the English naturalist who first soundly established the theory of organic evolution in his monumental work, *Origin of Species*. From December 1831 to October 1836 Darwin sailed in HMS *Beagle* as naturalist for a surveying expedition that visited the Galapagos and other islands. His observations on the relationships between geographically separated animals and time-separated animals led him to develop his principles of evolution. It was because Darwin provided a scientific explanation of how evolution occurred that he succeeded where Lamarck had failed in making the fact of evolution acceptable.

48 See, for example, Mandel'shtam's surviving drafts dedicated to Darwin: 'Instead of scribbling and compiling catalogues, Darwin offered a new principle: the principle of natural scientific patrol duty ... [The naturalist carries out his patrol duty from the captain's bridge]' (III, 174; 340).

49 The examples of Darwin as traveller are so numerous in Mandel'shtam that it is helpful to provide another citation so that we may see this comparison as a clearly reiterated pattern: 'Around-the-world voyages became pedagogically fashionable. Not only the aristocracy of the financial world, but the entire middle class now ought to provide their children with the opportunity to travel around the world ... The era beginning with Darwin's voyage on the *Beagle* and ending with the famous artist Claude Monet's around-the-world

journey on the *Brigitte* was a period of colossal apprenticeship in analytical observation' (III, 134; 331).
50 It is interesting to observe that even the carrier pigeon's flights in chapter 5 find their counterpart in the descriptions of Darwin's around-the-world correspondence, and more specifically in the mention of 'some Sir Eliot let us say, who once sent him a couple of pigeons as a gift' (III, 138; 334).
51 Since my work rests on the patterns in Mandel'shtam's descriptions rather than on the poet's actual synopsis of his ideas, it is helpful here to give another example of Darwin's wavelike organization (here a 'serial unfolding') of the widest geographical setting and the biological life therein:

> The book seethes with natural phenomena, but they are turned upside down only when absolutely necessary; they play an active role in the argument and then yield their place to their successors. Above all, Darwin prefers to use a *serial unfolding of signs* and the collision of intersecting series. His gradual accumulation of essential signs gives rise to his crescendoing scale.
>
> Darwin constructed his scientific arguments volumetrically. He extended the coordinates of his examples in length, width, and depth, using his original selection of materials to obtain his effects. (III, 177; 342)

52 This explains why Mandel'shtam always underlines that Darwin is a prosaic writer: 'the remarkable prosaic quality of Darwin's work' or 'He possessed the courage to be prosaic' (III, 136; 332), or 'Darwin's work is prosaic. Popular' (III, 170; 336). Darwin's insight stops here, whereas poetry continues its quest; its impulse of transmutability cannot stop.
53 In this context it becomes clear why Darwin is always presented as a scientist determined by his own time: for example, 'Charles Darwin's prose style could not have emerged at a more appropriate time ... No one can popularize Darwin's theory better than Darwin himself. It is essential that we study his scientific style, although it is futile to imitate it, for the historical milieu of which he was a part will never be repeated' (III, 140; 335). Dante, in contrast, transcends (or rather breaks through) his time:

> Dante's cantos ... are missions for capturing the future. They demand commentary in the futurum ...
>
> Dante is anti-modernist. His contemporaneity is continuous, incalculable and inexhaustible.
>
> That is why Odysseus' speech, as convex as the lens of a magnifying glass, may be turned towards the war of the Greeks and Persians as well as towards Columbus' discovery of America, the bold experiments of Paracelsus, and the world empire of Charles V. (II, 389; 420)

54 Similarly, in the penultimate chapter of *Journey to Armenia*, Mandel'shtam

speaks about the desire to escape the Russian language, and about the unexpected magic of discovering the pull of some unknown quality of the Armenian tongue:

> The Armenian language cannot be worn down; its boots are of stone. Naturally, its word is thick-walled, its semivowels layered with air. But is it all there due to its charm? No! Then, whence its attraction? How can you explain it, understand it?
>
> I experienced such joy in pronouncing sounds forbidden to Russian lips, mysterious sounds, outcast sounds, and perhaps on some deep level, even shameful sounds.
>
> There was some magnificent boiling water in a pewter teapot, and suddenly a pinch of black tea was tossed into it.
>
> That's how I felt about the Armenian language. (II, 170; 372)

Terras discusses the significance of Mandel'shtam's desire to forget the Russian language, but he sees this in a political, rather than a poetic, context (1973, 459). Also see here Mandel'shtam's poem 'To the German Language' (I, 190).

55 'Invigorating clarity, like a beautiful day during the temperate English summer, and a certain quality in the author which could be called good scientific weather, that is, a moderately elevated mood, work together in Darwin's writings to infect the reader with the same mood and to help him comprehend Darwin's theory' (III, 139; 335).

56 The following passage clearly illustrates that mutual reflexivity between the patterns of Darwin's writing and his relationship with his reading public: 'This laboratory was vast. It included stud farms, poultry yards, apiaries, and greenhouses belonging to specialist and amateurs ... Darwin's solidarity with the international elite of the world of natural sciences imparts a secure self-confidence to his style and lends his argumentation additional strength, the length of a comradely handshake. The naturalist is at home anywhere in the world' (III, 138; 334).

57 If the previous landscape echoed the patterns of description of Mandel'shtam's Rozanov and 'his philology of Russia's holy-fools,' the present landscape brings to mind 'the martial philology of Annensky,' who travels to the farthest reaches of the poetic boundaries.

58 In other words, the goal of Odysseus's journey.

59 Mandel'shtam describes this conflict between reason and faith in his depiction of a little imperial University of Sorbonne, inundated on all sides by the folklore of Christian scripture: 'The enormous explosive power of the book of Genesis fell upon the tiny island of Sorbonne from all sides' (II, 391; 422).

60 'I maintain that every element of the modern experimental method may be

found in Dante's approach to Biblical tradition. These include the creation of specially contrived conditions for the experiment, the use of instruments of such precision that there is no reason to doubt their validity, and clear verification of the results' (II, 391; 422).

61 We find in the drafts of the *Journey to Armenia*: 'Reality has the character of a continuum ... although that continuum cannot be shown by any means or way. Thus, a prose tale is nothing more than a broken sign of this continuum' (III, 166; 394).

62 It is difficult to outline Mandel'shtam's thought here with any more precision. His work has been interrupted. But in the drafts of the *Journey to Armenia*, at the same place where he speaks about the inability of prose to fill the gap, he indicates that only the wave theory of light can correspond to this gap: 'A permanent precise description of matter rests on the effect of light: the so called Tyndall effect (the oblique indicator of the molecule in the ultra microscope) ... but there everything must be done from scratch, describe the light, etc.' (III, 167; 394). This somewhat puzzling and unfinished thought becomes in the *Conversation about Dante* the leading metaphor of chapter 6, that is, 'the undulations of formulating procedure' of poetic texture, its musicality, its rhythm.

63 On the unusual musical sense in Mandel'shtam see Przybylski 1971, 103–25. For music in Dante see *De Vulgari Eloquentia* 2.4.2. Poetry is '*nihil aliud quam fictio rhetorica musicaque poetica.*'

64 Although Mandel'shtam's interpretation of the role of music in poetry is highly original, it nevertheless draws upon the strong medieval tradition so evident in Dante, a tradition with its roots ultimately in the Platonic and Pythagorean tradition (where number and music are the clearest indication of true being) and most creatively developed by Augustine *inter alia* in *De musica* 6 (*Patrologia latina* 32, 1161ff). Here Augustine develops a hierarchy of sounds, *ut a corporeis ad incorporea transeamus*, that allows one to pass from things corporeal to the incorporeal.

65 Mandel'shtam obviously intends to speak of the wave as sound, which on the higher level becomes wave as light. See earlier in chapter 6: 'Music and optics create the knot of the thing' (II, 393; 423).

66 It is also possible that Mandel'shtam is here referring to Pasternak's 1922 depiction of the content of the work of art: 'As the forest's noise, the book is born God knows where, and it grows, and rolls, awakening and brightening moment, *it starts talking with all the tree tops*, having finally arrived' (Pasternak 1982, '*Neskol'ko polozhenii*,' 111). Mandel'shtam, who watched Pasternak's work with much attention and competitiveness, must have realized the importance of this metaphor.

67 The interconnection and kindredness of the key characteristics – the musical essence of poetry, the region of faith, the notion of joy and gratitude – explain Mandel'shtam's otherwise bewildering insistence that Darwin's work is totally prosaic because he did not see the necessity for being grateful to anyone: 'The remarkable prosaic quality of Darwin's work was preconditioned, to a large extent, by history. Darwin purged the scientific language, eradicating every trace of bombast, rhetoric, and teleologic pathos. He possessed the courage of being prosaic precisely because he had so much to say and did not feel obliged to express rapture or gratitude to anyone' (III, 136; 332–3).

68 In his radio script 'Goethe's Youth' (written in 1935 during his exile in Voronezh) Mandel'shtam singles out this moment of the amphitheatre-like celebration as an insight into the essence of art, a thought that had caused profound excitement in young Goethe: 'Cannot this entry be explained by the great spiritual agitation that possessed Goethe during his travels through Italy? ... He walked around the circus along the top tier of benches, and it made a strange impression on him: one should never look at an amphitheatre when it is empty, only when it is thronged with people. When people see themselves assembled, they must be astonished – their multi-voicedness, multi-soundedness, their wave-like excitedness [*mnogoglasnyi, mnogoshumnyi, volnuiushchiisia*] – they must suddenly see themselves united in one noble whole, merged into a single mass, a single body as it were. Each head in the audience serves as a measure of the enormity of the entire building' (III, 79; 466). On Dante's heavenly rose in Mandel'shtam see Glazova, 1984, 290–4.

Chapter 6

1 Mandel'shtam, in fact, says precisely that in 'On the Nature of the Word': 'Furthermore, Acmeism is a social as well as a literary phenomenon in Russian history. With Acmeism a moral force was reborn in Russian poetry' (II, 258; 131).

2 Timenchik stresses this point when he quotes the story of Anna Akhmatova, who claims that Gumilev's disappointment in symbolism was a key to what was most important in his character: 'as a boy he believed in Symbolism, as people believe in God. This was the untouchable and sacred, but as he was getting closer to the symbolist and to the "Tower" [V.I. Ivanov], his faith shuddered; he felt that something in him was blasphemed' (Timenchik 1981, 176).

3 I am not arguing here that Bakhtin read Mandel'shtam or that Jakobson

was much impressed by Mandel'shtam's work. I want rather to stress that several key ideas of the formalists, when played out within a much wider intellectual framework, will actually generate the *heteroglossia* of Bakhtin, which, in turn, influences decisively the French semioticians turned poststructuralist. Something of a similar development is evident in Mandel'shtam's thought.

4 See Glazova 1984.
5 Certain aspects of tradition cannot be invented, Cavanagh's argument notwithstanding.
6 It is instructive to observe how the school of Soviet semiotics continued to be arrested by its focus upon applying what is known about poetic construction to the question of poetic communication. It is also curious to see how close and yet how different is the development of Tynianov's 'tightness of the poetic series' in Mandel'shtam and in the Russian school of semiotics. Thus, the Soviet semiotician Lotman takes Jakobson's position one step further and proposes that poetry increases the levels of information that it transmits by making 'every element in the linguistic utterance which it employs significant' (Lotman 1976, 36), as well as by developing additional levels of meaning along the axes of combination, where the associative elements are connected with each other in *both* automatic and deautomatized fashions (43). The levels of meaning, therefore, multiply exponentially because the pattern of combination, as well as the content of the utterance itself, presupposes and awakens associative parallels while at the same time departing from them. According to Lotman, poetry preserves an exponential explosion, as it were, of meaning. This approach comes very close to characterizing poetic meaning as the hidden source of public energy. However, from Lotman we learn about the patterns of *storing* meanings in poetry, not the patterns of their *communication* and their *effect*. If poetic expression is a deviation from our normal perspective, the question of how such a deviation in communication occurs still remains unanswered.
7 On the relationship between Mandel'shtam and Tynianov's concept of 'unity and density of the poetic sequence,' see also Ronen 1983, ix; Segal 1968; and Segal 1972.
8 Aquinas identifies the king with the soul as the substantial form of the body in *De regno ad regem Cypri* 1.12, in *Opuscula omnia* 1.338–9.
9 In the second part of the *Conversation about Dante* Mandel'shtam depicts the tragic implication of the reader's inability to catch up with the impulse. Speaking here more generally of the human experience, Mandel'shtam isolates the fear of impending and inescapable disaster as a loss of speed precisely at the moment of the highest impetus to accelerate. The impulse of

sanity, health, life leaves the sufferer behind no matter how hard he tries to catch up with it; the body submits to death no matter how much it tries not to, because it is irreparably out of tune with the swift passage of life:

> The density of the cello's timbre is best for communicating expectation and agonizing impatience. There is no power on earth which can hasten the movement of honey pouring out of a tilted jar ... A cello retards sound, no matter how it hurries. Ask Brahms – he knew it. Ask Dante – he heard it.
>
> ... the chase after time which is slipping away ... The same rhythm of the mad dash emerges here in disguise, in the mute wailing of the cello, which strives with all its might to break out of the situation and gives a sound picture of a still more terrifying, slow chase, breaking speed down into the most delicate fibres. (II, 397, 399; 427, 429)

This quotation is an example of Mandel'shtam's insistence that, although following the impulse is characteristic of poetic discourse, this duality (form, matter) is also a performance of the forces that constitute human life.

10 This thought is stated most clearly in the manuscripts of the *Conversation about Dante* when Mandel'shtam develops the description of Dante's turning and disappearing into an observation that Dante has vanished because he has become an 'actual instrument in the metamorphosis of literary time, in its gathering and unfolding' (III, 180; 444). We have already discussed the notion of time and its different status at each level of the transmutation of the poetic *materia*. It is clear, therefore, that what Mandel'shtam states in the manuscripts he also plays out in the final draft of the *Conversation about Dante*, namely, that the poet is apprehended as a part of the text's metamorphosis, that his presence in the text becomes inseparable from the impulse that characterizes the text's transmutability.

11 Here Mandel'shtam makes brilliant use of Dante's text. Quoting *Paradiso*, he plays on the notion of how much more immediate is the desire to receive and respond on the higher level of human development than on the lower level. The passage follows upon Mandel'shtam's postulation that Dante has given witness in his poetry to the 'reflexology of speech,' 'a science, still not completely established, of the spontaneous psycho-physiological influence of the word on those who are conversing, on the audience surrounding them, and on the speaker himself, as well as on the means by which he communicates his urge to speak' (II, 404; 434):

> Just as an animal covered
> with a cloth grows nervous and
> irritable, only the moving
> folds of the material indicating

> his displeasure, so the first
> created soul (Adam's) expressed
> to me through the covering
> (light) the extent of its
> pleasure and sense of joy in
> answering my question. (*Paradiso* XXVI, 97–102)

The reaction of Adam to the word he is about to utter is displayed as joy at being asked, a joy in turn reflected in the intensification of the reflected light in the first created soul, which is immediately compared to the movement of sackcloth, constricting and covering an animal. Thus, what is constriction in the purely animal world is the pure freedom of communication in the *Paradiso*. Constriction on the physical level is a capacity for expansion in the highest intelligible landscape. Nervousness, animal, sack are transformed into the startling and free interchange of light into planets and of planets into birds: 'In the third part of the *Commedia* (the *Paradiso*), I see a genuine kinetic ballet' (II, 404; 434).

References

For Mandel'shtam's writings the first reference is to the standard Russian edition of his works: *Sobranie sochinenii* [Collected Works], ed. G.P. Struve, N. Struve, and B. Filippova, vols. 1–3 (Washington 1967, 1971, 1969), vol. 4 (Paris 1981); the second is to the English translation. With the exception of *The Noise of Time*, the English translations of the prose works are from *Mandelstam: The Collected Critical Prose and Letters*, ed. Jane Gary Harris, trans. Jane Gary Harris and Constance Link (Ann Arbor 1979). The translation of *The Noise of Time* [*Shum vremeni*] is from *The Prose of Osip Mandel'shtam: The Noise of Time, Theodocia, Egyptian Stamp*, trans. Clarence Brown (Princeton 1965). For clarity I have occasionally adjusted the English translation, and in these cases I have noted in the citations that the translation has been altered.

Akhmatova, A. 1968. 'Mandel'shtam (Listki iz dnevnika)' [Mandel'shtam (Leaves from a Diary)]. In *Sochineniia* [Works]. Vol. 2. Munich. 166–87

Alter, Robert. 1978. 'Osip Mandelstam: The Poet as Witness.' In *Defenses of the Imagination: Jewish Writers and Modern Historical Crisis*. Philadelphia. 25–46

Aristotle. 1941. *The Basic Works of Aristotle*. Ed. Richard McKeon. New York

Averintsev, S.S. 1990. 'Sud'ba i vest' Osipa Mandel'shtama' [Osip Mandel'shtam's Fate and Fame]. In *Sochineniia* [Works], ed. Peter Nerler. 2 vols. Moscow. 1: 5–64

Baines, Jennifer. 1976. *Mandelstam: The Later Poetry*. Cambridge

Bakhtin, Mikhail. 1978. 'Discourse Typology in Prose.' In *Readings in Russian Poetics: Formalist and Structuralist Views*, ed. Ladislav Matejka and Krystyna Pomorska. Ann Arbor. 176–96

– 1982. *Formal'nyi metod v literaturovedenii* [The Formal Method in Philology]. Moscow

- 1988. 'From the Prehistory of Novelistic Discourse.' In *Modern Criticism and Theory*, ed. David Lodge
Bann, Stephen, and John E. Bowlt. 1973. *Russian Formalism: A Collection of Articles and Texts in Translation*. New York
Barnes, Christopher. 1989. *Boris Pasternak: A Literary Biography*. Vol. 1: *1890–1928*. Cambridge
Barnstead, J.A. 1986. 'Mandel'shtam and Kuzmin.' *Wiener Slawistischer Almanach* 18: 47–81
Barthes, Roland. 1970. *S/Z*. Paris
- 1977. *Image, Music, Text*. Ed. and trans. S. Heath. London / New York
- 1988. 'The Death of the Author.' In *Modern Criticism and Theory: A Reader*, ed. David Lodge. 167–95
Bergson, Henri. 1908. *L'Evolution créatrice*. Paris
Bloom, Harold. 1973. *The Anxiety of Influence: A Theory of Poetry*. New York
- 1975. *A Map of Misreading*. New York
Brodsky, Joseph. 1985. 'The Child of Civilization.' In *Less than One*. New York. 123–44
- 1996. 'Vershiny velikogo treugol'nika' [The Tops of the Great Triangle]. *Zvezda* [Star] 1: 225–33
Brown, Clarence. 1973. *Mandelstam*. Cambridge
Brown, Clarence, trans. 1965. *The Prose of Osip Mandel'shtam: The Noise of Time, Theodocia, Egyptian Stamp*. Princeton
- trans. 1988. *The Noise of Time and Other Prose Pieces*. Berkeley
Bukhshtab, B. 1971. 'The Poetry of Mandelstam.' *Russian Literature Triquarterly* 1: 262–82
Cavanagh, Clare Adele. 1988. 'Osip Mandel'shtam and the Modernist Creation of Tradition.' PH D dissertation, Harvard University
- 1990. 'Synthetic Nationality: Mandel'shtam and Chaadaev.' *Slavic Review* 49, no. 4: 597–610
- 1995. *Osip Mandelstam and the Modernist Creation of Tradition*. Princeton
Chukovskaia, Lidiia. 1976. *Zapiski ob Anne Akhmatovoi* [Notes about Anna Akhmatova]. Vol. 1. Paris
Cohen, Ralph, ed. 1989. *Future Literary Theory*. London
Culler, Jonathan. 1975. *Structuralist Poetics: Structuralism, Linguistics, and the Study of Literature*. Ithaca, N.Y.
- 1976. 'Presupposition and Intertextuality.' *Modern Language Notes* 91: 1380–96
- 1981. *The Pursuit of the Signs: Semiotics, Literature, Deconstruction*. New York
- 1982. *On Deconstruction: Theory and Criticism after Structuralism*. New York
- 1983. *Roland Barthes*. London

Dante Alighieri. 1961. *The Divine Comedy*. Trans. John D. Sinclair. 3 vols. New York
Davidson, Pamela. 1989. *The Poetic Imagination of Vyacheslav Ivanov: A Russian Symbolist's Perception of Dante*. Cambridge
Davydov, Sergej. 1985. 'From "Dominant" to "Semantic Gesture": A Link between Russian Formalism and Czech Structuralism.' In *Russian Formalism: A Retrospective Glance*, ed. Robert Jackson and Stephen Rudy. 93–113
De Man, Paul. 1982. 'The Resistance to Literary Theory.' *Yale French Studies* 63: 3–20
Derrida, Jacques. 1976. *Of Grammatology*. Trans. Gayatri Chakrovorty Spivak. Baltimore
Dolezel, Lubomir. 1979. 'In Defence of Structural Poetics.' *Poetics* 8: 521–30
– 1982. 'A Schema of Literary Communication.' Unpublished manuscript
Eagleton, Terry. 1986. 'The Revolt of the Reader.' In *Against the Grain: Selected Essays 1975–1985*. London
Eco, Umberto. 1979. *The Role of the Reader: Explorations in the Semiotics of Texts*. Bloomington, Ind.
Eikhenbaum, Boris M. 1978. 'The Theory of the Formal Method.' Trans. I.R. Titunik. In *Readings in Russian Poetics: Formalist and Structuralist Views*, ed. Ladislav Matejka and Krystyna Pomorska. Ann Arbor
Epstein, Michael. 1991. 'Tsadik i Talmudist: Sravnitl'nyi opyt o Pasternake i Mandel'shtame' [The Tsaddik and the Talmudist: A Comparative Essay about Pasternak and Mandelstam]. *Dvadtsat' dva* 77 (June–July): 186–209
Erlich, Victor. 1981. *Russian Formalism: History – Doctrine*. New Haven, Conn
Eshelman, R. 1983. 'Mandel'shtam and Mystification: Notes on His Early Concept of Intertextuality.' *Wiener Slawistischer Almanach* 12: 163–80
Fish, Stanley. 1976. 'How to Do Things with Austin and Searle: Speech Act Theory and Literary Criticism.' *Modern Language Notes* 91: 983–1025
– 1978. 'Normal Circumstances, Literal Languages, Direct Speech Acts, the Ordinary, the Everyday, the Obvious, What Goes on Without Saying and Other Special Cases.' *Critical Inquiry* 4: 625–44
– 1980. *Is There a Text in This Class?* Cambridge
– 1981. 'Why No One's Afraid of Wolfgang Iser.' *Diacritics* 11 (March) 2–13
Fitzgerald, F. Scott. 1925. *The Great Gatsby*. New York
Fleishman, L.S. 1982. 'Neizvestnaia stat'ia Osipa Mandel'shtama' [An Unknown Essay of Osip Mandel'shtam]. *Wiener Slawistischer Almanach* 10: 451–7
Freidin, Gregory. 1978. 'The Whisper of History and the Noise of Time in the Writing of Osip Mandel'shtam.' *Russian Review* 37, no. 4: 421–37
– 1980. 'Osip Mandel'shtam: The Poetry of Time (1908–1916).' *California Slavic Studies* 11: 141–86

- 1982. 'Mandel'shtam "Ode to Stalin": History and Myth.' *Russian Review* 41, no. 4: 400–26
- 1987. *A Coat of Many Colors. Osip Mandelstam and His Mythologies of Self-Presentation.* Berkeley

Frye, Northrop. 1963. *Fables of Identity: Studies in Poetic Mythology.* New York

Garvin, Paul L., ed. and trans. 1964. *A Prague School Reader on Esthetics, Literary Structure, and Style.* Washington

Gasparov, Boris. 1978. 'The Narrative Text as an Act of Communication.' *VLM* 9: 245–61
- 1987. 'Son o russkoi poezii (O. Mandel'shtam, "Stikhi o russkoi poezii," 1–2)' [A Dream about Russian Poetry (O. Mandel'shtam, "Verses about Russian Poetry," 1–2]. In *Stanford Slavic Studies*, 1: 259–306

Gershtein, Emma. 1983. *Novoe o Mandel'shtame* [New Notes on Mandel'shtam]. Paris
- 1987. 'Slushaia Mandel'shtama' [Listening to Mandel'shtam]. *Novyi mir* 10: 194–6

Gifford, Henry. 1979. 'Mandelstam and the Journey.' In *Osip Mandelstam: Journey to Armenia,* trans. Sidney Monas. 7–33

Glazova, M. 1984. 'Mandel'shtam and Dante: *The Divine Comedy* in Mandel'shtam's Poetry of the 1930s.' *Studies in Soviet Thought* 28: 281–335
- 1988. 'The Artist as Transgressor in Mandel'shtam's Poetry.' *Studies in Soviet Thought* 36: 1–61

Grigor'ev, A., and I. Petrova. 1977. 'Mandel'shtam na poroge tridtsatykh godov' [Mandel'shtam on the Threshold of the 1930s]. *Russian Literature* 5, no. 2: 181–99

Gumilev, Nikolai. 1962, 1964, 1968. *Sobranie sochinenii* [Collected Works]. Vols. 1, 2, and 4. Washington

Gydov, V.N. 1991. '"Dyshat' ne dlia sebia ..." (voronezhskii period Osipa Mandel'shtama)' ['To breathe not for oneself ...' (Osip Mandel'shtam's Voronezh Period)]. In *Slovo i sud'ba. Osip Mandel'shtam: Issledovanija i materialy.* Moscow. 278–86

Harris, Jane Gary. 1982. 'Mandelstamian *Zlost',* Bergson, and a New Acmeist Esthetic?' *Ulbandus Review* 2, no. 2: 112–30
- 1986. 'The "Latin Gerundive" as Autobiographical Imperative: A Reading of Mandel'shtam's *Journey to Armenia.*' *Slavic Review* 45, no. 1: 1–19
- 1989. Review of *Substantial Proofs of Being,* by Charles Isenberg. *Russian Review* 48, no. 1: 110–11

Harris, Jane Gary, ed. 1979. *Mandelstam. The Collected Critical Prose and Letters.* Trans. Jane Gary Harris and Constance Link. Ann Arbor

Heidegger, Martin. 1977. *Basic Writings.* Ed. and trans. David Farrel Krell. New York

Isenberg, Charles. 1977. 'Associative Chains in *Egipetskaja Marka.*' *Russian Literature* 5, no. 3: 257–76
- 1987. *Substantial Proofs of Being: Osip Mandelstam's Literary Prose.* Columbus, Ohio

Iser, Wolfgang. 1971. 'Indeterminacy and the Reader's Response in Prose Fiction.' In *Aspects of Narrative,* ed. J. Hillis Miller. New York. 1–46
- 1972. 'The Reading Process: A Phenomenological Approach.' *New Literary History* 3: 279–99
- 1978. *The Act of Reading: A Theory of Aesthetic Response.* Baltimore
- 1980. 'Interview.' *Diacritics* 10 (June): 57–86
- 1981. 'Talking Like Whales: A Reply to Stanley Fish.' *Diacritics* 11 (September): 82–7

Ivanov, Viacheslav Ivanovich. 1974. 'O granitsakh iskusstva' [Of the Boundaries of Art]. In *Sobranie sochinenii.* Brussels. 2: 627–51
- 1979. 'O veselom remesle i umnom vesel'i' [About Joyful Craft and Wise Joy]. In *Sobranie sochinenii.* Brussels. 3: 62–77

Ivanov, Viacheslav Vsevolodovich. 1973. 'Dva primera anagrammaticheskix postroenii v stikhax pozdnego Mandel'shtama' [Two Examples of Anagrammatic Structures in the Poems of Late Mandel'shtam]. *Russian Literature* 2: 81–7
- 1985. 'Temy i stili Vostoka v poezii Zapada' [Themes and Styles of the East in the Poetry of the West]. Afterword in *Vostochnye motivy: Stikhotvoreniia i poemy* [Eastern Themes: Short and Long Poems], comp. L.E. Cherkasskij and V.S. Muravjev. Moscow. 424–70
- 1988. 'Pasternak i opoiaz (k postanovke voprosa)' [Pasternak and Opoiaz (Towards a Formulation of the Question)]. In *Tynianovskii sbornik; Tret'i Tynianovskie chteniia* [A Collection of Essays in Honour of Tynianov. Third Volume], ed. M.O. Chudakova. Riga. 70–82
- 1990. '"Stikhi o neizvestnom soldate" v kontekste mirovoi poezii' ['Verses about the Unknown Soldier' in the Context of World Poetry]. In *Zhizn' i tvorchestvo O. E. Mandel'shtama* [Life and Work of O.E. Mandel'shtam]. Veronosh, 356–66
- 1991. 'Mandel'shtam i biologiia' [Mandelstam and Biology]. In *Osip Mandel'shtam: K 100–letiiu so dnia rozhdeniia. Poetika i tekstologiia. Materialy nauchnoi konferentsii 27–29 dekabria 1991* [Mandelstam Centenary Conference ... London 1991]. Moscow: 280–98

Jackson, Robert, and Stephen Rudy, eds. 1985. *Russian Formalism: A Retrospective Glance. A Festschrift in Honor of Victor Erlich.* New Haven, Conn.

Jakobson, Roman. 1921. *Noveishaia russkaia poeziia* [Contemporary Russian Poetry]. Prague
- 1960. 'Closing Statement: Linguistics and Poetics.' In *Style in Language,* ed. Thomas A. Sebeok. New York

- 1971. 'On Realism in Art.' Trans. Karol Magassy. In *Readings in Russian Poetics: Formalist and Structuralist Views*, ed. Ladislav Matejka and Krystyna Pomorska. Ann Arbor. 38–46
- 1980. *The Framework of Language.* Ann Arbor

Jakubinskij, Lev. 1916. 'O zvukakh stixotvornogo iazyka' [About the Sounds of Poetic Language]. In *Sborniki po teorii poeticeskogo iazyka, Vypusk pervyi.* [Essays in Theory of Poetic Language, First Edition]. Petrograd

Kablukov, S.P. 1979. 'Iz dnevnika S.P. Kablukova' [From the Diary of S.P. Kablukov]. Ed. A.A. Morozov. In 'Mandel'shtam v zapisiakh dnevnika S.P. Kablukova.' [Mandel'shtam in the Diaries of S.P. Kablukov]. *Vestnik Russkogo Khristianskogo Dvizheniia* 129: 135–55

Karabchievsky, Iuri. 1985. *Voskresenie Maiakovskogo* [The Resurrection of Maiakovsky]. Munich

Khardzhiev, N.I. 1973. 'Primechaniia' [Notes]. In O. Mandel'shtam, *Stikhotvoreniia* [Poems]. Biblioteka poeta, Bol'shaia seriia, 2nd ed. Leningrad. 249–316
- 1974/5. 'Vosstanovlennyi Mandel'shtam' [Recomposed Mandel'shtam]. *Russian Literature* 3, nos. 7/8: 19–22
- 1978. Notes in *Osip Mandel'shtam.* Moscow. 251–315

Khlebnikov, V.V. 1968, 1972. *Sobranie sochinenii* [Collected Works]. Vols. 1, 3. Munich

Kristeva, Julia. 1977. *Polylogue.* Paris

Kristeva, Julia, Jean-Claude Milner, and Nicolas Ruwet, eds. 1975. *Langue, discours, société.* Paris

Kuzin, B.S. 1983. 'Ob O.E. Mandel'shtame' [About O.E. Mandel'shtam]. *Vestnik Russkogo Khristianskogo Dvizheniia*, 40: 99–129
- 1987. 'Iz perepiski O.E. Mandel'shtama s B.S. Kuzinym' [From the Correspondence of O.E. Mandel'shtam and B.S. Kuzin]. *Voprosy istorii estestvoznaniia i tekhniki* [Questions in Natural and Technical History]. 127–44

Laferriere, D. 1977. *Five Russian Poems.* Jersey City, N.J.

Langerak, Thomas. 1991. '"Kak svetoteni muchenik Rembrandt ..." (Razgovor poeta s khudozhnikom)' ['Like Rembrant, martyr of chiaroscuro ...' (The Poet's Conversation with the Painter)]. In *Osip Mandel'shtam: K 100–letiju so dnia rozhdeniia. Poetika i tekstologiia* [Mandelstam Centenary Conference ... London 1991]. Moscow. 83–6

Lear, Jonathan. 1988. *Aristotle: The Desire to Understand.* Cambridge

Levin, Iuri. 1969. 'O nekotorykh chertakh plana soderzhaniia v poeticheskikh tekstakh. Materialy k izucheniiu poetiki O. Mandel'shtama' [About Certain Features of Content in the Poetic Texts. Materials towards the Examination of Mandel'shtam's Poetics]. *International Journal of Slavic Linguistics and Poetics* 12: 106–64
- 1975a. 'O sootnoshenii mezhdu semantikoi poeticheskogo teksta i vnetek-

stovoi real'nosti (Zametki o poetike O. Mandel'shtama)' [Of the Correspondences between the Semantics of the Poetic Text and Extratextual Reality]. *Russian Literature* 3, nos. 10/11: 147–72
- 1975b. 'Zametki, o "krymsko-ellinskikh" stikhakh O. Mandel'shtama' [Notes on O. Mandel'shtam's 'Crimean-Hellenic' Poems]. *Russian Literature* 3, nos. 10/11: 5–31
- 1982. '"Masteritsa vinovatykh vzorov ..." O. Mandel'shtama' [O. Mandelstam's 'Mistress of guilty glances ...']. In *Uchenyi material po analizu poeticheskikh tekstov*, ed. M. Iuri Lotman. Tallin. 168–79
Levin, Iu. I., D.M. Segal, R.D. Timenchik, V.N. Toporov, and T.V. Civ'ian. 1974/5. 'Russkaia semanticheskaia poetika kak potentsial'naia kul'turnaia paradigma' [Russian Semantic Poetics as a Potential Cultural Paradigm]. *Russian Literature*, 3, nos. 7/8: 47–82
Levinton, G.A., and Timenchik, R.D. 1978. 'Kniga K.J. Taranovskogo o poezii O.E. Mandel'shtama' [The Book of K.J. Taranovsky about the Poetry of O.E. Mandel'shtam]. *Russian Literature* 6, no. 2: 197–211
Literaturnye Manifesty. 1: *Ot Simvolizma k Oktjabriu* [Literary Manifestos. Vol. 1: From Symbolism to October]. 1969. Munich
Livingstone, Angela, ed. 1985. *Pasternak on Art and Creativity*. Cambridge
Lodge, David, ed. 1988. *Modern Criticism and Theory: A Reader*. London
Lotman, Eurii. 1971. *Struktura khudozhestvennogo teksta* [The Structure of the Artistic Text]. Moscow. Rpr. Brown University Slavic Reprints 9. Providence, R.I.
- 1976. *Analysis of the Poetic Text*. Ed. and trans. D. Barton Johnson. Ann Arbor
- 1984. 'Semantika konteksta i podteksta v poezii Mandel'shtama' [Semantics of Context and Subtext in the Poetry of Mandel'shtam]. *International Journal of Slavic Linguistics and Poetics* 29: 133–42
Mailloux, Steven. 1989. *Rhetorical Power*. Ithaca
Mandel'shtam, Nadezhda. 1970a. *Vospominaniia* [Memoirs]. New York
- 1970b. *Hope against Hope: A Memoir*. Trans. Max Hayward. New York
- 1972. *Vtoraia kniga* [Second Book]. Paris
- 1974. *Hope Abandoned*. Trans. Max Hayward. New York
- 1987. *Kniga tret'ia* [Third Book]. Paris
Mandel'shtam, Osip. 1967, 1971, 1969. *Sobranie sochinenii v trekh tomakh* [Collected Works in Three Volumes]. Ed. G.P. Struve and B.A. Filippova. Washington and New York
- 1979. *Mandelstam: The Collected Critical Prose and Letters*. Trans. Jane Gary Harris and Constance Link. Ann Arbor
- 1981. *Sobranie sochinenii. 4: dopolnitel'nyi* [Collected Works. Vol. 4: Addendum]. Paris
- 1982. 'Pshenitsa chelovecheskaia' [Grain of Humanity]. *Wiener Slawistischer Almanach* 12: 163–80

- 1987. *Slovo i kul'tura* [Word and Culture]. Ed. P.M. Nerler. Moscow
- 1990. *Sochinenija* [Works]. Ed. P.M. Nerler. Moscow

Margolina, S. 1989. *Mirovozzrenie Osipa Mandel'shtama* [The Intellectual Vision of Osip Mandel'shtam]. Marburg

Meijer, J.M. 1979. 'The Early Mandel'shtam and Symbolism.' *Russian Literature* 7: 521–36

Miller, J. Hillis. 1989. 'The Function of Literary Theory at the Present Time.' In *Future Literary Theory*, ed. Ralph Cohen. New York

Miller, Owen J. 1978. 'Reading as a Process of Reconstruction: A Critique of Recent Structuralist Formulations.' In *Interpretation of Narrative*, ed. M.J. Valdés and O.J. Miller. Toronto. 19–27

Monas, Sidney, trans. 1979. *Osip Mandel'shtam: Journey to Armenia*. San Francisco

Morozov, A.A. 1967. 'Primechaniia' [Notes]. In *Osip Mandel'shtam: Razgovor o Dante* [Osip Mandel'shtam: Conversation about Dante]. Moscow. 71–84
- 1979. 'Introduction.' In 'Mandel'shtam v zapisiakh dnevnika S.P. Kablukova.' [Mandel'shtam in the Diaries of S.P. Kablukov]. *Vestnik Russkogo Khristianskogo Dvizheniia* 129: 133–5

Mukařovský, Jan. 1964. 'Standard Language and Poetic Language.' In Paul L. Garvin, ed. and trans., *A Prague School Reader on Eesthetics, Literary Structure, and Style*. Washington. 19–35
- 1977. 'On Poetic Language.' In John Burbank and Peter Steiner, eds, *The Word and Verbal Art: Selected Essays by Jan Mukařovský*. New Haven, Conn. 1–65

Nietzsche, Friedrich. 1992. 'The Birth of Tragedy from the Spirit of Music' [1872]. In *Critical Theory since Plato*, ed. Hazard Adams. New York. 628–34

Nilsson, Nils Atke. 1974/5. 'Mandel'shtam's Poem "Voz'mi na radost"' [Take for the Joy].' *Russian Literature* 3, nos. 7/8: 133–58
- 1985. 'Frozen Time as a Paradigm in Modern Slavic Poetry (Mandel'shtam, Kocbek, Milosz).' *International Journal of Slavic Linguistics and Poetics* 31/32: 283–85

Pallas, Peter Simon. 1793. *Voyages de M. P.S. Pallas, en differentes provinces de l'empire de Russie, et dans l'Asie septentrionale*. Paris
- 1812. *Travels through the Southern Provinces of the Russian Empire, in the Years 1793 and 1794*. London

Parnakh, V. 1934. *Ispanskie i portugal'skie poety, zhertvy inkvizitsii* [Spanish and Portuguese Poets, Victims of the Inquisition]. Leningrad and Moscow

Pasternak, Boris. 1959. *Doctor Zhivago*. Trans. Max Hayward and Manya Harari. London
- 1966. *Doctor Zhivago*. Trans. Max Hayward and Manya Harari. London
- 1981. *Perepiska s Ol'goi Freidenberg* [Correspondence with Olga Freidenberg]. New York

- 1982. *Vozdushnye Puti: Proza raznykh let* [Aerial Paths: The Prose of Different Years]. Moscow
- 1985. *Pasternak on Art and Creativity*. Ed. A. Livingstone. Cambridge

Poliakova, S.V. 1992. *Osip Mandel'shtam; nabliudeniia, interpretatsii, neopublikovannoe i zabytoe* [Osip Mandel'shtam: Observations, Interpretations, Unpublished and Forgotten]. Ann Arbor

Pollak, Nancy. 1987. 'Mandel'shtam's Mandel'stein (Initial Observations on the Cracking of a Slit-Eyed Nut, or a Coule of Clinks in the Schnell).' *Slavic Review* 46, nos. 3–4: 450–70
- 1995. *Mandelstam the Reader*. Baltimore

Pomorska, Krystyna. 1968. *Russian Formalist Theory and Its Poetic Ambience*. The Hague/Paris

Potebnja, Alexandr. 1922. *Mysl' i iazyk* [Thought and Language]. Moscow

Pratt, Mary Louise. 1977. *Toward a Speech Act Theory of Literary Discourse*. Bloomington, Ind.

Prince, Gerald. 1973. 'Introduction à l'étude du narrataire.' *Poétique* 14: 178–96

Przybylski, Ryszard. 1971. 'Osip Mandel'shtam i muzyka' [Osip Mandel'shtam and Music]. *Russian Literature* 1: 103–25
- 1987. *An Essay on the Poetry of Osip Mandel'shtam: God's Grateful Guest*. Trans. Madeline Levine. Ann Arbor

Ricoeur, Paul. 1974. 'Metaphor and the Main Problem of Hermeneutics.' *New Literary History* 6: 95–110
- 1978. 'The Metaphorical Process as Cognition, Imagination and Feeling.' *Critical Enquiry* 5: 143–59
- 1991. *A Ricoeur Reader: Reflection and Imagination*. Ed. Mario J. Valdés. Toronto

Riffaterre, Michael. 1978. *Semiotics of Poetry*. Bloomington, Ind.

Rilke, Rainer Maria. 1946. *Selected Letters*. Trans. R.F.C. Hull. London

Ronen, Omry. 1973. 'Leksicheskii povtor, podtekst i smysl v poetike Osipa Mandel'shtama' [Lexical Repetition, Subtext and Meaning in the Poetics of Osip Mandel'shtam]. *Slavic Poetics: Essays in Honour of K. Taranovsky*. Paris. 367–87
- 1979/81. 'K siuzhetu "Stikhov o neizvestnom soldate" Mandel'shtama' [Towards the Plot of 'The Poems about the Unknown Soldier' of Mandel'shtam]. *Slavic History* 5: 214–22
- 1983. *An Approach to Mandel'shtam*. Jerusalem
- 1994. 'O "russkom golose" Osipa Mandel'shtama' [About 'the Russian Voice' of Osip Mandel'shtam]. In *Tynianovskii sbornik: Piatye Tynianovskie chtenija*. [Tynianov issue. Fifth Tynianov Symposium]. Riga

Rusinko, E. 1982. 'Acmeism, Post-symbolism, and Henry Bergson.' *Slavic Literature* 41, no. 3: 496–510

Segal, D.M. 1968. 'Nabljudeniia nad semanticheskoi strukturoi poeticheskogo proizvedeniia' [Observations on the Semantic Structures of the Poetic Text]. *International Journal of Slavic Linguistics and Poetics* 11: 159–71
- 1972. 'O nekotorykh aspektakh smyslovoi struktury "Grifel'noi ody" O. Mandel'shtama' [About Certain Aspects of the Meaningful Structure of 'G.O.' of Osip Mandel'shtam]. *Russian Literature* 2, no. 5: 49–102
- 1973. 'Mikrosemantika odnogo stixotvoreniia' [The Microsemantics of One Poem]. In *Slavic Poetics: Essays in Honour of Kiril Taranovsky*. Ed. Roman Jakobson. The Hague. 395–405
- 1974/5. 'Pamiat' zreniia i pamiat' smysla (Opyt semanticheskoi poetiki. Predvaritel'nye zametki)' [The Memory of Sight and the Memory of Meaning (The Experience of Semantic Poetics. Initial Notes)]. *Russian Literature* 3, nos. 7/8: 121–31
- 1975. 'Fragmenty semanticheskoi poetiki O.E. Mandel'shtama' [A Fragment of O.E. Mandelshtam's Semantic Poetics]. *Russian Literature* 3, nos. 10/11: 59–146
- 1983. 'Poeziia Mikhaila Lozinskogo: simvolizm i akmeizm' [The Poetry of Mikhail Lozinsky: Symbolism and Acmeism]. *Russian Literature* 13, no. 4: 333–414
Shklovsky, Victor. 1965. 'Art as Technique.' Trans. in Lee T. Lemon and Marion J. Reis, eds, *Russian Formalist Criticism: Four Essays*. Lincoln, Neb. 3–24
Shtempel', N.E. 1978. 'Mandel'shtam v Voronezhe' [Mandel'shtam in Voronezh]. *Novyj mir* 10: 207–34
Steiner, Peter. 1977. 'Poem as Manifesto: Mandel'shtam's "Notre Dame".' *Russian Literature* 5, no. 3: 239–56
- 1984. *Russian Formalism: A Metapoetics*. Ithaca, N.Y.
Stepanov, N. 1968. 'Tvorchestvo Velimira Khlebnikova' [Creative Works of Velimira Khlebnikov]. In V.V. Khlebnikov, *Sobranie sochinenii* [Collected Works]. Vol. 6. Munich. 33–64
Struve, N. 1982. *Osip Mandel'shtam*. Paris
Taranovsky, K. 1972. '"Dva molchaniia" Osipa Mandel'shtama' ['Two Silences' of Osip Mandel'shtam]. *Russian Literature* 2: 126–31
- 1976. *Essays on Mandel'shtam*. London
Terras, V. 1966. 'Classical Motives in the Poetry of Osip Mandel'shtam.' *Slavic and Eastern European Journal* 10, no. 3: 251–67
- 1972/3. 'The Organic Tradition in Russian Literary Criticism.' *Russian Literature* 2, no. 5: 35–53
- 1973. 'Osip Mandel'shtam i ego filosofiia slova' [Osip Mandel'shtam and His Philosophy of the Word]. *Slavic Poetics: Essays in Honour of K. Taranovsky*. Paris. 456–60

Thomson, R.D.B. 1991. 'Mandel'shtam's *Kamen*': The Evolution of an Image.' *Russian Literature* 30, no. 4 (15 November): 501–30
Timenchik, R.D. 1974. 'Zametki ob akmeizme' [Notes about Acmeism]. *Russian Literature* 3, nos. 7/8: 23–46
- 1977. 'Zametki ob akmeizme II' [Notes about Acmeism II]. *Russian Literature* 5, no. 3: 281–300
- 1981. 'Zametki ob akmeizme III' [Notes about Acmeism III]. *Russian Literature* 9: 175–90
- 1988. 'Tynianov i "literaturnaia kul'tura" 1910-kh godov' [Tynianov and Literary Culture of 1910–1920]. In *Tynianovskii sbornik: Tret'i Tynianovskie chteniia* [Tynianov issue. Third Tynianov Symposium], ed. M.O. Chudakova. Riga. 159–73
Toddes, E. 1974. 'Mandel'shtam i Tiutchev.' *International Journal of Slavic Linguistics and Poetics* 17: 59–85
Todorov, Tzvetan. 1975. La lecture comme construction.' *Poétique* 24: 417–25
Toporov, V.N. 1979. 'Dve glavy iz istorii Russkoj poezii nachala veka: I V.A. Komarovskii – II V.K. Shileiko (k sootnosheniju poetiki simvolizma i akmeizma)' [Two Chapters from Russian History of the Beginning of the Century: I V.A. Komarovskij – II V.K. Shilejko (Towards the Correspondences between the Poetics of Symbolism and of Acmeism)]. *Russian Literature* 7: 249–326
- 1991. 'O "psikhofiziologicheskom" komponente poezii Mandel'shtama' [On the 'Psychophysiological' Component of Mandel'shtam's Poetry]. In *Osip Mandel'shtam: K 100-letiiu so dnia rozhdeniia. Poetika i tekstologiia. Materialy nauchnoi konferentsii 27–29 dekabria 1991* [Mandelstam Centenary Conference ... London 1991]. Moscow. 7–27
Toynbee, Paget. 1968. *A Dictionary of Proper Names and Notable Matters*. Ed. C.S. Singleton
Tsvetaeva, Marina. 1961. 'Pis'ma k A. Bakhrakhy' [Letters to A. Bakhrakh]. *Mosty* [Bridges]. Book 6. Munich
- 1979. *Izbrannaia proza v dvukh tomakh, 1917–1937* [Selected Prose in Two Volumes, 1917–1937]. New York
- 1980. *Selected Prose*. Ed. and trans. J.M. King. Ann Arbor
Tynianov, Yurij. 1924. *Problema stixotvornogo iazyka* [The Problem of Verse Language]. Leningrad
- 1927. 'Oda kak oratorskii zhanr' [Ode as the Oratory Genre]. In *Poetika*. Vol. 3. Leningrad
- 1977. 'Promezhutok' [Interval]. In *Poetika. Istorija Literatury Kino* [History of Cinemagraphic Literature]. Moscow. 189ff
- 1981. *The Problem of Verse Language*. Ed. and trans. Michael Sosa and Brent Harvey. Rpr. Ann Arbor

Vejdle, V. 1961. 'O poslednikh stikhakh Mandel'shtama' [About the Last Poems of Mandel'shtam]. *Vozdushnye puti* [Aerial Ways] 2: 70–86

Venclova, Tomas. 1985. 'A.A. Fet: Moego tot bezumstva zelal' [A.A. Fet: That One Wished My Madness]. *Russian Literature* 17, no. 2: 87–110

– 1986. *Neustoichivoe ravnovesie: vosem' russkikh poeticheskikh tekstov* [The Unstable Balance: Eight Russian Poetic Texts]. New Haven

Zeeman, Peter. 1988. *The Later Poetry of Osip Mandelstam: Text and Context.* Amsterdam

Zhirmunsky, V. 1928. 'Vokrug "Poetiki" Opoiaza' [Around the Poetics of Opoiaz]. In *Voprosy teorii literatury* [Questions of Literary Theory]. Leningrad

Zholkovsky, A.K. 1979. 'Invarianty i struktura teksta. II. Mandel'shtam: "Ia p'iu za voennye astry' [Textual Invariants and Structure. II. Mandel'shtam: 'I drink for the military asters']. In L. Fleishman, O. Ronen, and D. Segal, eds., *Slavica Hierosolymitana* 4: 159–84

Index

Because of the extensive use of imagery and metaphoric terminology in Mandel'shtam's prose writings this index should be read in conjunction with the detailed table of contents, which provides a key to the structure of Mandel'shtam's poetics

absence. *See* blank
acmeism, 6, 15, 26, 29, 30, 32, 41, 113–14, 115, 154 n 19, 155 n 4, 173 n 1
Acropolis. *See* cathedral; Gothic cathedral
address, in poetry, 55, 56, 66–7, 75, 80, 85, 92, 105–6, 134
addressee, 11, 55, 56, 60, 62, 66, 67, 68, 71, 72, 73, 79, 80, 81, 85, 86, 91, 92, 97, 99, 100, 105, 107, 108, 123, 124, 127, 133–4, 167 n 32
Akhmatova, Anna, 3, 113
anger [zlost'], 43–4, 48, 156 n 15, 158 n 29
Annenskii, Innokentii, 40, 41, 46, 47, 156 n 19
annihilation, 26, 42
Aquinas, Thomas, 119, 129, 163 n 4, 174 n 8
Arab theme, 77, 89, 90–1, 92, 168 n 37
Aragon, 6

Aristotle, 20, 77, 101, 118–19, 120, 121, 131, 156 n 17
arrest, 4
Aseyev, 6
authoritativeness in poetry. *See* imperative nature of poetry
Averintzev, Sergei, ix–xii, xiv, 10
Averroes, 77

babble. *See* noise, noise of language
Bach, J.S. 79, 99
Bakhtin, Mikhail, 115, 162 n 10, 173 n 3
Barthes, Roland, 8, 115, 116, 133–4, 141–3, 144
bee (instinctual self), 83–6, 151 n 13, 155 n 9
Belyi, Andrei, 7, 65, 164 n 13
Bergson, Henri, 33, 40, 43, 50–1, 132, 154 nn 16–17 (ch 2), 154 n 2 (ch 3), 163 n 7
biology, 71–4, 76, 87–8, 94–8, 132,

162 n 11, 167 n 32, 169 nn 47–9, 170 nn 50–3, 173 n 67
blank, 8–9, 13–28, 56, 62–3, 64, 74–6, 135, 151 n 19, 151 n 21, 152 n 27, 152 n 30, 155 n 7, 155 n 10, 162 n 8, 164 n 14, 167 n 29. *See also* nothing, nothingness
Blok, Aleksandr, 49, 50, 51, 154 n 3, 156 n 20, 159 n 39
Bloom, Harold, 141, 143–4
Brodsky, Joseph, 145, 151 n 16, 154 n 1, 165 n 18
Brown, Clarence, 8, 10, 13, 48, 155 n 8, 162 n 12
Buffon, Compte Georges Louis Leclerc de, 87, 88
Bukhshtab, Boris, 10, 150 n 6, 153 n 13

carpet, fluid, or flying carpet, 34, 52, 58, 90–1
catastrophe, essence of, 49–51, 57, 82, 158 nn 31–2, 158 n 36, 166 n 26
cathedral, 19, 20, 23, 30, 31, 55
Catullus, 44, 50, 79–80
Cavanagh, Clare, 111, 114, 115
Chaadaev, Peter, 18–23, 25, 32, 41
chemistry, 102–3, 105, 116–17, 171 n 60
Chénier, André, 14–18
Christian art, 23–4, 26, 152 n 29
Christianity, 18, 22–8, 42, 68, 130
classical morality, rationality, 16–17
classical tragedy, 16
colour, coloration, 87–93, 107–9, 137, 167 n 31, 167 n 34, 168 n 38, 168 n 41, 168 n 42
command. *See* imperative nature of poetry
conductor's baton, 103–5, 106
crack [*proval*]. *See* gap

crystallographic figure or theme, 32, 82–3, 84, 132, 167 n 29
Culler, Jonathan, 123–4, 133, 142, 143, 144

Dante Alighieri, 27, 32, 38, 51, 52, 68 ff passim, 163 n 7, 170 n 53, 172 n 64, 175 nn 10–11
Darwin, Charles, 91, 94–100, 125–7, 131, 169 nn 47–9, 170 nn 50–3, 171 nn 55–6, 173 n 67
death, 4, 22–8, 30, 59, 76–7, 81, 165 n 22
defamiliarization, deautomatization 44–5, 122–4
Derrida, Jacques, 8, 9, 13–14, 149 n 2
dialogue, dialogical nature of poetry, 54–6, 101, 102, 105–7, 138
differentiation (along the journey), 53, 62, 64, 68, 70, 93, 108–9, 140. *See also* metaphoric transformation
diffusion (of light, warmth), 33–4, 36, 38, 40, 43, 50–1, 154 n 2. *See* waves
Dionysiac/Dionysian powers, elements, 15, 17, 24, 25, 59, 150 n 11, 156 n 13
dualism, 15, 21–8, 34, 35, 37–8, 41, 42–8, 50, 51, 56, 57, 154 n 2, 163 n 5, 163 n 7. *See also* hybridization

education, 78–9, 165 n 19
Eikhenbaum, Boris M. 7, 46, 121, 122
Eliot, T.S., 114
expression, 15, 35, 48, 51, 52, 53, 54, 81–3, 87–8, 121, 122, 123, 127–8, 131, 134, 136, 147, 150 n 9, 158 n 36, 166 n 25, 166 n 28, 167 n 31, 174 n 6
extermination, exterminated tradition, 8, 14, 26, 115, 116

Fish, Stanley, 133
Fleishman, L., 49, 158 nn 32–3
formalists, 6, 7, 118, 121–7, 128, 155 n 5, 162 n 10
Foucault, Michel, 118
Freidin, Gregory, 9, 10, 150 n 5, 151 n 16, 155 n 8, 165 n 18
Frye, Northrop, 5
futurism, 6, 113, 151 n 21, 154 nn 18–19, 159 n 38, 162 nn 9–10

gap, 74–6, 80–2, 88, 134, 164 n 14
Gershtein, Emma, 9, 162 n 1
Geryon, 90, 91
ghost, 80–1, 134
Goethe, Johann Wolfgang von, 132, 173 n 68
Gothic cathedral, 15, 17, 19, 20, 23, 29, 30–1, 55, 132, 151 n 18. *See also* cathedral
Gumilev, Nikolai, 3, 15, 113–14, 152 n 2, 155 nn 4–5, 155 n 7, 158 n 31, 161 n 2, 161 n 6, 163 n 6

Harris, Jane, 10, 150 n 7, 157 nn 14–15, 160 n 1, 161 n 4
Hegel, G.F.W., 6
Heidegger, Martin, 13, 41, 149 n 2
Hellas (as soil), 22, 23, 24, 29, 151 n 25
Hellenism, 18, 23, 24, 25, 43, 47, 65, 151 n 25, 152 n 26, 155 n 12
Heracles, 65
Hofmann, Iosif (musician), 58–9
Holland, Norman N., 133
home, homespun essence, domesticity, xi, 7, 45–6, 156 n 21
hybridization, 69–72, 138, 154 n 3, 159 n 37, 163–4 n 10
hypnotic power of poetry, 16, 17, 40, 41, 42, 55–6, 150 n 8, 155 n 8

Iakhontov, Vladimir, 35, 36, 49, 57, 59, 161 n 3
imagination. *See* colour, coloration
imperative (obligatory) nature of poetry, 16, 17, 23, 36, 38, 44, 52–3, 60, 62, 79–80, 103–10, 156 n 21
impressionism, 86, 89–94 passim, 169 n 49
impulse [*poryv*], 69–72, 98–101, 103, 104, 114, 118, 120, 125–7, 128, 129, 138, 146–7, 156 n 13, 160 n 42, 169 n 46
inner reality (of the word), 34, 35, 36, 37, 45, 46, 98, 161 n 3. *See also* space
intensification (of the word), 40, 41, 50. *See* authoritativeness in poetry
intertextuality, 77–8, 115, 137, 140–7, 164–5 n 17
Iser, Wolfgang, 13, 14, 41, 133, 152 n 27
Ivanov, Viacheslav I., 3, 152 n 26, 155 n 12, 159 n 37, 163 n 3, 164 n 12
Ivanov, Viacheslav V., 10, 132, 155 n 12

Jacob's ladder, 19, 23. *See also* Gothic cathedral
Jakobson, Roman, 6, 17, 123, 124, 127, 141, 154 n 18, 173 n 3
Jewishness, 8, 14, 37, 46, 130, 136, 155–6 n 12

Kant, Immanuel, 6
Khazina. *See* Mandelsh'tam, Nadezhda Iakovlevna
Khlebnikov, Velemir, 57, 151 n 21, 161 n 3, 166 n 26
Khruchenykh, A., 122, 151 n 21, 152 n 1
kindredness, 64–7

Komissarzhevskaia, Vera, 35, 36
Kristeva, Julia, 115, 141–4
Kubelik, Ian, 58–9
Kuzin, B.S., 132, 162 n 11, 167 n 32

Laing, R.D., 14
Lamarck, Jean-Baptiste de, 72, 76, 77–9, 80, 87, 88, 108–9, 131, 132, 165 nn 19–20
Levin, Iuri, 6, 10, 150 n 9, 155 n 12
light waves, 69, 92–3, 94–7, 100, 137, 172 n 62, 172 n 65
Linnaeus, Caorolus, 87, 88, 95, 131
literariness, 7, 121
logos, forming principle, 68–72, 156 n 12

Maiakovsky, Vladimir, 3, 60, 65, 151 n 19
Mallarmé, Stéphane, 47
Mande'shtam, Nadezhda Iakovlevna, 3, 4, 6, 22, 113, 163 n 3
materia. *See* poetic *materia*
metaphoric transformation, 9, 10, 11, 12, 13, 15, 19, 20, 27, 29, 30–2, 38–9, 48–9, 60–7, 71, 81–2, 89, 90–1, 92, 98–9, 120, 130, 162 n 13
metre, 18, 21; Alexandrine, 18; iambic, 17, 18
Middle Ages, 101, 117, 131–2, 163 n 4, 172 n 64
Mikhoels, Solomon, 35, 37, 46
Miller, Owen J., 135, 162 n 8
miniature, 88–9, 91–2
Monet, Claude, 86
Mukařovský, Jan, 127–9
music, 14, 22, 23, 30, 49–50, 51, 52, 78, 99–117, 146, 172 n 63, 175 n 9. *See also* noise; ringing (of the image)
mute (or voiceless) thought, sound, 20, 21–2, 23, 27, 69–70, 77, 120, 128, 156 n 14

Nadson, Semion, 57, 59–60, 161 n 3
Nietzsche, Friedrich, 13, 16, 17, 23, 150 n 11
noise, noise of language, 8, 9, 33, 39, 50, 52, 77–80, 137, 156–7 n 21, 159 n 38, 160 n 40
nothing, nothingness, 13, 18, 19, 41–2, 43, 53, 55–6, 151 n 21, 162 n 9, 163 n 5

Odysseus (Ulysses), 94–7, 98, 169 n 44, 170 n 53, 171 n 58
Oedipus, 142–3
orality, 7, 37
organ (musical-sexual pun), 78–9, 81–2
organic life, 68–9, 73–4, 76, 83–8, 94–8, 164 n 11, 165 n 19, 166 n 27, 167 n 31
Orpheus, 25, 42, 172 n 66
outer solidity, 34, 35, 36, 37, 57, 58, 158 nn 29–30
Ovid, 44

Pallas, Peter Simon, 87, 88, 108–9
part. *See* miniature
Pasternak, Boris, 3, 12, 50, 128–30, 136, 137, 160 nn 40–1, 166 n 27, 172 n 66
People's Will Party, 57
Persephone, 17, 151 n 12
Phaedra, 24
physics, 68, 95, 100–1, 118, 154 n 18, 171 n 60
physiology of reading, 9, 60–1, 63, 162 n 15
Plato, 141, 163 n 4, 166 n 24

plough (as poetry), 30–1
poetic *materia*, 69–110 passim, 118, 121, 124, 130, 138, 145–7, 175 n 10
Pollack, Nancy, 9, 10, 111, 136, 137, 150 n 5, 153 n 9, 167 n 13
postmodern poetics. *See* poststructuralism
poststructuralism, 7–9, 12, 14, 115–18, 125, 126, 132, 140–7, 173–4 n 3
Potebnija, Alexander, 7
Pound, Ezra, 114
Prometheus, 23
Przybylski, Ryszard, 10, 172 n 63
Psyche, psyche, 17, 33, 112, 153 n 13
Pushkin, Aleksandr, 18, 24, 42, 129, 144–5

rage. *See* anger
reader-reception, receptivity, 13, 52, 54–60, 62, 133–40, 160 n 1, 162 n 2
reading process, 54–9, 72, 85–6, 88–93, 99–100, 106–9, 133–40
reflexology, reflexology of speech, 9, 60–1, 110, 124, 146–7, 162 n 15, 175 n 11
rhythm, 18, 122
ringing (of the image), 33, 38, 44, 49, 50, 52, 78, 137, 156–7 n 21, 159 n 38, 160 n 40, 164 n 11
romanticism, 17, 22, 23, 27, 143, 159 n 38
romantic, poetry. *See* romanticism
Rome (as stone), 23, 24, 25, 29, 151 n 26, 163–4 n 10
Ronen, Omry, 10, 152 n 2, 153 n 15, 155 n 8, 155 n 11, 158 n 35, 158 n 37, 160 nn 43–4, 165 n 18
Rozanov, I.N., 31–2, 40, 41, 45, 46, 92, 153 n 10, 156 n 19, 171 n 57

Rudakov, Sergei, 9, 162–3 n 1
rupture, 15, 16, 17, 23
Russian Revolution, 42, 49, 50, 159 n 39
Russian spirit, 18–21, 24–5, 31–2, 153 n 12

Saussure, Ferdinand de, 122
Shklovsky, Viktor, 6, 7, 44, 121–2, 123, 156 n 18
Signac, Paul, 89, 92
siren-piano. *See* blank
Skriabin, Alexsandr, 18, 22–6
soil, 23, 30, 58–9. *See also* vegetation; stone
solidity. *See* outer solidity
Sologub, Fiodor, 41, 47, 58–9, 161 n 5, 161 n 7
space (inside/outside the word), 35, 37
speed. *See* colour; wave
Stalin, Josef, 3, 4, 131
stone, 15, 17, 19, 23, 29–32, 72, 74–6, 81–3, 152 n 4, 164 n 11, 164 n 13, 167 n 29. *See also* Gothic cathedral; Jacob's ladder
structuralism, 127–30
student. *See* education
surface consolidation. *See* outer solidity
symbolists, 3, 26, 29, 60, 113–14, 131, 145, 155 n 5, 155 n 8, 156 nn 13–14, 158–9 n 37, 159 n 38, 173 n 2

Taranovsky, Arsenii, 10, 164–5 n 17
teacher. *See* education
theatre, 34–8, 46, 49
time, 19, 20, 21, 25, 30–1, 78, 81, 156 n 16, 164 n 15, 165 n 18

Timenchik, R.D., 10, 150 n 10, 154 n 19
Tiutchev, Fiodor, 30, 47, 152 n 3
tongue-tied, 8, 14, 59, 161 n 5, 162 nn 6–7
Toporov, V., 10, 29, 59
transformation. *See* differentiation
transmutations. *See* turns
Trotsky, L., 7, 121
Tsvetaeva, Marina, 3, 7, 98, 112–13, 144–5, 150 n 6
turns, transmutations, 71–2, 82–110 passim, 134, 138, 139, 163 nn 9–10, 168 n 36, 175 n 10
Tynianov, Yurij, 6, 122, 124–6, 149 n 4, 153 n 15, 154 n 20, 155 n 5, 174 nn 6–7

Ulysses. *See* Odysseus
unity of thought, 18–19, 20, 21, 23, 24, 25, 33–4, 62, 124, 137, 154 n 16, 154 n 20. *See also* differentiation; metaphoric transformation

vegetation, 23, 30, 63–5. *See also* organic life
Villon, François, 54, 55
Virgil, 75, 144

wave (word), 34, 51–2, 61, 68, 90–1, 93–9, 100, 102, 112–26, 134, 137, 158 n 34. *See also* light waves

Zholkovsky, Aleksandr, 10, 154 n 21, 158 n 29, 160 n 45